P9-DOC-871

HOUSES, HISTORY
and
PEOPLE

HOUSES, HISTORY and PEOPLE

RICHARD PRATT

Published by
M. EVANS AND COMPANY, INC.,
New York
and distributed in association with
J. B. LIPPINCOTT COMPANY,
Philadelphia and New York

For Anne

Copyright © 1965 by Richard Pratt

*All rights reserved under International and
Pan American Copyright Conventions*

Library of Congress Catalog Card Number: 65–21773

*Text printed in the United States of America
Illustrations printed in the Netherlands*

Designed by Luc Bouchage

PHOTO CREDITS

Frontispiece by Ezra Stoller.

Douglas Armsden, 102, 103, 106; Charles Baptie, 94, 95, 97; Brooks Studio, 218 tr; Jim Burns, Clemson News Bureau, 21; English Life Publications Ltd., Derby, 15 br; Frick Art Reference Library, 159 t; Louis H. Frohman, 92 tl; Herbert Georg Studios, 173; Historical Society of Pennsylvania, 56; Joe Horton, 121; Cortlandt V. D. Hubbard, 53, 55; Leonard V. Huber, 193; The Hughes Company, 86; Joslyn Art Museum, Omaha, 231; Kaufmann & Fabry Co., 228; Knight Photo Company, 109 tr; Knutson-Bowers, 207; Paul E. Lefebvre, 37; Lloyd Studio, 233 bl; Marler, 219; Herman F. Marshall, 77, 84; M. Richard Marx © 1961 Automobile Club of Southern California, 171; Frank Lotz Miller, 192; Minnesota Historical Society, 201, 202; Museum of Fine Arts, Boston, 31; Sydney W. Newbery, English Life Publications, Ltd., 10, 13, 15; Newman's Photo Service, 144; Jessie O'Connell, 217; Harold Phelps, Arkansas Publicity and Parks Commission, 147 t; Photo-Art Commercial Studios, 182; Photographers Associates, 231 tl; Plimoth Plantation Inc., 24, 27; Richard Pratt, 11 t; Ezra Stoller Associates, 59, 60, 61, 63, 64, 67, 70, 71, 75, 128, 129, 131; Sullivan Photo Service, 90 tl; R. K. Sunderbruch, 232 tl, tr; Taylor & Dull, 79, 80, 82; Laurence E. Tilley, 32, 33, 37, 38, 39, 46, 48, 49, 51, 136, 141; Virginia Historical Society, 21 tr; Virginia Museum of Fine Arts, 21 tl; Thomas L. Williams, The National Park Service, Colonial National Historical Park, Yorktown, Va., 17, 21 br; Yale University Art Gallery, Gift of Isaac Lothrop of Plymouth, Mass., 52.

FOREWORD

Houses *are* history. In an intimate physical sense they are just about as close to history as it is possible to get. In them it is possible to look at history face to face. It is possible to *touch* it.

Places are history too,—Jamestown, Plymouth, Valley Forge. But houses and places can't create history by themselves. Only the lives, deeds, and words of the men and women connected with them can do that.

History occasionally seems to come alive, in words written and spoken. But what makes it seem to come alive most vividly is when in certain houses and certain places we consider what certain men and women did and said in those houses and those places.

For this reason houses can be documents of great poignancy. Also, of course, they can be buildings of great beauty. They can be as beautiful as Gunston Hall and as poignant as the only house that Lincoln ever owned, in Springfield, Illinois. They can contain the whole long history of a family and community full of history, as the Quincy Homestead does. Or they can recall, as Oakley does in its paradise of birds, the brief but immensely productive sojourn of an Audubon in Louisiana.

No wonder that dozens of books have been written about houses of American history, with dozens more still to be written; each one with a special aim of its own. The aim here is to tell some American history in terms of the extraordinary country-wide collection of some sixty houses and other landmarks with which The National Society of the Colonial Dames of America is concerned. Known among themselves as the "Dames," that is how they will be designated here. The book is about them only to the extent of bringing their historical activities out from behind the scenes, where for years the Dames have worked their wonders.

They speak of themselves as a historical society. As such the Dames discover and bring out books of reference, unpublished manuscripts, diaries, journals, and other sources of authentic colonial history. They seek and preserve old records, family Bibles, wills, deeds, vestry books, church registers, seals and inscriptions, including those found in colonial cemeteries. They build monuments to mark the sites of notable events in colonial times. They affix descriptive tablets to historic buildings, to the homes of colonial heroes, to colonial state houses, churches, and forts. They investigate, restore, and preserve historic houses, fill them with furniture of their period, and open them to the public, holding in them exhibitions of historical relics and works of art.

One of the most endearing things about the Dames is that they wisely extend their interest beyond the colonial period. They follow this country's architectural frontiers for a full hundred years after the Declaration of Independence, and by including in their collection the English ancestral home of George Washington, they make it possible for this book to open with a house that was built before there was a "colonial" settlement on the North American continent. Yet the 1540 Sulgrave Manor in Northamptonshire leads as surely into the colonial period as the happenings of that period lead right up to the 1875 Hotel De Paris in Georgetown, Colorado, one of the latest buildings in this book.

In the collecting of material for this book the Dames proved themselves to be generous and invaluable collaborators. Their Historical Activities Committee, its chairman, Mrs. J. W. E. Moore, and its members in the various states, provided local information and performed local research which often would have been unobtainable from other available sources. They identified the furnishings in all the photographs and they read the manuscript with zealous scrutiny. For all of which the author is profoundly grateful.

CONTENTS

I

Seventy-two miles from London toward Coventry, the manor lies eight miles from Banbury, famous since the 17th century for its cakes and for the cross the Puritans destroyed in 1602. It is built of the local limestone not unlike that of the Cotswold hills to the southwest. In the gable above the entrance Lawrence Washington placed the royal arms, in plaster, marked with the initials E.R. for Elizabeth Regina, who is said to have stopped by one day when she was a child. There is a beautiful rose garden containing all the famous roses of English history—the red of Lancaster, the white of York, the Crusaders' rose of Damascus, and many others. The kitchen (below) is one of the most authentic Tudor kitchens in England, with a huge fireplace equipped to roast anything from deer, lamb, pig to gamebirds. Of the three fireplace ovens, one is a charcoal brazier, one is for roasting, and one for baking. In winter curtains are hung from the ceiling to conserve heat and make the kitchen cozy.

THE SULGRAVE MANOR STORY

The People

Lawrence Washington, builder of Sulgrave

Elizabeth Gough, his first wife

Amee Pargiter, his second wife

Robert Washington, elder son of Lawrence and Amee, second owner of Sulgrave

Lawrence Makepeace, grandson of the builder, third owner of Sulgrave

John Washington, great-grandson of the builder, first Washington emigrant and great-grandfather of George Washington

Henry VII, Henry VIII, Elizabeth I, James I, Charles I, Oliver Cromwell, Sir Walter Ralegh, William Shakespeare, Sir Francis Drake, Captain John Smith, Captain Christopher Newport, William Strachey

A contemporary and fellow-townsman of Columbus, John Cabot left Genoa at fifteen, learned seafaring out of Venice, came to England in the 1480's, and became a Bristol mariner. In 1497, under a patent from Henry VII to explore the coast of North America, he first came to what he called his "new-founde-land," then sailed down to what is now Bar Harbor, before returning to England. And in the King's account book for the day Cabot came to report to the Crown were the following entries:

To the damsel that danceth	£ 12
To the man who found the new island	10
To Jake Haute for tennis play	9
To a woman with a red rose	2 shillings.

Then in 1498, the year of Columbus' third voyage (on which he sighted South America), "the man who found the new island" for Henry VII sailed again from Bristol, and this time supposedly explored the American coast as far south as the Chesapeake, though there is no record of his returning to England.

Into this era of American discovery and exploration a baby boy named Lawrence Washington was born about 1500 at Wharton in Lancashire. A little less than three hundred years later, in a letter to Sir Isaac Heard, George Washington, Lawrence's most celebrated descendant, recalled that he had been told the family had come from one of the northern counties of England. According to Douglas Southall Freeman, Washington "was not sure whether it was Lancashire or Yorkshire or a region still farther North . . . Genealogy seemed to him as of 'very little moment.'"

That being the case, Washington would not have been much impressed by the fact that his family line has now been pretty surely, though not quite positively, traced back to a John de Wessington who lived about 1260 near the border of Lancashire and Westmorland. Hardly anyone, however, with an interest in personal records could fail to be impressed by the monumental and fascinating Washington genealogy amassed by Charles Arthur Hoppin, which has been such a help here with what Hoppin calls the "Sulgrave Washingtons," whose head was the baby Lawrence. For it was within the period of the Sulgrave Washingtons, from Cabot's discoveries to the settlement of Jamestown and Plymouth, that the English colonization of America was born, bred, and brought into being. And it was directly from the Sulgrave Washingtons that Lawrence's great-grandson became the first Washington emigrant to America and the great-grand-father of our country's first President.

When Lawrence was a boy of about nine, Henry VIII became King, and as a young man Lawrence acted as a manager for Sir William Parr, uncle of Catherine Parr, who became the King's last Queen.

Parr had large interests in Northamptonshire, and about 1530 Lawrence moved there and married Elizabeth Gough, widow of a rich wool stapler of Northampton town. How much the widow's fortune affected Lawrence's financial welfare doesn't seem to be a matter of record, but he seems to have prospered as a wool merchant (his uncle, Sir Thomas Kytson, was the great wool magnate of England in his time, and in very good standing with the King). Lawrence's cousin, Sir John Spencer, of nearby Althorp, was reputed at one time to have herds totaling twenty thousand sheep. In Hoppin, Lawrence is spoken of as "Lawrence Washington of Northampton and Gray's Inn," so it would appear that at some point he took training in the law.

Lawrence was several times mayor of Northampton, and there is record of the fact that on July 15, 1539, he witnessed a will at Northampton in which occurs the sentence: "I bequeathe to Mayster Wasynton a gown furyd wyth foxe." As mayor he would have been addressed as "Mayster" (master). He was also one of the early Protestants of England. In other words, by 1539 he was a man of means and station, with rich and influential relatives and friends. Shortly before that his wife had died childless and he had taken the lease of a property called Millefeldes, adjacent to the Priory of St. Andrews at Sulgrave, one of the estates of Sulgrave Manor.

Then in 1539 came the dissolution of the monasteries, and Lawrence quickly seized the chance to buy from the Crown both the manor and the estate he had under lease. The price he paid was about 325 pounds, and the deed was witnessed by the King himself. In this connection, it may be of interest to note that a large part of the monies acquired by the Crown from the sale of the monasteries all over England found its way into funds that were later used to finance the early efforts to colonize America.

Not long after Lawrence became lord of the Manor of Sulgrave, he married another widow named Amee Tomson, née Pargiter, who began bearing him children apace (eventually four sons and seven daughters). At the same time, either because of this growing family, or simply because he had the money and liked to build, Lawrence was building onto the Manor, not stopping until 20 years later. And largely due to the way they built in Tudor times, Sulgrave has been able to survive as well as it did the long periods of painful abuse and neglect it suffered during the ensuing centuries.

Admittedly, at various times Sulgrave has been added onto and subtracted from. It is smaller now than it was when Lawrence Washington finished his work on it. A Queen Anne wing was built onto the Tudor portion. The Tudor roof is typically steep, and the Elizabethan red-brick chimney stacks are characteristically set at an angle, in contrast with the Queen Anne chimney stacks of solid stone. In other words, the house in its various parts illustrates the transitions that took place—chiefly Tudor—between the feudal perpendicular Gothic style and the Palladian influence brought into England in 1615 by Inigo Jones. Apart from the differences in their outward appearance, these transitional styles marked a swing away from the military austerities of the feudal style to greater and greater domestic comforts and conveniences in plan and appointments. What Lawrence Washington did at Sulgrave was repeated a hundredfold in various parts of England as the monasteries were picked up and turned into great country homes. And the building ideas inherent in these transitional styles were to find their way to the English colonies in America as the first manifestations of conscious architecture in this country.

At a considerable distance from Sulgrave, while Lawrence Washington was first enlarging the Manor, a Spaniard, Hernando de Soto, with several hundred soldiers, was exploring the North American continent from Florida to the Blue Ridge, to the Gulf near Mobile, thence north again,

This portrait of George Washington, which hangs in the Oak Parlor, was painted in 1792 by Archibald Robertson, on commission from the Earl of Buchan.

crossing the Mississippi River below Memphis, and on through the Ozarks to Oklahoma (as if any of these names would occur to anyone for years to come). He finally returned to the Mississippi, where he died of a fever in 1542, leaving no permanent settlements of any kind or even temporary ones as far as can be seen—only a saga of indefatigable search.

Some time before Elizabeth was crowned in 1558, she is supposed to have stopped at Sulgrave. There is a large oak cupboard at the top of the staircase, around which various legends have grown up. "The most persistent," according to *Sulgrave Manor and the Washingtons*, "is that Queen Elizabeth hid there as a child." "There is no accounting for tradition," says Hoppin with the spoil-sport skepticism of the true genealogist. The Royal Family have sponsored the restoration from the beginning, and have visited it many times. One day in September 1937, the late Queen Mary stopped by, had her picture taken in the doorway, and presented Sulgrave Manor House with a charming pearwood snuffbox with George Washington's profile carved on the cover.

Ten years after Elizabeth became Queen, Lawrence's oldest son, Robert, who was living at Sulgrave with his first wife, Elizabeth Light, became the father of his first son, Lawrence, an event of importance in the direct male line to George Washington himself. Sixteen years later Lawrence the builder, died, leaving his estate to Robert. That same year, Shakespeare, at 20, who had already been married for two years to Anne Hathaway, moved from nearby Stratford to London and the beginnings of glory.

In March of this year, 1584, a friend of Shakespeare's and a favorite of Elizabeth's, Sir Walter Ralegh, was granted a patent from the Queen for the exploration and colonization of North America. And in July, coming with the wind up the Carolina coast, he turned into Albemarle Sound and landed on Roanoke Island. Giving the whole vast continent westward the name "Virginia" in honor of his Virgin Queen, he returned almost at once to England to acquaint her in September with the success of his expedition.

The following April he sent a colonizing expedition which landed in July on the island, where a settlement was created which lingered on for five years, but through such vicissitudes that when the help that had been held up by the Spanish Armada finally arrived in August 1590, the colony had vanished without a trace, leaving little but the legend of Virginia Dare, the first English child born in America. Ralegh's final expedition, sent out by him in 1602 in a desperate last search for survivors, found nothing.

The defeat of the Armada by the English fleet in the summer of 1588 in the Channel, together with the peace of 1604, uneasy as it was, gave impetus to English plans for colonizing in North America. The rivalry with Spain for possession was still intense, but Spain's power to prevent English ships from freely crossing the Atlantic was very much lessened, even though not entirely eliminated.

After the death of Elizabeth in 1603 and the accession of James I, Englishmen of every rank, from the King down, began to have the colonization of "Virginia" on their minds more and more, either as organizers, financiers, or possible colonists. By right of discovery they believed it to be theirs, south roughly to Florida, north to the St. Lawrence, and "sea to sea," as the wording went. They had begun to realize that this could be one of the biggest things that had ever happened to England, and at the same time to themselves. Many English merchants and nobles were convinced that organized colonization was the next step, and together they petitioned the King for a crown patent, conferred in April, 1606, under whose terms two Virginia companies were established. One was the London Company, authorized to settle "South Virginia," the other the Plymouth Company, authorized to settle "North Virginia." The lands of the two companies overlapped, creating in effect a neutral zone that ran roughly between where New York City and Washington, D. C., are now.

By August the Plymouth Company was ready to send out its first expedition, which had the bad luck to be captured by the still-privateering Spaniards in the West Indies. In October a second was dispatched, which worked its way down the coast of Maine, exploring, but returned to England without making a settlement.

Then five days before Christmas, three ships of the London Company sailed out of Plymouth, under the command of Captain Christopher Newport, bound for the Chesapeake. These ships were the *Susan Constant*, of 100 tons carrying 71 people, the *Godspeed*, of 42 tons carrying 52 people, and the *Discovery*, of 20 tons and only 49 feet in length, with 21 aboard; 144 in all, *and all men.*

In August of 1608 a congregation of dissidents from the Church of England, who had established themselves at Scrooby, Nottinghamshire, emigrated to Holland rather than submit to the impositions being placed upon the Church by the Crown. Under the leadership of William Brewster and John Robinson they remained in Amsterdam and then in Leyden until 1620, when, as Pilgrims, they made their momentous voyage on the *Mayflower*, an account of which appears in the Plymouth chapter.

On June 2, 1609, the bark *Sea Venture* sailed out of Plymouth, and instead of steering by way of the West Indies and with the winds up the coast, the customary route, made straight across for Jamestown. On board was a Jacobean historian in his late thirties, named William Strachey, who was going out to become the secretary of Virginia, a job, as A. L. Rowse points out in his biography of William Shakespeare, that John Donne had badly wanted. In the neighborhood of Bermuda, the *Sea Venture* encountered an unusually violent storm which caused the little ship to be blown ashore on the island, miraculously without any loss of life. This was described vividly at length in a letter from Strachey to a "Noble Lady" in London, but appeared "still better and more vividly," as Mr. Rowse puts it, "in rivetting fashion in *The Tempest*." For the play contains so many of the details of Strachey's letter that no doubt can exist as to where Shakespeare found his inspiration. The play was performed November 1, 1611, "at Whitehall before the King's Majesty." Strachey's *Historie of Travaile into Virginia Britannia* did not achieve publication until 1849.

In 1610 Robert Washington, the inheritor of Sulgrave, with the consent of his eldest son Lawrence, arranged the sale of Sulgrave Manor to his nephew, Lawrence Makepeace, a grandson of Lawrence the builder, with the stipulation that Makepeace would not take possession until Robert's death. This occurred eight years later, ending seventy-nine years of occupancy by the Washington family.

In the meanwhile Lawrence had died, two years before his father, but had begotten no less than eight sons and nine daughters by his wife, Margaret Butler, a direct descendant of the Plantagenets. This connection with that early English royal house was eventually passed on, through Margaret's fifth son, Lawrence, to our first President, a fact of which George Washington appeared to have been oblivious.

14

The entry leads into the great hall, above, eighteen by twenty, paved with blue Hornton stone, with a great open fireplace at one end, over which hangs the treasure of the room, if not the whole manor, the Gilbert Stuart portrait of Washington. Emblazoned on the windows are the Washington arms as well as those of the families into which they married. An immense Tudor refectory table is just right for the room, and a big Elizabethan wall cupboard (out of sight) is filled with Washington relics. In the great chamber upstairs, the beautifully carved Elizabethan bed, the Elizabethan chest carved with palm leaves on the four uprights and lions' masks on the panels, the small chest carved to illustrate "Nonesuch", King Henry VIII's favorite palace destroyed in King Charles I's reign, all are rare museum pieces as are materials of the period which furnish the other bedrooms of the manor.

15

This latest Lawrence, born in 1602, was the first member of his family to have graduated at Oxford; and, after winning his M.A. in 1626, he remained at the university, becoming lector of Brasenose and then one of the proctors of Oxford. He had already been named a fellow of the college, but had resigned his fellowship, due to an Oxford rule, a year after his marriage to Amphillis Twigden. During that year, 1632, his son John had been born.

After taking holy orders, Lawrence became rector, in 1633, of All Saints, Purleigh Parish, Essex. Things didn't go well, and in 1643, according to Freeman and Hoppin, triumphant Puritans relieved him of his rectorship, claiming him to be a "common frequenter of Ale-houses, not only himself sitting daily tippling there, but also encouraging others in that beastly vice." While due to friends he was allowed to preach at Little Braxted, Essex, he must have been ruined financially, according to Hoppin, and in January 1652 he died at fifty-four.

By the time Lawrence's son John "was twenty-three or twenty-four," again according to Freeman and Hoppin, "he had learned something of shipping and seamanship. In 1656, on invitation of Edward Prescott, owner of the ketch *Sea Horse of London*, he journeyed to Danzig, joined the vessel, sailed with her to Lübeck and Copenhagen and, at Elsinore, agreed to a partnership voyage with Prescott to Virginia." And there he arrived the same year, with results we already know.

By 1659, when Abel Makepeace sold it, Sulgrave Manor lost its last connection with any part of the Washington clan—at least until the spirit of that famous name was revived in it a few days before the First World War.

Sulgrave was bought in 1914 by the British-American Peace Centenary Committee as a gift to the American people, commemorating the hundred years of peace since the Treaty of Ghent. The first amount subscribed was £12,000, the purchase price £8,400 (about $42,500 in 1914), leaving less than enough to start restoration, which of course couldn't have been started in any case, because of the First World War. However, on July 25, only a matter of days before the Germans marched into Belgium, in a moving ceremony at Sulgrave, the Duke of Teck (brother of Queen Mary, and Honorary President of the British-American Peace Centenary Committee), handed the keys of Sulgrave Manor to the American Ambassador, Walter Hines Page.

One of the Dames, Mrs. T. Harrison Garrett, of Maryland, who represented the Society at the ceremony, has described how much this was made an American occasion. "The special train [from London to Sulgrave] was decorated with our flags, as were both the village and the church of the Washington family. I need not describe the Manor," Mrs. Garrett went on to say (having brought back some pictures). "But in all these years it has been much altered and now has practically fallen to pieces."

Between 1914 and 1924 the Dames sent $27,000 toward the purchase, partial restoration, and maintenance of Sulgrave Manor; English men and women from the royal family down gave over $150,000 toward purchase and restoration.

On June 21, 1921, Sulgrave Manor was formally opened and dedicated, restoration funds having been subscribed after the war; and the work of restoration entrusted to Sir Reginald Blomfield was well under way, though not altogether completed until 1929. However, with scarcely any money earmarked for maintenance, it would have been impossible to keep the house open to the public if the Dames in 1924 hadn't set out to raise $100,000 for this purpose. They planned to use the device of asking each of their (then) 9,000 members to gather ten donations of a dollar each. They even bettered their mark by $12,000. In 1927 they raised about $15,300 more from the display at the Sesquicentennial Exposition of a scale-model reproduction of the Manor. In 1931 the Dames gave $58,936 toward restoration. Since then the fund has grown to more than $250,000, thereby endowing the Manor as an open house of rare distinction and beauty for all the foreseeable future, the finest American landmark in England.

This painting of the arrival of the settlers at Jamestown in 1607 is by the late Griffith Baily Coale and hangs in the State Capitol at Richmond, Virginia.

THE SETTLEMENT OF JAMESTOWN

The People

Captain John Smith, explorer, colonizer, soldier of fortune
Gabriel Archer, lawyer and explorer
George Percy, sailor, author, son of the 8th Earl of Northumberland
William Strachey, Tudor historian and colonial secretary
Sir Thomas Gates ⎫
Lord Delaware ⎬ *early governors*
Captain George Yeardly ⎭
John Rolfe, tobacco planter
Pocahontas, his wife
Nathaniel Bacon, Jr., leader of the rebellion
Sir William Berkeley, First Royal Governor

In these excerpts from George Percy's *Observations*, the story of the voyage and the landing in Virginia can be told with the true flavor of the times.

"On Saturday the twentieth of December in the yeere 1606, the fleet fell from London, and the fifth of January we anchored in the Downes: but the winds continued contrarie so long, that we were forced to stay there some time, where wee suffered great stormes, but the skilfulnesse of the Captaine wee suffered no great losse or danger . . .

"The three and twentieth day [of March] we fell with the Iland of Mattanenio [Martinique] in the West Indies. The foure and twentieth day we anchored at Dominico, within fourteene degrees of the Line, a very faire Iland, the Trees full of sweet and good smels; inhabited by many Savage Indians. . . .

"The tenth day [of April] we set saile, and disimboged out of the West Indies, and bare oure course Northerly. . . . The six and twentieth day of Aprill, about foure a clocke in the morning, wee descried the Land of Virginia. The same day wee entred into the Bay of Chesupioc directly, without any let or hinderance. There wee landed and discovered a little way, but wee could find nothing worth speaking of, but faire meddowes and goodly tall Trees, with such Fresh-waters running through the woods, as I was almost ravished at the first sight thereof . . .

"The nine and twentieth day we set up a Crosse at Chesupioc Bay, and named that place Cape Henry. Thirtieth day, we came with our ships to Cape Comfort; where we saw five Savages running on the shoare. . . .

"The twelfth day [of May] we went backe to our ships, and discovered a point of Land, called Archers Hope, which was sufficient with a little labour to defend our selves against any Enemy. The soile was good and fruitfull, with excellent good Timber. . . . If it had not beene disliked, because the ship could not ride neere the shoare, we had setled there to all the Collonies contentment.

"The thirteenth day, we came to our seating place in Paspihas Countrey, some eight miles from the point of Land, which I made mention before: where our shippes doe lie so neere the shoare that they are moored to the Trees in six fathom water.

"The fourteenth day, we landed all our men, which were set to worke about the fortification, and others some to watch and ward as it was convenient. . . .

"The fifteenth of June we had built and finished our Fort, which was triangle wise, having three Bulwarkes, at every corner, like a halfe Moone, and foure or five pieces of Artillerie mounted in them. We had made our selves sufficiently strong for these Savages. We had also sowne most of our Corne on two Mountaines. It sprang a mans height from the ground."

What different fate the future might have held for Jamestown if the ships could only have anchored nearer the shore at "Archer's Hope" is futile conjecture now, but from another account written at the time it becomes clear that the Jamestown terrain was going to prove far from ideal.

"This Iseland . . . is low ground, full of Marches and Swomps, which makes the Aire, expecially in the Sumer, insalubritious and unhelthy: It is not at all replenished with springs of fresh water, and that which they have in their wells, brackish, ill sented, penurious, and not gratefull to the stumack . . ."

It was a foretaste of dissensions that were to follow the landing that Captain Smith, as important a figure as he was in the expedition, arrived at Jamestown in confinement, and remained for several weeks under guard. His leadership, however, was essential to the enterprise, and he was released, with results that he described, among others, in his *Generall Historie*.

"Now we so quietly followed our businesse, that in three moneths wee made three or foure Last of Tarre, Pitch, and Sope ashes; produced a tryall of Glasse; made a Well in the Fort of excellent sweet water, which till then was wanting; built some twentie houses; recovered our Church: provided Nets and Wires for fishing; and to stop the disorders of our disorderly theeues, and the Salvages, built a Blockhouse in the neck of our Isle, kept by a Garrison to entertaine the Salvages trade, and none to passe nor repasse Salvage nor Christian without the presidents order. Thirtie or forty Acres of ground we digged and planted. Of three sowes in eighteene moneths, increased 60 and od Piggs. And neere 500 chickings brought up themselves without having any meat given them: but the Hogs were transported to Hog Isle: where also we built a block-house with a garison to give us notice of any shipping, and for their exercise they made Clapbored and waynscot, and cut downe trees."

After being injured in a gunpowder explosion in the fall of 1609, Smith returned to England, leaving George Percy as Deputy Governor. Due in part to the loss of Smith's leadership the winter that followed was known throughout Jamestown history as the "Starving Time," here described by Percy.

"Now all of us att James Towne beginneinge to feele that sharp pricke of hunger which noe man trewly descrybe butt he which hath Tasted the bitterness thereof A worlde of miseries ensewed as the Sequell will expresse unto you in so mutche thatt some to satisfye their hunger have robbed the store for the which I caused them to be executed. Then haveinge fedd uponn horses and other beastes as long as they Lasted we weare gladd to make shifte with vermine as doggs Catts Ratts and myce All was fishe thatt came to Nett to satisfye Crewell hunger as to eate Bootes shoes or any other leather. . . .

"And now famin begineinge to Looke gastely and pale in every face thatt notheinge was spared to mainteyne Lyfe and to doe those things wich seame incredible. . . .

"To eate many [of] our men this starveing Tyme did Runn away unto the Salvages whome we never heard of after."

It is hardly surprising that the survivors of that disastrous winter were ready by spring to abandon the colony, and they would undoubtedly have done so had Sir Thomas Gates not arrived in May with provisions of a sort in two small boats he had built in Bermuda, where he had been in the wreck of the *Sea Venture*. With him, of course, came William Strachey, whose letter to London about the wrecking was to result in the writing of *The Tempest*.

In describing how Jamestown looked on his arrival, Strachey said he found the palisades torn down, "the portes open, the gates from the hinges, the church ruined and unfrequented, empty howses rent up and burnt, the living not able, as they pretended, to step into the woods to gather other fire-wood; and, it is true, the Indian as fast killing without as the famine and pestilence within."

All in all, it *did* seem better to everybody to abandon the colony, and on June 7 they set sail and started down the James, only to get word somehow that Lord Delaware had arrived at Point Comfort on his way to Jamestown with 150 settlers and plenty of provisions. So hastily returning to the settlement, they were back there waiting when Delaware dropped anchor off the island on the tenth.

Delaware returned to England in March, 1611, and Sir Thomas Dale, a tough military administrator, arrived in May. Among the laws he at once introduced and enforced was one that vividly describes the conditions he was determined to clear up.

"There shall be no man or women, Launderer or Launderesse, dare to wash any uncleane Linnen, drive bucks [wash clothes], or throw out the water or suds of fowle cloathes, in the open streete, within the Pallizades, or within forty foote of the same, nor rench, and make cleane, any kettle, pot, or pan, or such like vessell within twenty foote of the old well, or new Pumpe: nor shall any one aforesaid, within lesse then a quarter of one mile from the Pallizadoes, dare to doe the necessities of nature, since by these unmanly, slothfull, and loathsome immodesties, the whole Fort may bee choaked, and poisoned with ill aires, and so corrupt (as in all reason cannot but much

After carrying six hundred Dames from Richmond to the dedication ceremonies of their memorial church at Jamestown, the steamer Pocahontas stopped at Westover on the return trip for the Dames to be entertained at tea at William Byrd's beautiful old Georgian mansion.

infect the same) and this shall they take notice of, and avoide, upon paine of whipping and further punishment, as shall be thought meete, by the censure of a martial Count. . . .

In April of 1614, in the church at Jamestown, Pocahontas was married to one of the original settlers, John Rolfe, who had done more than any other to develop the successful cultivation of tobacco in the colony, and whose marriage did much to improve relations with the Indians.

In 1616 a new frame church was built, and in 1619 Captain George Yeardly, on a visit to England, was knighted by James I, and appointed the new Governor of Virginia. When he returned in April, he became the first exponent of a new and more liberal governmental policy, espoused in England by the colonies' backers, among them the Earl of Southampton, Shakespeare's great friend.

Soon after his return, Yeardly performed a momentous act by calling for a legislative assembly, which on July 30, 1619, convened in the church at Jamestown, remaining in session until August 4. It was the first example of representative government in America.

This was in one way a red-letter year, for it was decided in London by the Company that the following year in May and June, the first contingents of ninety "young maidens" would arrive to become wives of the settlers (the church becoming the scene of marriage after marriage), and these arrivals were to be followed by more and more young women. According to the minutes of the Company, it was wished that "A fitt hundreth might be sent of woemen, Maides young and uncorrupt to make wifes to the Inhabitantes and by that meanes to make the men there more setled & lesse moveable who by defect thereof (as is credibly reported) stay there but to gett something and then to returne for England, which will breed a dissolucon, and so an overthrow of the Plantacon."

But it was also a black-letter year, for John Rolfe relates in a letter to Sir Edwin Sandys, a director of the Company in London, that about "the latter end of August, a Dutch man of Warr of the burden of a 160 tunes arrived at Point-Comfort, the Comandors name Capt Jope, his Pilott for the West Indies one Mr Marmaduke an Englishman. They mett with the Trer [another ship] in the West Indyes, and determyned to hold consort shipp hetherward, but in their passage lost one the other. He brought not any thing but 20 and odd Negroes, which the Governor and Cape Marchant bought for victualles (Whereof he was in greate need as he pretended) at the best and easyest rates they could."

In a letter from the Governor and Council in Virginia to the royal authorities in England, January 18, 1639, the Royal Governor John Harvey wrote " . . . there are twelve houses and stores built in the Towne, one of brick by the Secretayre, the fairest that ever was knowen in this countrye for substance and uniformitye, by whose example others have undertaken to build framed howses to beautifye the place, consonant to his majesties Instruction that wee should not suffer men to build slight cottages as heretofore.

"Such hath bene our Indeavour herein that out of our owne purses wee have largely contributed to the building of a brick church, and both masters of shipps and others of the ablest Planters have liberally by our persuasion underwritten to this work."

This was presumably the church whose brick tower still stands—the third.

Jamestown had taken the Cromwellian wars, the beheading of Charles I, the Commonwealth Government in England, and the ascension of Charles II all in her stride, but she was being outstriven by the plantation economy which fitted so well the needs of Virginia's further colonization and development. So by 1676, the town economy was not going too well, and considerable feeling was being aroused by Governor Berkeley's seeming unconcern for the needs and protection of the proletarian planters. It was at this point that Nathaniel Bacon, Jr., openly rebelled against the Governor, marched into Jamestown "with his Small tired Body of men," sent the Governor scurrying to the Eastern Shore, and set fire to the town, burning the church, state house, houses, and all. A few weeks later Bacon died a natural death, and Governor Berkeley returned, but it was the beginning of the end to oppressive and unpopular government in Virginia.

The full length portrait of Sir Thomas Dale (artist unknown) is at the Virginia Museum of Fine Arts. George Percy's portrait above, is at the Virginia Historical Society, in a copy by Herbert Luther Smith.

The ancient tower of the first church built upon our soil by Englishmen still stands. Adjoining it the Dames reconstructed the rest of the original 1639 church within whose walls American government began. In 1907 the Dames presented it to the Association for the Preservation of Virginia Antiquities in a ceremony in connection with the Tercentenary Celebration at Jamestown.

The state house and church were rebuilt, and some of the residential town; but when in 1698 it all burned down again, that was the end; it was decided to move everything to Middle Plantation, which is to say, Williamsburg. Archer's Hope, which came so close to being the site of Jamestown, was to become more important than Jamestown as a port for Williamsburg.

Colonial capital and leading town of Virginia for nearly a hundred years, Jamestown as described by Hugh Jones a few years later is solemn and rather sad, "consisting at present but Abundance of Brick Rubbish, and three or four good inhabited Houses . . .," the Governor having "removed the Residence of the *Governor*, with the Meeting of the *General Courts* and *General Assemblies* . . . seven miles from *James Town*, in a healthier and more convenient *Place*, and freer from the Annoyance of *Muskettees*."

At the Seventh Council of the Dames, in 1903, it was decided that the National Society should erect a permanent memorial at Jamestown to celebrate the tercentenary of the first permanent English settlement in America.

Still standing at the Jamestown site was the old church tower, all that remained of the 1640 brick church burned during Bacon's rebellion in 1676. It was suggested by the Association for the Preservation of Virginia Antiquities, which owns the site of the church and the twenty-two acres surrounding it, that the Dames rebuild the church as their memorial. The Dames agreed to this suggestion, and under the guidance of the four authorities[*] best equipped to deal with the archaeological, historical, and architectural problems involved, the ancient church was faithfully reproduced and ready for the presentation ceremony, which was to take place on May 11, 1907, two days before the tercentenary date.

The tower was left untouched, and the foundations of the 1640 church, as well as the earlier one, were carefully preserved and left open to view, under glass, within the memorial structure.

True 17th-century salt-glazed brick of the right size and color, which could never have been imitated, was discovered by the Dames' committee in charge, in the ruins of two brick houses contemporary with the church. And the ruins of the 17th-century Smithfield church, 30 miles down the James, served as the model for the restoration, with its round-arched windows, moulded brick mullions, and corbelled buttresses.

"For several days before the eleventh, Dames from all quarters were arriving in Richmond." And to let one of the Dames who was there go on to describe the expedition: "On the morning of the eleventh, an army of Colonial Dames, six hundred strong boarded the *Pocahontas* and sailed away to old Jamestown. Although the day dawned with lowering skies and some rain, the heavy clouds were soon scattered by fresh winds and the trip down the river, upon whose lovely shores are Shirley, Berkeley, Upper and Lower Brandon, and many another historic country seat, was altogether delightful."

Among the other "historic country seats" was Westover, one of the greatest, the home then of Mrs. William M. Ramsey. Mrs. Ramsey, sometime before, through the Virginia Society, had invited the Dames, on their way back from Jamestown to Richmond, to disembark at the Westover wharf for tea in her house and garden. By prearrangement, a paper on which was written the number of Dames in the party was to be placed in a bottle and tossed overboard as the *Pocahontas* passed Westover on the way down the river in the morning. A boy in a rowboat would be waiting to pick up the bottle and take it to Mrs. Ramsey. Whatever her feelings were when she learned that in a few hours she would be entertaining "an army of Dames six hundred strong," she was a least given that much time to make her preparations.

[*]Samuel H. Yonge, United States Engineer in charge of James River, and author of *The Site of Old Jamestown*; Glenn Brown, of the American Institute Architects in Washington, Edmund M. Wheelwright, architect, of Boston, and William G. Stanard, of Richmond, genealogist and Secretary of the Virginia Historical Society.

A columnist on the old *Outlook* magazine was on hand at the memorial to report the ceremony, and in the *Outlook* he describes the landing of the Dames that day at Jamestown.

"They came up in procession from the small open wharf—first, the Richmond Blues, their high plumed casques tossing in the spring breeze; then a white-robed choir, singing the Jamestown hymn; then the Dames, in line—a notably fine looking body of women. It had a quaint effect as of an old world pilgrimage, full of color and music, as it marched through the handsome wrought iron gates set up at the church entrance two days before, and under the shadow of the old tower, to the grassy open spot set apart for the presentation."

The choir sang the hymn, "O God of Bethel, by whose hand," set to the music of the Elizabethan composer Thomas Tallis, which was followed by a prayer. Then the National President of the Dames, Mrs. William Ruffin Cox, of Virginia, made the presentation of the Memorial to the Association for the Preservation of Virginia Antiquities, and the formal deed of gift was read by General Francis Henry Appleton, of Boston. In the absence of Mrs. Joseph Bryan, President of the Association, Mr. Bryan, acting for his wife, accepted the church "in an eloquent and appropriate address," after which Mrs. Barrett Wendell, Chairman of the Jamestown Memorial Committee, introduced Dr. Thomas Nelson Page, the orator of the day.

"Virginian as I am in every fibre of my being," the doctor declaimed toward the close of his oration, "I declare my belief before the high God that this spot belongs by indefeasible title to all the people of this country, and that there is no power under heaven to defeat their claim."

To the tune of "Old Hundredth," the Dames marched back to the *Pocahontas* and steamed up the James to tea at Westover. Embarking again, for the remainder of the trip to Richmond "the choir entertained the company with a number of part songs, and later with some familiar evening hymns."

The Mayflower, with her shallop sailing alongside, leaving the Provincetown anchorage for Plymouth Harbor. Below, the chart made from the 1614 surveys of the fabulous Captain John Smith, which proved invaluable to the Pilgrims.

THE VOYAGE OF THE MAYFLOWER

The People

William Bradford, historian and principal leader of the Pilgrims
William Brewster, elder and spiritual leader
John Carver, first governor of the colony
Edward Winslow, diplomatic leader
Captain Myles Standish, military leader
Captain Christopher Jones, master of the Mayflower
Captain John Smith, previous visitor to Plymouth

Bradford, Brewster, and Carver were leaders of the famous Scrooby congregation of religious dissenters which in 1607 and 1608 emigrated under horrible circumstances from England to Holland, where they could worship as they wished. After a brief spell in Amsterdam, the group of about 125 moved to Leyden, where they stayed "some eleven or twelve years," and where Winslow joined them sometime before 1617.

When about seventy of the Pilgrims, in July 1620, set sail in the little ship *Speedwell* for Southampton to join the *Mayflower*, a fifth leader, John Robinson, who would have liked to go along, felt it his responsibility to remain with those who preferred to make Holland their home. He died there five years later, and the Pilgrims who stayed gradually became as Dutch as the Dutch.

During the last few years in Leyden the Pilgrims had been debating where to go before the twelve-year truce between the Netherlands and Spain came to an end, and with it possibly also the right to their freedom of worship. Some who had been reading Sir Walter Ralegh's *Discovery of The Large, Rich and Beautiful Empyre of Guiana* "were earnest for . . . some of those fertile places in these hot climates." But in the end it was decided that the climate of Virginia would better "agree with our English bodies"—Virginia then being in English minds virtually the whole of North America.

Various negotiations were undertaken with the Virginia Company in London regarding charters and assurances of religious freedom, none of which achieved any finality; and even the agreement finally made with a group of London merchants, who would "adventure the money" for the voyage over, was still in a state of vagueness when the voyage actually began, with a fantastic series of misadventures at the very outset.

Captain Christopher Jones had brought the *Mayflower*, chartered by the Pilgrims, down from London with about sixty passengers for Virginia; some of them "Saints," as the Puritans called themselves, and the rest "Strangers," as the Puritans called everyone else.

When the *Speedwell*, which was to be the *Mayflower's* consort, tied up alongside on July 26, a redistribution of people from one ship to another gave the *Mayflower* ninety passengers and left the *Speedwell* with thirty. What with one thing and another, mostly retrimming the *Speedwell*, trying to overcome her leakiness, it was August 5 before the two ships started off.

All went well for five days, after which the *Speedwell* was found to be leaking so badly that both ships put into Dartmouth harbor, where the *Speedwell* was thoroughly overhauled at a cost of twelve days' time. Then off again. Four days later the *Speedwell* was again taking on water, and it was decided to put into Plymouth, send the *Speedwell* back to London with some eighteen or twenty of her passengers who had had enough, and take the dozen or so others onto the *Mayflower* with part of the *Speedwell's* cargo. By the time this was all accomplished it was September 6, just a month since the Southampton departure. And now, with about a hundred men, women, and children aboard, and a fine gale of wind, Captain Jones sailed out of Plymouth roadstead and set his course for the "northern coasts of Virginia."

Jones had been master and part owner of the *Mayflower* for several years. His vessel was about twelve years old, and was 90 feet in length with a beam of 26. She was known as a "sweet ship," meaning that the usual filth of a ship's bilges was in the case of the *Mayflower* somewhat neutralized by the seepage from the casks she carried when she was in the wine trade. It has been suggested that this "sweetness" may have accounted for the lack of sickness among the ship's company on the voyage.

Except for the death of a seaman and his burial at sea, the first half of the voyage, considering everything, was comparatively uneventful, providing a good opportunity to get a glimpse of the principal passengers.

The most important was William Bradford, who brought his wife Dorothy with him, and one child; a son followed along later. Bradford was born in Yorkshire in 1590. As a child he was trained as a farmer. At twelve he took to the Bible with such fervor that, in spite of his youth, he joined a group of Puritans who met for prayer and discussion at the home of William Brewster in the nearby village of Scrooby. The congregation that grew out of these meetings, held in secret, became his life. His history, *Of Plymouth Plantation*, which he wrote between 1630 and 1650, has been called by Samuel E. Morison one of the greatest books of the 17th century, critics ranking his name "little lower than those of Milton, Bunyan and of King James' translators of the Bible.

Next in importance, taken from a listing made by Bradford in 1647 and 1648, were "Mr. Edward Winslow, Elizabeth his wife and two menservants called George Soule and Elias Story; also a little girl was put to him called Ellen, the sister of Richard More." To this Bradford adds, "Mr. Edward Winslow his wife died the first winter, and he married with the widow of Mr. White and hath two children living by her, marriageable, besides sundry that are dead."

Winslow was born in 1595 in Worcestershire. In Leyden he was associated with William Brewster's printing establishment. In the colony he was the principal negotiator, not only with the Indians but with the Company back home in England. He knew the wilderness better than anyone else in the colony, and in 1632 was apparently the first Englishman to visit Connecticut.

Again from Bradford's list: "Mr. John Carver, Katherine his wife, Desire Minter, and two man servants, John Howland, Roger Wilder, William Latham, a boy, and a maidservant and a child that was put to him called Jasper More." Adding: "Mr. Carver and his wife died the first year, he in the spring, she in the summer. Also his man Roger and the little boy Jasper died before either of them, of the common infection. Desire Minter returned to her friend and proved not very well and died in England. His servant boy Latham, after more than twenty years stay in the country, went into England and from thence to the Bahama Islands in the West Indies; and there with some others was starved for want of food. His servant John Howland (who in a storm on the voyage fell overboard from the Mayflower, but miraculously catching a length of rigging hanging from a yardarm, was hauled back on board) married the daughter of John Tilley, Elizabeth, and they are both now living and have ten children, now all living, and their eldest daughter hath four children: and their second daughter one, all living, and other of their children marriageable. So fifteen are come of them."

Born in 1576, John Carver was one of the oldest of the Pilgrims and the only one who was really well-to-do. A London merchant, he came to Leyden about 1610. He was the chief organizer of the London contingent which came to Southampton on the *Mayflower*. He was the charterer of the *Mayflower*, and the first Governor of the colony.

Still again from Bradford's listing, which in its entirety is a capsule personal chronicle of the colony, we have "Mr. William Brewster, Mary, his wife, with two sons whose names were Love and Wrestling. And a boy was put to him called Richard More, and another of his brothers. The rest of his children were left behind and came over afterwards. Mr Brewster," Bradford goes on to say, "lived to a very old age: about 80 years he was when he died, having lived some 23 or 24 years here in this country. And though his wife died long before, yet she died aged. His son Wrestling died a young man unmarried. His son Love lived till this year 1650 and died and left four children, now living."

Nine years older than Carver, Brewster was briefly at Cambridge, was the chief member of the Scrooby congregation, and in Leyden printed a number of religious books and tracts. The sole religious leader of the colony until 1629, he was never ordained, so confined his ministry to services of prayer and praise only.

"Captain Myles Standish and Rose his wife . . . his wife died in the first sickness and he married again and hath four sons living and some are dead."

Standish was born about 1584 in Lancashire, became a soldier of fortune, and was engaged by the Pilgrims to be their military leader. Though they would have called him a "Stranger," he became one of the most useful and loyal members of the colony. He died in 1656.

"John Alden was hired for a cooper at Southampton where the ship was victualed, and being a hopeful young man was much desired but left to his own liking to go or stay when he came here; but he stayed and married here."

"Mr. Mullins and his wife, his sons and his servant died the first winter. Only his daughter Priscilla survived, and married with John Alden; who are both living and have eleven children. And their eldest daughter is married and hath five children."

A man who would have liked to come along, if the Pilgrims had met his terms, was Captain John Smith. In 1614 he had already been where they were going to end up. He had charted the coast line, and given the whole region the name of New England. But as he said, it was cheaper for the Pilgrims to purchase his map than hire his person. And how he would have got along with their "ostentatious godliness" is another matter. These Puritans were not like the Jamestown crowd.

Halfway across the Atlantic the *Mayflower* encountered a succession of heavy gales, and the discomforts of a cold, wet, overcrowded ship kept the passengers and crew alike in a constant state of misery. In the midst of all this, Elizabeth, the wife of Stephen Hopkins, gave birth to a son they called Oceanus, who became a seaman and died in Barbados.

Finally, on November 10, came the cry of "Land Ho!" from the lookout, and soon it was possible in the dawn's early light to see the Cape Cod sand cliffs a little below where Wellfleet is today.

The granite canopy, designed by McKim, Mead & White, to protect Plymouth Rock, and presented by the National Society of the Dames to the State of Massachusetts, commemorating the third centennial of the landing from the Mayflower.

If, as was likely, Captain Jones had been heading for the mouth of "Hudson's River," his land-fall was only 45 miles off course, which wasn't too bad, considering the kind of navigational equipment and geographical knowledge available in the early 1600's. And the fact that he immediately turned southward would indicate that the Hudson was his target. It is fascinating to contemplate the consequences if Jones had hit it. For according to Bradford's account it was also the Pilgrim's intention "to find some place about Hudson's River for their habitation." But the shoals and breakers and adverse winds off Monomoy, on the lower tip of the Cape, with which the *Mayflower* met up in midafternoon, left all those intriguing consequences in the realm of conjecture once and for all.

As Bradford says, considering "the dangerous shoals and roaring breakers . . . and the wind shrinking upon them withal, they resolved to bear up again for the Cape and thought themselves happy to get out of those dangers before night overtook them, as by God's good providence they did. And the next day they got into the Cape Harbor where they rid in safety."

This was November 11, sixty-five days out of Plymouth, and, in view of the season, a very good passage. But it was to be a month to the day before a little boat called a shallop, brought over on the *Mayflower* and now carrying a party from the ship, led by Bradford and Standish, was to land on the Rock.

It was a month of getting the dismantled shallop ashore and putting it together; a month of explorations, on foot, by long boat, and by shallop, looking for a site on which to settle; a month of unaccustomed cold and bleakness, of sickness and death. One death was the probable suicide by drowning of Dorothy Bradford while her husband, the historian, was away on the last expedition, which led to the landing. It was also a month in which Francis Billington, the bad boy of the Pilgrim band, came close to blowing up the *Mayflower* by shooting off a musket right next to an open barrel of gunpowder in his father's cabin.

After landing from the shallop on the 11th of December and looking around, the party decided they had found the most suitable site, and returned in the shallop to the *Mayflower*, still at anchor in what is now Provincetown Harbor. Here the Pilgrims heard of the place, named Plimouth by Captain Smith in 1614, which was going to be their home. And Bradford heard of Dorothy's drowning. He doesn't say a word about it in his history, but goes right on to describe the next move.

"On the fifteenth of December they weighed anchor to go to the place they had discovered, and . . . on the sixteenth day . . . they arrived safe in the harbor. And afterwards took better view of the place, and resolved where to pitch their dwelling; and the twenty-fifth day began to erect the first house for common use to receive them and their goods." The rest is many-times-told history.

If Bradford, or anybody, had even mentioned the Rock in their writings at the time, it would have saved historians and others a lot of trouble. But just as the Pilgrims, from the very real records they have left of their accomplishments, are a symbol of the ideas and doings they have come to typify, now, after centuries of hearsay, backed by some pretty sound circumstantial evidence, the Rock has become a symbol too. It would be very difficult to dislodge it from the hold it has on people's minds.

Over the years the physical Rock has had to take a lot of pushing around from place to place. But at last it lies about where it did in Pilgrim days, now flanked by a heavy granite seawall and fronted by a strong steel grating which together protect it from the action of the sea, yet allow the waves to wash around it. From above it is looked at by hundreds of thousands of people a year though a large rectangular railed-in opening. The paved platform around the opening is surmounted by a classical granite canopy supported by 16 monolithic columns of granite, creating an edifice 34 feet long, 18 feet wide, and more than 25 feet high. In itself the canopy is a promise of the Rock's permanence as a symbol of the Pilgrims' devotion to the self-government for which they lived and died. Designed for the Dames by McKim, Mead and White, it was placed there by the Dames and presented by them to the State of Massachusetts to commemorate the three-hundredth anniversary of the landing of the Pilgrims.

The canopy was dedicated November 29, 1921, on a day for which William Bradford had written a description three hundred years before when he said, "They that know the winters of that country know them to be sharp and violent, and subject to cruel and fierce storms." The storm that day was so "cruel and fierce," that instead of dedicating the canopy at the site, the ceremonies were held in the First Parish Church.

Moored near the Rock is the replica of the *Mayflower*, built in England and sailed here along the route of the original voyage. Nearby are two reconstructions of the first Pilgrim houses, and two miles away is a remarkable reconstruction of the Pilgrim village, complete with Pilgrim activities, all a carefully researched project called Plimouth Plantation. Though the Pilgrims didn't celebrate Christmas Day, that is the best season of the year to see what the weather was like when they landed.

II

THE QUINCY HOMESTEAD STORY

The People

Edmund Quincy I, the Emigrant
Edmund Quincy II, the Colonel
Edmund Quincy III, the Judge
Edmund Quincy IV, the Squire
Dorothy Quincy, "Dorothy Q,"
    Edmund III's daughter
Dorothy Quincy, "Miss Dolly,"
    Edmund IV's daughter
Captain Francis Goelet, a visitor in Boston
John Hancock, patriot, first Signer
Henry Flynt, Harvard tutor

The Copley portrait of Dorothy Quincy Hancock.

Edmund I, whose descendants, by their style, their patriotic, political, and social graces, and often by the beauty of their women, left their mark on American history, was born in 1602 in England, where he married Judith Pares in 1623, had a daughter Judith in 1626, and had a son Edmund II in 1627. In 1633 the four of them, with five servants, came to Boston on the *Griffin*. Already by 1634 Edmund was representing Boston on the First Colonial Court, and through 1637 was active on various town committees.

In 1636 he and his close friend, the courageous William Coddington, were given grants of five hundred adjoining acres each at Mount Wollaston. These became the site of Braintree in 1640, and of Quincy in 1792.

For many years it was supposed that a farmhouse Coddington built on his property was the nucleus, seventy years later, of the present Quincy homestead, built in 1706 by Edmund Quincy III. As of 1965, this had not been certified. Nor is it known whether the first Edmund built anything on his five hundred acres before he died, nor even exactly when he died, though it was sometime in the late thirties or early forties.

As a Puritan rebel, Coddington sold his farm in 1638, and with Anne Hutchinson followed Roger Williams to Rhode Island when Anne was banished from Massachusetts Bay for preaching that faith alone was necessary for salvation—and there he founded the town of Newport.

Edmund II then occupied the family property and in 1648 married Joanna Hoar, whose brother was the third president of Harvard. Edmund became a colonel in the local militia and "one of the three richest men in Braintree." When Joanna died in May 1680, he married Elizabeth Eliot, the widowed daughter-in-law of John Eliot, called Apostle to the Indians, who translated into the Algonquin Indian language the first Bible printed in this country.

Five years later, Judge Samuel Sewall wrote in his famous diary: "Lodged in Lower Room of Unckle Quinsey's new house," and in 1697, when Colonel Edmund died, Sewall called him "a true New England man & one of our best friends." Whatever happened to Uncle Quincy's house nobody knows. Archaeological research may prove it to be the one onto which the colonel's son built his own.

31

The Quincy Homestead in Quincy, Massachusetts, stands today as the most fitting memento possible of a truly distinguished early American family. Surrounded now by a bustling city, it leads a charming existence in the protection of its little park and the wise and watchful ministrations of the Massachusetts Dames. In the Quincy parlor, with its wondrous imported post-colonial wallpaper, the three tables are in the Queen Anne style. The card table at the right has extended corners for wine glasses and candlesticks and recesses in the top for gambling money. The one at the left has an unusual serpentine top. The drop-leaf tea table is between a pair of the parlor's set of Chippendale style chairs. An outstanding feature of the room's outstanding furniture is the mid-18th-century mahogany secretary bearing the signature of I. Winslow. It has a series of secret compartments—small boxes behind the central cupboard of the desk section; the whole piece in unusually good condition. At the far end of the room, a very early spinet, with baluster legs. The simplicity of the comfortable old kitchen, like the study of Tutor Flynt above it, makes a charming contrast to the fine stylishness with which the rest of the house is furnished, upstairs and down.

In any event, when Edmund III, the judge-to-be, was 24, in 1706, a handsome house did begin to make its appearance on the property. It still stands, the point and purpose of this story; though it is almost certainly more of a house now than it was when it was built. Edmund was seven years out of Harvard, and had been five years married to Dorothy Flynt, when he arranged with a man named John Marshal to start construction. Marshal, in his way, was also a diarist. "We raised Mr. Quinzey's house," he wrote for June 14. On July 29, "I layed the foundation of Mr. Quinzey's chimnies," and on August 17 he was "colouring the pedements at Mr. Quinzey's most part of day."

Edmund's son, Edmund IV, was born four years before the house was built, and a daughter, Elizabeth, in 1706. The first child born in the homestead was Dorothy, whose portrait, painted when she was "thirteen summers, or something less," with "girlish bust" and "lips that lover has never kissed," inspired her great-grandson, Oliver Wendell Holmes, to write, in 1871 at sixty-two, one of his most popular poems, "Dorothy Q." The portrait having been slit by a British officer's sword, Holmes wrote, "I will heal the stab of the Red-Coat's blade, / And freshen the gold of the tarnished frame, / And gild with a rhyme your household name."

From the poem, which asks the question: "Shall I bless you, Dorothy, or forgive / For the tender whisper that bade me live?", these two stanzas portray the poet's concern with his birthright.

> O Damsel Dorothy! Dorothy Q.!
> Strange is the gift that I owe to you;
> Such a gift as never a king
> Save to daughter or son might bring, —
> All my tenure of heart and hand,
> All my title to house and land;
> Mother and sister and child and wife
> And joy and sorrow and death and life!
>
> What if a hundred years ago
> Those close-shut lips had answered No,
> When forth the tremulous question came
> That cost the maiden her Norman name,
> And under the folds that look so still
> The bodice swelled with the bosom's thrill?
> Should I be I, or would it be
> One tenth another, to nine tenths me?

In April of 1725, Sewall set down in his diary that "Mr. Colman married Mr. Edmund Quincey of Boston and Miss Elizabeth Wendell of New York. The parents of the Bridegroom & Bride were present: I and my wife, Dan Oliver Esq. and his wife, Mr. Cooper and many more were present . . . I set out for Plimouth with Mr. Sam Mather, dined at Col. [Josiah] Quincey's with the Weddingers."

Shortly after, the couple took a town house in Boston where Edmund, his brother Josiah, and their brother-in-law Edward Jackson, who had married Dorothy Q., became partners in shipping enterprises which in 1748 brought them a bonanza when one of their merchantmen captured a prize that netted the partners 300,000 pounds.

The Quincy-Jackson ship *Bethell*, "14 guns, 37 men and boys, off the Isle St. Marys in Lat 30° N," in dead of night, met up with the Spanish privateer *Jesus, Maria & Joseph*, with 26 guns and 110 men. The smaller *Bethell* poked out "Quaker" guns made of logs, lined the deck with dummies to make her seem much larger in the dark, then steered straight for the Spaniard, calling on her to surrender, which she did without a shot.

Boarding her, the Boston men imprisoned the captives and sailed the prize home. One hundred and sixty-one chests of silver, two of gold, a cargo of cochineal, and a lot besides. In Boston the *Bethell* crew, brandishing their pistols and cutlasses, escorted their booty through cheering crowds to Josiah's wine cellar for safekeeping. There they returned two chests of silver to save face for the Spanish captain, who promptly gave a big party for his captors.

When the partners divided the spoils, Josiah and Jackson retired, whereas Edmund invested his portion in a venture with two of his sons, which in a few years left him high and dry, and faced with the necessity in 1755 of selling the homestead. Fortunately, Dorothy's husband bought it, "to keep it in the family," and it remained the Quincys' home, with Edmund IV in residence, until Dorothy's death in 1762, when it was sold, out of the family, to a Boston baker.

Yet the thirty-seven years from Edmund's marriage to the family's final departure from the homestead were generally happy and often very gay. Of the nine children, the five daughters in the 1750's were growing into womanhood. Elizabeth married Samuel Sewall, a grandson of the diarist. Esther married another Sewall; Sarah married a Greenleaf; and Dorothy, the baby, "Miss Dolly," who became a famous colonial flirt, married John Hancock; while the lovely Catherine never married.

Long afterward, one day in 1822, when John Adams, who lived nearby, walked past the homestead with the daughter of Josiah Quincy (the Quincy who for so many years was president of Harvard), the second President of the United States said to Miss Quincy, "Sixty years ago, I used to visit the family of your name who resided here . . . Mrs. Sewall, Mrs. Hancock and their sisters were then unmarried, and more beautiful women I have never seen in Europe or America."

It was about the time of which Adams was speaking that Captain Goelet, a young, rich, and roistering New York merchant and ship owner, was keeping Boston up until three, four, and five in the morning while one of his ships was being readied to take him to London. No matter how late the party at night, he was always ready for another the next morning, such as driving one of the Wendell girls in a chaise to a Cambridge inn for an early afternoon "turtle frolic," attended by about twenty couples, among whom were Catherine and Sarah Quincy. He tells in his journal of playing the harpsichord with the Quincy girls, and of going down to the homestead for a "feast of fish."

"The country house is a neat building," he writes, "and finely accommodated for company, with a fine hall and large rooms. About ten yards from the house is a beautiful canal, which is supplied by a brook well stocked with silver eels." [This was "Mr. Quinzeys mill dam" that Mr. Marshal was writing about in his diary in March 1710: "Both days very cold I wrought at Mr. Quinzey's dam."] Fifty years later Captain Goelet and the Quincy girls caught "a parcel of eels and had them dressed for supper . . . The house has a beautiful pleasure garden adjoining it," Goelet goes on to on to say, "and on the back is a beautiful orchard with fine fruit trees."

The Captain doesn't mention either the oldest or the youngest members of the homestead household, the two most important. The former was tutor Henry Flynt, the brother of Edmund's wife Dorothy, who stayed at the house so much of the time that a bedroom and study were built on especially for him. Born in 1675, he graduated from Harvard in 1693, and died in 1760. A tutor at Harvard (what would be called a don or a fellow at Oxford or Cambridge), and sometimes called Father Flynt, he was a college character there for more than fifty years.

When the college was closed, he would get jobs like negotiating treaties with the Indians, but was "always back at college when first bell rang at end of summer vacation," according to one of his colleagues. In Sibley's *Harvard Graduates* it is related how in the old days whenever two or three Harvard men got together, stories were told of Father Flynt, his hospitality and parsimony, quick temper, warm heart, ripe learning, antique manners, and ancient phrases. In appearance he was "rather short and thickset."

While holding a class in his chamber one morning, he happened to glance in a mirror and behind him saw one of his students lift a keg of wine from a table and "take a satisfying drink from the bung hole . . . I thought," said Tutor Flynt, "I would not disturb him while drinking, but as soon as he had done, I turned around and told him he at least ought to have the manners to have drunk to somebody."

The boys were always playing tricks on him, like leaving a snake in his room, but "he was always the one to plead for offenders in faculty meeting, saying that 'wild colts often make good horses.'"

To the students of a graduating class who wanted to leave him something as a sign of their admiration, he said he was single, had a well-filled library, and needed nothing. So they had a solid silver chamber pot made, "of the appropriate dimensions," and in a fine red morocco case they presented it to Tutor Flynt on the morning of Commencement Day. He kept it in his room at Quincy, but when the family moved out in 1762, two years after his death at the homestead, it was taken to Boston, where it disappeared during the Revolution. Somewhere in England today, no doubt.

The baby of the household was born in the Boston town house in 1747, the year before the *Bethell* incident. This Dorothy is nowadays often confused with her aunt, "Dorothy Q." of the poem. In her lifetime she was always Miss Dolly or Dolly, and, having grown up in a household famous for its flirtations, it is hardly surprising that Dolly was already quite a coquette by the time she was twelve, although much too young to have been at the party at her Uncle Josiah's just before his house burned down—a party described by John Adams in his diary when he was twenty-two.

"Here are two nights and one day and a half spent in a softening, enervating, dissipating series of hustling, prattling, poetry, love, courtship, marriage. During all this time I was reduced into the course of unmanly pleasures . . . forgetful of the glorious promises of fame, immortality, and a good conscience." This was five years before John married Abigail Smith, who was only fifteen at the time of the two nights John spent at the party.

When the Quincys in 1763 left the homestead for the last time, they went to live in Boston, where the next year Dolly met John Hancock for the first time. Five years later Edmund's wife Dorothy died and Dolly went to live with Aunt Lydia, Hancock's foster mother, who became the chaperone and encourager of the courtship. This began about 1771, for in a letter that year from Samuel Salisbury to his brother Stephen, the town gossip related, "'Tis said that John Hancock courts Dolly Quincy. 'Tis certain he visits her and has company in private every evening."

The wedding didn't take place for four more years—years when the nation was rapidly rushing into the Revolution. But in August 1775, that tumultuous time, Dolly and John were married, not in Boston, or Quincy, or in Massachusetts at all, but at the home of John's friend Thaddeus Burr in Fairfield, Connecticut. Dolly's father, who had just fled Boston with his unmarried daughter Catherine to his married daughter Sarah Greenleaf's home in Lancaster, Massachusetts, couldn't make the long trip to give his Dolly away in Fairfield. But the married couple together wrote to him of their plans: two days in Fairfield, then by way of New York to Philadelphia for the opening of Congress.

In 1780 Edmund IV was back in Boston with his daughter-in-law, living on what is now the corner of Pie Alley and Washington Street. The family financed a dry-goods store for him, which he ran with little success. In 1785, at eighty-two, Edmund remarried, and in 1788 he died.

At the homestead in Quincy, the brook is gone now, and the "beautiful canal," and of course with them the silver eels, but the house still stands in its little park of trees, looking as handsome as it looked to Captain Goulet back in those entertaining times. In custody of the Massachusetts Dames, who maintain and furnish it in true Quincy style, it is there for anyone to enjoy inside and out.

In a simplicity characteristic of the owner, the house stands on its steep hillside site where it has come to rest. On the downhill side is an authentic 18th-century parterre garden executed by the Dirt Gardeners of Providence from a plan made and given to the house by the late Alden Hopkins, resident landscape architect of Colonial Williamsburg, and a direct descendant of the Hopkins family. Stephen Hopkins is quoted on the sundial: "A garden that might comfort yield"' and the peonies, mock orange and centifolia roses in the pictures that follow are from this garden.

THE HOPKINS HOUSE STORY

The People

Stephen Hopkins, statesman, politician, patriot
Samuel Ward, Hopkins' political rival

Providence ("God's merciful providence") was settled and given its name in 1636 by Roger Williams, after his banishment from Massachusetts. He was followed there by William Coddington, but the two men failed to hit it off together. Coddington went on to purchase the island of Aquidneck from the Narragansetts, and to found the the settlement of Portsmouth in 1638, and Newport a year later.

The religious freedom inaugurated by Williams, which made the colony of Rhode Island stand out in this respect from all the others, also encouraged her citizens to place a very high value on their liberties, and they were looked upon by the people of the neighboring colonies as a contentious lot. As a result of all this, Rhode Island was never admitted to the New England Confederation. And as a side result, considerable strife developed within the colony itself from time to time.

The rivalry that grew up between the joint capitals of Newport and Providence, as the latter began to surge ahead in importance and power, flamed for almost thirteen years, from 1755 to 1768, into one of the bitterest political feuds in colonial history. The man who played the leading role was Stephen Hopkins, who had just been elected Governor for the first time.

In the keeping room, the curly maple counting desk whose fan doors with the carved "full sun" pattern help to make it a remarkable piece, is about 1725-1740 and is on loan from the Rhode Island School of Design. The flintlock blunderbuss above the fireplace is marked "Tower." The armchair is an early American slat-back with rush seat and "sausage" stretchers.

In 1742, Hopkins had bought the little side-hill house at Town Street and Bank Lane, now South Main and Hopkins, which had been built in 1707 (the year he had been born), and which he enlarged to its present size the year after he bought it. He had married Sarah Scott in 1726, when he was nineteen; of their two daughters and five sons, one daughter and one son died early. Of the three sons who went to sea, John died of smallpox in Spain, Silvanus was tortured to death by the Indians, and George was captain of a ship that sailed out of Charleston, South Carolina, the year before the Revolution, and was never heard from again. The other daughter Lydia married a Captain Tillinghast of Newport, so only the surviving son Rufus carried on the name of Hopkins. The loss of three sailor sons in a single year hastened Sarah's death, and later Hopkins married Miss Anne Smith, a Quaker, whereupon he formally joined the Society of Friends.

Self-educated, he became one of the most enlightened and looked-up-to men of his day. He was the leading contributor to the creation of the public library that is now the Providence Athenaeum. He was the Chief Justice of the Superior Court and the first Chancellor of Brown University, a position he held for life. He was ten times Governor of Rhode Island, a member of the First and Second Continental Congresses, and a signer of the Declaration of Independence—which act he performed when he was afflicted with palsy. "My hand trembles," he said, "but my heart does not."

George Washington once stopped by unannounced to pay his respects, causing the neighbors to hurry to Hopkins' stepdaughter, who kept house, to offer their fine linen, china, and silver for the occasion. "Thank you," she told them, "but what is good enough for my father is good enough for George Washington."

For a man of such high qualities, achievements, and esteem, he was able to employ on a rough-and-tumble political level the contentiousness that was said to characterize the colony. This he did to an extraordinary degree in the famous long feud with Samuel Ward. And to get as close to the conflict as possible, here is how it was summed up on the spot in 1768 in the Newport *Mer-*

38

As a leading authority on colonial houses has enthused, "The shell cupboard over the fireplace in the parlor is distinctive of Rhode Island and is a superlative accomplishment in interior design." The two Queen Anne chairs beside the drop-leaf table belonged to Stephen Hopkins as did mahogany mirror with gold leaf beading around the old bevelled glass. This piece is also Queen Anne.

cury, in that periodical's "Review of the Politics of Rhode Island for the last Ten Years".

"The rival candidates for Governor, Messrs. Samuel Ward and Stephen Hopkins, each entered the field of political opposition as early as the year 1758, at which time Hopkins was Governor. Ward came up as his opposing candidate, and had for his support, the southern interest, principally; he was the candidate of the aristocracy, at the head of which, stood Newport; and Hopkins was as warmly supported by the democracy, at the head of which stood the town of Providence. Hopkins obtained his re-election, and was again re-elected in the year 1759-60 and '61. Ward succeeded in 1762, and Hopkins in 1763.

Finally in the spring of 1767, when Governor Hopkins was elected by a larger majority than ever before, he proposed that henceforth Ward nominate a man for governor from the Hopkins party and Hopkins a candidate for Deputy Governor from the friends of Ward, thus providing a union of the two parties—a compromise that was accepted. Political peace was established. The two men shook hands, became friends, and were later chosen together as delegates to the Continental Congress.

Hopkins, on top of everything else, had great business acumen and figured importantly with the three Brown brothers, Nicholas, John, and Moses, who were the financial, mercantile, and industrial hierarchy of the colony. In the spring of 1769 he collaborated with the brothers and others in an elaborate scientific observation of the Transit of Venus, indicating a strong inclination on his part to scientific activities. All in all an extraordinary man.

His house is now owned by the State, but has been placed in the custody of the Rhode Island Dames, who use it as their headquarters and maintain it as a museum filled with furnishings of historic value and interest, as the pictures and captions make clear.

On the downhill side of the house is a delightful 17th-century parterre garden designed by the late Alden Hopkins, who was resident landscape architect of Colonial Williamsburg and a direct descendant of the Governor.

THE FORT CONDE-CHARLOTTE HOUSE STORY

The People

Jean Baptiste le Moyne, sieur de Bienville, French colonizer
General James Wilkinson, soldier, intriguer
Jonathan Kirkbridge, builder

A passer-by with any knowledge of period styles would place this house in the 1850's. But that is only the way it is dressed. For while the clothes it is wearing were put on in 1854, when it became the residence, there on Theatre Street in Mobile, of a man named Jonathan Kirkbride, its ante-bellum costume covers the remarkable remains of what was originally a French military magazine for the storage of arms and ammunition—dated about 1715.

It was built within the stockaded enclosure of Bienville's early Fort Louis de la Mobile of 1711. Still earlier, in 1702, Bienville had built, at the mouth of the Dog River, the first Fort Louis, but when this flooded out he built a second one here on safer land where modern Mobile now stands. This second fort of log stockades was put up for temporary protection until a proper masonry fort could be built alongside. When that great bastioned affair of solid brick was finished and named Fort Condé after the celebrated general, Prince de Condé, the stockades were undoubtedly taken down, leaving the brick and timber magazine standing just outside the new fortification which would certainly have its own magazine within.

This original magazine was heavily built of odd-sized brick and whipsawn timbers still visible in the structure's present incarnation. The house has never had a cellar, due to the fact that its old brick floor is two feet thick. At some point after its magazine days, it was fitted with cells and otherwise altered as necessary to become a jail for civilian offenders, and so it remained through the English take-over after 1763, when the name Fort Condé was changed to Fort Charlotte after the consort of George III, who bore her husband fifteen children. And so it remained, supposedly, through the Spanish occupation from 1780 to 1813 when General Wilkinson seized the fort and the town of Mobile for the United States.

It took from 1821 to 1823 to tear down the fort. All that Mobile brick and oyster-shell lime mortar! But the old magazine-jail was left standing. At least it could be used; the fort was just in the way of the growing city. Then shortly after the fort had been demolished, a contractor from Vermont, named Peter Hobart, bought the magazine, and while the records are not clear, he either made it over into a court house or a dwelling for himself—maybe both. At any rate, he held it until 1854, when Kirkbride bought it and remodeled it in the image of that time and that place.

When the Alabama Dames bought the Kirkbride house in 1957, they decided to do a French room in Empire, and English room in the style of Chippendale, an American room of the period 1813-1825, and a Confederate room with furnishings that would have been in a Southern parlor at the outbreak of the Civil War.

To make the house even more a museum, a special museum room was prepared in which a section of the old brick floor can be seen, laid up in its oyster-shell lime mortar, and a model of Bienville's old Fort Louis de la Mobile, constructed from the original French drawings.

Houses sometimes have history thrust upon them.

The Fort Condé-Charlotte House stands on colonial fortifications which are some two hundred and fifty years old. Its interiors have been magnificently restored and refurnished by the Alabama Dames. The portrait on the right-hand wall is of Marine Lt. Thomas Richer Swift, painted about 1810 by John Wesley Jarvis.

41

In the center of the Hanover House drawing room, on the antique Chinese rug, the walnut tea table is Queen Anne, and the two rush-seat ladder-back chairs, black with gold trim, are William and Mary, as is the fine English marquetry chair at the far right. Next to it is an early 18th-century concertina card table with a William and Mary brass candle holder, and above it an English Queen Anne mirror in burl walnut veneer with gilt gesso trim. The slat-back fireside chair, black with gold trim, is William and Mary. The crewelwork curtains were designed in the French manner especially for this Huguenot house, and executed by members of the Spartanburg Dames. What saved the house from destruction on its original site on the Santee River when that land was about to be flooded, was the report to the U.S. Department of the Interior made by the late Thomas T. Waterman, architect and historian. "Hanover," he said, "is the only house in the proposed region of inundation the loss of which can be considered of national importance."

42

THE HANOVER HOUSE STORY

The People

Pierre de St. Julien, Huguenot emigrant from Vitre, France
René Ravenel, an old friend and fellow emigrant from Vitre
Paul de St. Julien, grandson of Pierre and builder of Hanover
Mary Amy Ravenel, granddaughter of René and wife of Paul
Mary de St. Julien, daughter of the St. Juliens
Henry Ravenel, "Henry of Hanover," great-grandson of René and second owner of
   Hanover
Stephen Ravenel, son of Henry, third owner
Daniel James Ravenel, brother of Stephen, fourth owner
Henry Le Noble Stevens, grandnephew of Daniel, fifth owner
Henrietta S. Gaillard, Henry's wife

When Louis XIV in 1685 revoked the Edict of Nantes, French Protestants were forbidden to leave the country; an order that was obviously impossible to enforce. And although the King promised them the right of free worship and freedom from molestation, he had no intention of keeping his word. Instead he instituted a sly system of persecutions and indignities, and the Huguenots, who were the Calvinist Protestants of France, became the principal victims. The form of harassment most repugnant to the Huguenots was the *dragonnade*—the enforced billeting of the roughest soldiers, especially the rowdy dragoons, in the Huguenot homes, and the condoning of their misconduct.

The King's idea, or that of his advisers, was that these tactics would cause mass conversions to Catholicism. What they caused instead was the mass emigration of Huguenots, so that entire cities and regions were depopulated and ruined. It was one of the worst of the King's many mistakes. The Huguenots fled principally to the Protestant German states, to England, and to the British colonies in America—mostly to the Carolinas and to Pennsylvania and New York.

Among the most prominent Huguenots who came to the Carolinas in 1686, right after the revocation, were the families of Pierre de St. Julien and René Ravenel. It was Pierre's grandson Paul, who in 1716 began to build the house called Hanover. This was to honor the House of Hanover, always friendly to the Huguenots, which began that same year, in the person of George I, its rule of England, though George ruled from the Principality of Hanover and never learned to speak English.

In 1663 Charles II had granted to eight Lords Proprietor, led by Sir John Colleton, Sir William Berkeley, and Sir Anthony Ashley Cooper, later Earl of Shaftesbury, the whole region between 31° and 33° north (roughly from Florida to a little north of Charleston) and extending "westward to the South Seas." Charleston had been settled where the Ashley and Cooper rivers come together six years before the St. Juliens and Ravenels arrived, and almost at once Pierre received from the Proprietors a grant of three 1,000-acre tracts of land on the west branch of the Cooper, a region now covered by the waters of Lake Moultrie, part of a large hydroelectric scheme. It was on one of these 1000-acre tracts that in 1716 the Paul de St. Juliens began building their house.

The first kiln-load of bricks that Paul processed would have been enough to build the house the way he'd planned—brick up to the second floor—but he made the basement walls so thick that before he had even reached the first floor he had used up the whole batch. As Henry Ravenel, the chronicler, remarks in *Ravenel Records*, "the cellar walls and cross walls are thick enough to hold up a small Eiffel Tower." And by the time he had finished the foundations and built the chimneys, he had found it necessary to process two more full kiln-loads. So he gave up the idea of brick to the second floor and settled for frame.

It is not a large house as great Carolina plantation houses go, but it is a lot larger within than it looks from without. Undoubtedly this is due to the two king-size chimneys at either end, which dwarf the house in between; and undoubtedly too the house was built in between after the chimneys were up.

This repeated setting-up of the kiln made the building of the house an interminable operation, what with the primitive methods employed in getting out the boards and framing timbers. All the lumber had to be whipsawed under the old saw-pit process: a team of two men to a saw, one in the pit and one above on a trestle spanning the pit. Two hundred feet of boarding a day was about the best a team could turn out. One of the finishing touches to the exterior was a plaster collar just under the crown of each chimney, and on the right-hand chimney Paul scratched the words *peu a peu*—"little by little the bird builds its nest." Poor Paul still had the inside of his nest to feather! But he finally got it nicely furnished.

And he had a chance with his family to enjoy his charming house for more than twenty years. He died in 1741 and left the house to his oldest daughter Mary, who in 1750 married Henry Ravenel. As the *Ravenel Records* remarks, "It got into the Ravenel *family*," where it was to remain for another hundred and fifty-four years.

Henry already owned two Ravenel plantations, Brunswick and Pooshee, but he liked to be known as Henry of Hanover, and made Hanover so much his home that according to one of his chroniclers "the Henry Ravenels became more closely identified with Hanover than any of its many occupants. Their sixteen children were born there, and although only six of these lived to maturity, two of them, René and Paul de St. Julien Ravenel, left a long line of distinguished descendants."

Henry himself left a journal of sorts, and a few entries from it serve to give the tone and temper of the times:

"Henry Ravenel married to Mary de St. Julien the 13th of September, 1750. We came to live at home, called Hanover, the 13th of April, 1751, and went back to Pooshee the 9th of June, and my wife was delivered of a son on the 26th of said June. Then we came home again the second time the 1st of October, 1751. On Friday, the 27th of March, 1752, we whent back to Pooshee (Cous Petr St Julien died that evening)."

"Harry very sick with a scarlet fever and I with a hard fever the next day. On Monday, the 30th, in the evening, my wife miscarried of a boy, and lay very ill with the fever and a pain in one shoulder for five weeks."

"On Monday, the 20th of July, there rose a smoak and very black clouds, with thunder and lightning, which made the earth so dark that I could scarce desern my wife from the front porch to the back, and then we had a great shower of rain as ever I saw."

44

"On Tuesday, the 14th of July, 1752, met at Somerton's old Ditch Mr. René Ravenel, Doctr Keith, Messrs Daniel, James, Daniel and Heny Ravenel, Benj. de St. Julien, and laid out a road thro' the Swamp at the Indian Field, 20 degrees N. E., and just as we had eat dinner a fine shower of rain drove us all home."

"On Wednesday the 22nd, we met again (Heny St Julien and Doctr Keith excepted), and put up stakes both sides the path 20 feet wide, (and all came and dined with me at Hanover)."

"June 18th, Friday, mov'd from Hanover to Chs Town with my family to Live."
"Very Cool and dry weather all September, and very hott all the Month of October, the Thermomitor at 82 and 86 several days; very rainy from 1st August."
"November 20, Come up with my Family from Town to live at Hanover again."

Henry's four sons were all great horsemen and fought with General Francis Marion in the guerilla warfare that made Marion famous as the "Swamp Fox." Marion, too, was a planter before the outbreak of the Revolution, when he joined up with the regiment of General William Moultrie (who married the niece of the builder of Hanover). Confronted with a formidable force, Marion would retire to the swamps, only to reappear at some distant unexpected point to take the enemy by surprise. As a breaker-up of British communication lines and capturer of scouting and foraging parties, the nuisance value of Marion was incalculable, and, serving with him, men like the Revenels, who knew the swamp lands by heart, were in their element.

When Henry of Hanover died in 1785, his son Stephen bought the place from the other heirs, and with his bachelor uncle Daniel Ravenel lived there until his death. It passed to Daniel, and, on *his* death, it went to Henry Le Noble Stevens (he was Daniel's grandnephew) in 1833. During the next twenty-six antebellum years with the Stevenses, Hanover reached the height of its prosperity and good times. Then came the war, and in 1862, at the second battle of Bull Run, a great victory for the Confederates, Henry was killed. Worse than the war for Hanover was the Reconstruction, and for a while Hanover went from bad to worse, but it remained in the Ravenel family until 1904.

In 1941, when the now-decrepit Hanover was about to be destroyed, the South Carolina Public Service Authority, after a plea from President Roosevelt, provided the necessary funds for Clemson College, the only college in the state with a school of architecture, to move the old house from its Low Country home to a place on its campus, far across the state in the Up Country. Moved and restored with skill and care, all it lacks is a setting of live oaks and Spanish moss. And it *took* skill and care to bring the whole right-hand chimney top intact, with *peu a peu* inscribed in the plaster by Paul de St. Julien, grandson of the Huguenot emigrant from Vitre.

The interior restoration of Hanover House has been undertaken by the Spartanburg Committee of the South Carolina Dames, who are furnishing it as it would have appeared in the first half of the 18th century.

This ancient and most appealing gambrel-roofed weathered shingle house was built in 1728 at what is now Swansea, Massachusetts, between Fall River and Providence.

The oak spinning wheel has always been in the house, a possession of the Martin family, who lived here for more than 200 years. Among the other interesting pieces is an American Windsor chair, slightly older than the house, a Colonial tip-top table and the Queen Anne style armchair of maple marked 1710. The canes beside the door all belonged to Martins and some are of the 18th century.

THE MARTIN HOUSE STORY

The People

Robert Martin, first arrival
Johanna, his wife
Abraham Martin, Robert's bachelor brother, second arrival
Richard Martin, another brother, third arrival
John Martin, Richard's son
Johanna Esten, John's wife
John Martin II, their second son, and builder of the house (1674-1757)
Marcy Hayward, the builder's first wife
Marcy Thurber, his second wife

On the ship with Robert and Johanna Martin, which arrived in the colonies in the spring of 1635 were Robert's sister Elizabeth with her husband Joseph Upham and their four children, the whole contingent under the spiritual guidance of the Reverend Joseph Hull. The ship carried twenty-one families, all from the village of Badcombe in Somersetshire. She had sailed on March 20 from Weymouth, England, and on May 6 put in at Weymouth, Massachusetts. This was as much a coincidence as the *Mayflower's* setting out from Plymouth, England, and landing at Plymouth in America.

Though his colonial occupation here was to be that of surveyor, Robert had put himself down on the passenger list as "husbandman," which was common practice during the Cromwell years when higher rankings among the emigrants ran the risk of scrutiny.

Robert's bachelor brother Abraham arrived a few months later, and in September he was among the first proprietors to draw house lots in Hingham, where he is known to have worked as a weaver until 1644, when he took part in the movement to Rehoboth.

Rehoboth was a tract of land ten miles square that lay between the Taunton and Narragansett Rivers about thirty miles south of Weymouth and Hingham. The southeastern section now contains the suburbs of Fall River, and the northwestern part the suburbs of Providence. It was bought from the Indian Massasoit by a company of settlers from Weymouth and Hingham, among whom were the Martin brothers. Their leader was the Reverend Samuel Newman, who had arrived from England in 1636, and by 1643, becoming dissatisfied with his pastorate at Weymouth, arranged the purchase of this little territory the Indians called Seekonk. And it was he who christened it Rehoboth, Hebrew, roughly, for, wide-open spaces. This kind of resettlement inlandward from the increasingly populated shores of Massachusetts Bay had many individual variations, but Rehoboth was close to the classic pattern. In the southeastern corner of the tract was the 1632 settlement of Swansea, which was set off from Rehoboth in 1668.

About 1660 Robert Martin died childless in Rehoboth, and in 1663 the third brother, Richard, arrived from England with his son John. No record of a wife or further children. In June 1669

In the dining room is an English gate-leg table with oak Windsor chairs and a noteworthy collection of pewter. The musket and powder horn were carried in the Revolutionary War by the Thomas Martin who was born in this house in 1759. A simple dwelling house, the home of a simple unpretentious family.

Richard was appointed by the General Court of New Plymouth Colony as Surveyor of Highways for Rehoboth, and his name appears as a contributor to the colonist campaign in the bloody, bitter, and senseless King Philip's War. When Abraham died in 1670, Richard was the principal heir, and when Richard died in 1694 he left most of his holdings in Rehoboth to his son John.

We are getting gradually closer to the Martin house, for back in 1671, John Martin had married Johanna Esten, and on March 15, 1674, their second son John, who was to be the builder of the house, was born. Son John married Marcy Hayward, who died in 1710, and in 1713 he married another Marcy, widow of Richard Thurber. And it was with the second Marcy in 1728 (the same year that Bishop Berkeley [of the next chapter] was to build Whitehall, fifteen miles away at Middletown), that John left Rehoboth for Swansea, ten miles away, and built the house that was to remain in the family for the next two hundred and seven years. It was willed by a Martin descendant to the Massachusetts Dames, who maintain it devotedly, for the pleasure of the public, in the spirit of the early Martins.

In 1880 the family historian wrote: "Few members of the family at any time attained political notoriety. Nor did any of them arrive at eminence in literature or science. Through successive generations they have been honest yeomen, good and useful members of society, acting well their part in the sphere of life in which they were placed, and from their manliness and probity, winning the respect and confidence of the community in which they lived."

"Yeoman . . . A workingman without a master, early admitted to political rights, the yeoman was thought to give great strength to English society." Columbia Encyclopedia.

In New England they built for themselves the best unpretentious houses in the early colonies, of which the Martin house is a charming survival.

THE WHITEHALL STORY
The People

Rev. Dr. George Berkeley, Dean of Londonderry, owner of the house
His wife
Henry, their infant son
John James and Richard Dalton, "Gents of Honour and Fortune"
John Smibert, the painter

George Berkeley was born in 1685 in Dublin, where he was educated at Trinity College, becoming first a scholar, then a fellow. His field was philosophy, in which some of his best work was done before he was thirty. In his early forties it became his dream to establish a college in the Bermudas to convert and educate Indians from America. When he was given to believe that he would receive financial support from Parliament for his project, he decided to come to America and wait here for the money. The naiveté of this decision was to cause him considerable concern during his brief sojourn in this country. As it turned out, we now not only have a charming house to mark his distinguished Irishman's visitation, but other everlasting tokens of his distinguished character.

Newport was expecting the Dean. In a letter from London dated August 28, 1728, Jaheel Brenton had learned that Berkeley was to be in America shortly with plans for a college [in the Bermudas] to make "the gospel of Jesus Christ more known than it had been hitherto among the natives of the Continent," adding that he would be in the company of John James and Richard Dalton, "Gents of Honour and Fortune," who, having traveled through the more polite parts of Europe, "will have the pleasure of communicating their experiences to the uncultivated parts of America."

On January 23, 1729, the Reverend John Comer of Newport set down in his diary: "This day Dean George Berkeley arrived here with his spouse and a young ladie in Companie, in order to find a suitable place in America to settle a Colledge; he was 4 months and 16 days to Virgine where he made but a short stay; so to Newport he was 5 months [eight weeks was average]—he is reported a man of moderation."

The "young ladie" was Miss Handcock from Dublin, a friend of Mrs. Berkeley's, coming to visit her cousins, the Newport Coddingtons. Also in the party, bound for Boston, was John Smibert, the painter who was to become one of the best known colonial artists.

The two young gentlemen, James and Dalton, had disembarked at Jamestown to visit in Virginia, sending the Berkeley party on to Newport.

The following are brief excerpts from lengthy letters.

G. B. *to Sir John Percival*
Newport in Rhode Island.   February 7th, 1729

My Lord,
Though I am at present in no small hurry and have been so ever since my landing, with visits and business of several kinds, yet I would not omit the first opportunity of paying my duty to your Lordship and acquainting you with our safe arrival in this Island. We came last from Virginia where I received many unexpected as well as undeserved honours from the Governor and principal inhabitants. The same civil kind treatment attends us here. We were a long time blundering about the ocean before we reached Virginia, but our voyage from thence hither was as speedy and prosperous as could be wished. Mr. James who proposeth to continue in Virginia till Spring and Mr. Dalton who pursueth his journey to this place by land, will both repent of their choice when they find us arrived so long before them. . .

Your most devoted and most humble servant,
Geo. Berkeley

On February 18 Berkeley bought the farm of Joseph Whipple, about four miles east of Newport on the road to Providence, in what is now Middletown, and began building his house. By April 9 the work was finished and the Berkeleys moved in, naming their new home Whitehall.

G. B. *to Thomas Prior*
                                                April 24th, 1729

Dear Tom,
I can by this time say something to you from my own experience of this place and people. The inhabitants are of a mixed kind, consisting of many sects and subdivisions of sects. Here are four sorts of Anabaptists, besides Presbyterians, Quakers, Independents, and many of no profession at all.

The climate is like that of Italy, and not at all colder in the winter than I have known it everywhere north of Rome. The spring is late. But to make amends, they assure me the autumns are the longest and finest in the world; and the summers are much pleasanter than those of Italy by all accounts, foreasmuch as the grass continues green, which it doth not there.

This island is pleasantly laid out in hills and vales and rising grounds, hath plenty of excellent springs and fine rivulets and adjacent islands.

The town of Newport contains about six thousand souls, and is the most thriving flourishing place in all America for its bigness. It is very pretty, and pleasantly situated. I was never more agreeably surprised than at the sight of the town and the harbour.

Your affectionate and humble servant
George Berkeley

From a letter written June 27, to Sir John Percival: "For my amusement in this new world I have got a little son whom my wife nurses." This son was Henry.

G. B. to Thomas Prior

Rhode Island, March 9, 1730

Dear Tom,
My situation hath been so uncertain, and is like to continue so till I am clear about the receipt of his Majesty's bounty . . .

My design still continues to wait the event, and go to Bermuda as soon as I can get associates and money (which my friends are now soliciting in London).

I live here upon land I have purchased, and in a farmhouse that I have built on this Island. It is fit for cows and sheep and may be of good use for supplying our College at Bermuda.

Mr. James, Dalton, and Smibert, etc. are at Boston, and have been there for several months . . .

No more at present but that I am, dear Tom,

Your affectionate humble servant,
Geor. Berkeley.

To Sir John Percival

Rhode Island, July 20, 1730

My Lord,
I already informed your Lordship that I hold myself in readiness to go to Bermuda . . . Bermuda after all is the proper place, for, besides that the 20000 pounds were addressed for by Parliament and granted by the Crown for that individual spot, there are other reasons which lie against placing the College here, particularly the extreme dearness of labour and the difficulty of getting Indians, the number whereof is very inconsiderable in this part of America, having been consumed by wars and strong liquors, not to mention some other particulars wherein I take Bermuda to have the advantage.

As for the raillery of European wits, I should not mind it if I saw my College go on and prosper . . . If [Parliament] let it drop, the disappointment may be to me, but the censure, I think, will light elsewhere . . .

Your Lordship's most obedient and
Most humble Servant
G. Berkeley

The fireplace tiles in the "Red Room" are 18th-century Delft. Above the 17th-century Connecticut chest is a rare mezzotint portrait of Rev. Dr. Honeyman by S. Oakey. The high back chair is 18th-century English Windsor.

In the Whitehall parlor (or "Green Room"—from color of woodwork) the curtains are of 18th-century bourette with contemporary fringe. Far window shows curtain down. The chairs are 18th-century Windsors from England as is the 17th-century Bible box.

This painting by John Smibert entitled "The Bermuda Group" depicts the artist standing at the left, Dean Berkeley standing right. Thomas Moffatt, Smibert's nephew, stands next to his uncle; John James is the other man standing. Seated, from left to right, are Richard Dalton, Berkeley's secretary in America, Miss Handcock, a friend of the Berkeley family, and Anne Forster Berkeley, the Dean's wife, with their son Henry, born in America in 1729.

To Sir John Percival

Rhode Island, 2nd March, 1731

My Lord,

I have received such accounts on all hands both from England and Ireland that I now give up all hopes of executing the design which brought me into these parts. I am fairly given to understand that the money will never be paid. And this long continued delay and discountenance hath made those persons who engaged with me entirely give up all thoughts of the College . . . My thoughts are now set towards Europe, where I shall endeavour to be useful some other way . . . .

My wife is big with child and so far gone that we cannot safely put to sea least she should be brought to bed on shipboard. As soon as this event is over and she and her infant can put to sea, I propose with God's blessing to return. I pray God preserve your Lordship and good family and remain with sincere affection and respect,

My Lord,

Your Lordship's most obedt
and most obliged humble
Servant

G. Berkeley

In April Mrs. Berkeley gave birth to a daughter, christened Lucia. The baby died September 6. And on September 7, in a letter to a friend in New Haven, Berkeley wrote, "I am now upon the point of setting out for Boston in order to embark for England." He and his wife and son left Newport on the ninth, sailed from Boston on the 21st, and arrived in London the first of November. Before he left he divided his library between Yale and Harvard. The Whitehall property he gave to Yale with the stipulation that the income from it should be used for "Premiums and a Scholarship: The first endowment for a fellowship for graduate studies ever provided in an American college," according to Professor Witherspoon's Berkeley birthday address at Berkeley College, Yale, in 1963.

In 1734 he was made Bishop of Cloyne, in County Cork, where he died in 1753. While his house is still owned by Yale, the Rhode Island Dames have it in their custody on a 999-year lease. Whitehall has a very charming small 18th century garden designed by Mrs. Stanley D. Hart, a Dame, a member of the Whitehall committee, and of the Newport Garden Club which lovingly maintains the garden. And in nearby Newport, as a further memento of the Dean's visit, is the organ he gave to Trinity Church, one of the two oldest church organs in American and still making music.

Stenton Mansion stands in what is now a little Philadelphia park, a fragment of Logan's five-hundred-acre estate; its style, a stately Georgian carried out by Logan with elegant Quaker restraint. There is a beautifully maintained garden, beyond which is the Logan graveyard where several members of the Logan family are buried.

THE STENTON STORY

The People

James Logan, merchant, scholar, builder of Stenton
William Penn, the proprietor
Hannah Callowhill, Penn's second wife
Sarah Read, Logan's wife

How Pennsylvania developed is as pertinent to the Stenton story as Penn's persuading Logan to come with him to the Province. So the story begins when William Penn was born in London, son of the Admiral William Penn who appears so frequently in Pepys and who was knighted in 1660 by Charles II. In 1662 the son was expelled from Oxford for Quakerism and sent by his father to France as a possible cure, a maneuver which didn't work. As an active proponent of freedom of conscience, he spent some time in the Tower, where he wrote his famous tracts, *Innocence With Her Open Eyes* and *No Cross, No Crown*. His father died in 1670 with the Crown owing him 16,000 pounds, and in 1681 Charles II, partly perhaps as repayment, made William Penn absolute proprietor of the colony to which the King himself gave the name of Pennsylvania.

James Logan, who became Penn's right-hand man, was born in the town of Lurgan, near Lough Neagh in central Northern Ireland in 1674. Son of an Edinburgh graduate, "he was so thoroughly tutored in Greek and Latin by his father that he became head master of the Bristol [England] Friend's School at the age of nineteen." Also in Bristol, working in a linen draper's establishment, by the time he was twenty-five he developed his mercantile talent to a degree that equaled his classical learning. At the same time he became proficient in French, Italian, and Spanish.

He was a boy of eight, still in Ireland when Penn, on October 27, 1682, sailed up the Delaware in the little ship *Welcome*, to the site of Philadelphia, laid out for him earlier that year by one of his commissioners, Thomas Holme. The next day he received the territory from the Duke of York's agent, and on November 2 proclaimed in Assembly that the "Duke's laws were to be in force until the people decided otherwise." Quaker immigration began at a great rate—though from the outset freedom of worship was granted to all.

Penn returned to England in August 1684 to defend his southern boundary against Lord Baltimore; but after James II had been deposed, Penn, as a friend of that King, was accused of treason, and his colony was held by the Crown from 1692 to 1694, after which it was restored.

Due to some difficulties in the province, Penn returned to Philadelphia in 1699 in the *Canterbury* with his second wife, Hannah. Also with him was James Logan, whom he had engaged in Bristol as his secretary. The young Scotch-Irish Quaker had agreed, without the least hesitation, it seems, to come with Penn for a few years to America. As it happened, in less than two years Penn was to go back to England to stay, and Logan, whom he was to leave here as his agent, was to remain in Pennsylvania fifty years more, until he died. "He was to become the dominant figure in almost every phase of Pennsylvania life between the time of William Penn and that of Benjamin Franklin."

Logan not only served Penn as private secretary, but often enough served Penn's wife, although in a different manner. From Pennsbury, the great Penn country seat up the Delaware above Bristol (now reconstructed), where Penn was nursing a swollen leg all through the summer of 1700, Hannah would write to Logan in Philadelphia, "Must desire thee to send the two pair of pewter candlesticks, some great candles . . . and a dozen pounds smaller ditto . . . Call Betty Webb to thy assistance: let her send two mops to wash house with, four silver salts, and the two-handled porringer that is in my closet, the looking glass that is in the hall, if it can be carefully put up, the piece of dried beef; and if any ship with provisions come from Rhode Island, I would have thee buy a firkin, two or three, as price and worth are, of good butter, also cheese and candles, etc., for winter's store."

Still, by the time Penn left the following year, Logan had proved himself such a capable and effective administrator that Penn didn't hesitate to make the young man Clerk of the Council, Secretary of the Province, Commissioner of Property, and Receiver-General of quitrents and other moneys.

Just before Penn's departure, as, the Logan authority quoted throughout this chapter, Tolles states, "called a great Indian council at Pennsbury to say goodby to his red-skinned friends, and at that council fire he pointed Logan out to them as the person he particularly entrusted to take care of them in his behalf. Logan was faithful to the trust. Hardly a single important Indian council was held in Pennsylvania [many of them at Stenton] in the next half century at which he was not present as the principal negotiator. No one in the British colonies was more skillful, more respected as an Indian diplomat. He was the real executor of Pennsylvania's remarkably successful Indian policy."

Always dabbling on the side in commercial ventures, Logan was now making bigger and bigger investments in ships and in trading to the West Indies, England, and the Continent; and in 1712 he began turning his attention as well to the very lucrative trade in furs. Soon his was the largest single operation in the city, dealing with fur traders who were "a parcel of brutish fellows," as Logan called them. "He was forever having to sober them up when they got drunk in town," we are told, "pay their gambling debts, bail them out of jail; and finally, when they died, hopelessly in his debt, he was often forced to attach their paltry possessions to recover a little of what he had advanced them over the years." The fortune he built up in furs he later invested in lands, so that when he died he was the proprietor of nearly 18,000 acres in Pennsylvania and New Jersey, not to mention his iron "plantation" at Durham on the upper Delaware, and his handsome estate of Stenton. He became Chief Justice of Pennsylvania, and one of the most politically powerful figures in the Province.

"My dearest love," Logan, now forty, began his letter to Quakeress Sarah Read, hardly more than a child, and very virtuous, "To tell thee how much I admire, value, and love thee and thy excellent virtues is needless, for thou canst not be insensible of it. I look on thee as one capable to bring a man the greatest blessing in thy person that he is capable of receiving in the world . . . and how eager one in my circumstances, who rates thee at the highest, would be to possess such a blessing may easily be judged."

Logan had been smitten twice before, but his suits had been unsuccessful. Not this one, however, and in December the two were married in the Great Meetinghouse; Sarah later bearing him seven children, of whom four survived.

For more than ten years after their marriage James and Sarah stayed on in Logan's Philadelphia town house on what is now Logan Square, where their first five children were born. While Logan had bought what he called a "plantation" shortly after his marriage—five hundred acres near Germantown, and five miles from the city, there seems to be no mention in his letters of a house there until 1722, when he wrote from the plantation that he had been "called hither last

The great entrance hallway above, with its herringbone floor of Stenton bricks and its simply detailed paneling and fireplace, leads into the stair hall that is lit by an oversize window of hand-blown glass on the landing of the finely balustraded staircase. On the left, the North Parlor is where the Logan family gathered to entertain their friends, among them the most prominent figures of their day. The carved Philadelphia Chippendale chair is an especially rare example and belonged to the Logan family, as did the 1756 Philadelphia walnut stool by John Elliot. "J.L. 1728" is east in the fireback from Durham Furnace.

Back of the North Parlor is the first floor bedroom, in which it is said seventeen Logan children were born, being conveniently next to the kitchen. The candlestand between the wing chair and the warming pan is a fine one with urn-shaped pedestal and birdcage. The early American cradle is said to have held many a Logan baby. The bed, with beautiful reeded posts and Marlborough feet, was made by Thomas Tufts, a famous Philadelphia cabinetmaker. The paneling is all original, and the fireback is another in which J.L. 1728 is cast.

55

James Logan, the builder

night to attend my mother"; the implication being that he had built a farmhouse as part of a working farm. In 1724 he wrote that his daughter Sally was "very busie at the Plantation in the Diary in which she delights." But still no indication that the mansion had been started.

Yet back in 1720, complaining of rheumatism in his back, he wrote to a friend, "To that plantation I have proposed to myself shortly to retire." Not until January 1725 did anything definite appear in his correspondence. It was then that he wrote to James Greenshields: "Kind Cousin . . . I now propose to quitt [public duties] & change them for a retired life on ye Plantation I have mentioned which I have since enlarged & am building on it a conveniency for my family."

In a letter to Hannah Penn in England, on November 1 of that same year, he indicated that Sarah was just as anxious as her husband that he retire from town. "honored Mistress," he wrote, "My wife of ye 12th of ye 9th month brought me a son named Charles after her father & brother, earnestly beseeched that I may be allowed to live with her on our Plantation near Germantown under no other obligation to public affairs than to ride once a week to town to advise and assist in your affairs for which she hath a great Zeal, yet more for her husband's peace."

Stenton was plainly coming along by the spring of 1728 for it was then that Logan said as much in a letter to John Penn, William Penn's son, Proprietor of the Colony since his father's death in 1718. "All therefore that is left for me in ye remainder of Life allotted to me, which I think cannot be long, is to retire & study to be easie, that my spirit may the better be supported to render my days more useful to my children in their education. I have accordingly resolved to hasten the finishing of my house in our Plantation & there bury myself from the sight of men as far as I can while living for company unless it be a few particular becomes daily more disagreeable."

There is clear evidence that finally, that fall, Stenton was ready for its windows and its door hardware. Here is a letter written to Nehemiah Champion that November: "What now particularly induced me to this essay, is to putt a little money into thy hands to purchase ye necessaries of a house I am building mentioned in ye inclosed List which I desire thee to procure for me at ye best hand & to ship them by the first vessel bound hither after your next fair. Pray be careful that the nails be tough, small—well drawn, those from London generally are finer & less clumsy than yours, but those called clasp-headed they say are always of good iron & well made & accordingly bear a somewhat better price. I would have ye locks of good workmanship and neat, but nothing more than common in such work, ye knobs or handles I suppose are now generally guttered & I believe wreath'd for giving ye surer hold, I take that fashion to be the best, tho' perhaps somewhat dearer. Pray endeavour that ye Locks differ in their wards, that one key may open no more than its own . . .

"For ye glass, I request that great care may be taken in applying to an honest Glazier that may be depended on. I would have ye strongest & clearest that can be bought at about 5d [pence] or under 6d a foot cutt exactly of ye Dimensions given, none of ye Squares warping or bending & very Carefully put up in boxes, as also on board out of danger of breaking. In ye size, I say I would have ye utmost exactness because ye sashes will be mostly made before the glass comes & therefore they will admit of no alteration. I intended ye frames should be made for glass of 8 inches by 11 exactly, but I find ye Carpenter has somewhat exceeded, which renders this small enlargement of ye glass absolutely necessary unless ye wood should be left too big & unsightly."

In spite of all his precautionary injunctions, when the glass panes came they were "wavy." Furthermore, as Logan notes, many were too small.

From a letter to Thomas Story written the following September, we gather that he was still not in the house because it was not yet fully plastered. Of its appearance he modestly said it was "not unsightly, if it stood better," meaning no doubt on an eminence. Sometime between that winter and the next, the moving-in had been accomplished, for the first letter in the Logan Letter Book is dated December 1730.

After Logan's death in 1751, the house went to Logan's eldest son William, who moved in with his family in April 1753. When William and his wife died in 1776, it was inherited by their son George. In 1782 Dr. George Logan moved in with his bride Deborah Norris, known as "the saucy Debby." In the meanwhile many Charleston notables, refugees from the British occupancy, were invited by Dr. Logan to make themselves at home in Stenton. Although uninvited, General Sir William Howe commandeered the mansion before the Battle of Germantown. At a later date the mansion was honored by a visit from the victorious General Washington; Jefferson was a frequent visitor; and Benjamin Franklin was, of course, a constant caller.

Deborah lived there until her death in 1839, eighteen years after her husband's. And as recorded by Sarah Wister Starr, Stenton then became the property of Deborah's only surviving child, Albanus, who married Maria Dickinson, daughter of the distinguished jurist John Dickinson. Stenton was left to their son, Gustavus George, and of the six children he and his wife had there, it was the surviving four who sold to the City of Philadelphia the property of which the mansion and the barn were a part. In 1910 the city placed the property in the custody of the Pennsylvania Dames, in whose care it still remains.

The scholarly attainments of the many-sided man who built this stately mansion are nicely pointed up by Gummere, who, after saying that Logan was an easy writer and speaker of Latin, read Greek comfortably, and was qualified by the age of thirteen for any university in Britain or Europe, tells of Logan sending his eldest son William back to Bristol for schooling. "William was urged (by his father) to finish, by the age of sixteen, Vergil's *Aeneid, Eclogues*, and *Georgics*, Cicero's *De officiis*, Thomas a Kempis, the *Consolation* of Boethius, some Tacitus, Seneca, Juvenal, Persius, and the Greek New Testament."

Among countless other accomplishments Logan was the first to establish the fact of sex in Indian maize, which earned him a long letter of praise, in Latin, from Linnaeus, to which he replied, of course, in Latin. And almost until the day he died, his mind remained alert as he lived among the 3,000 books of his library in Stenton, according to Tolles, the most distinghised of all colonial libraries.

We hear from Gummere that he was inclined to be "crotchety," that he was a fervid supporter of aristocratic causes, and an ultraconservative. But "there were few colonial Americans so versatile as Logan, in learning, statecraft, science, business, and application of the classical tradition to contemporary life." He was a most eminent Philadelphian, his house a most eminent Philadelphia mansion.

THE VAN CORTLANDT HOUSE STORY

The People

Olaf, or Oliver, the first Van Cortlandt to arrive in Nieuw Amsterdam
Stephanus, elder son of Olaf
Jacobus, much younger son
Frederick, son of Jacobus, and beginning builder of house
James, son of Frederick, and finishing builder of house
Augustus and Frederick, two of James' younger brothers; General Washington, and
*   behind the scenes, crowds of other Van Cortlandts, Philipses, Jays, Schuylers, Van*
*   Rensselaers, Livingstones, Beekmans, etc.*

Olaf Van Cortlandt, of Wyk, Holland, came ashore at Nieuw Amsterdam clad in the uniform of the West Indies Company constabulary. It was the same summer that Peter Minuit, the purchaser of Manhattan Island, was caught in a West Indies hurricane and lost at sea. He had also been a West Indies Company man, in a higher echelon than Olaf, but it was Olaf who really put Manhattan on the map.

Nieuw Amsterdam in 1638, from all accounts, was a place where an enterprising Dutchman could start making a fortune; but not as a soldier. So as soon as he could, Olaf transferred out of his constabulary uniform into the lace-collar clothes of the Company's civilian service. In 1642 he was married in the Dutch Church to a Belgian girl called Anne Loockermanns, and the next year they had a son called Stephanus who became in 1677 the first native-born mayor of British New York, serving two other terms in 1686 and 1687. Stephanus married a Schuyler, built Van Cortlandt Manor at Croton-on-Hudson, which the Rockefellers have restored, and by 1697 had holdings of land, up, and down, and back from the Hudson, 87,000 acres in all.

By 1648, Olaf was free and clear of the Company, and his first move on his own was to open a brewery. With that under way, he branched out into all kinds of business activities, from trading in lumber and furs, to buying land, to merchandising, importing, exporting; but mostly land. He was burgermeester seven times before the British took over the government in 1666, and an alderman under British rule. He died a very rich man, leaving three prosperous merchant sons, and four very well-married daughters.

Olaf's second son married very well indeed. The girl Jacobus won against considerable competition was the beautiful heiress Eva Philipse, adopted step-daughter of the Bohemian emigrant Frederick Philipse, who came over listed as architect-carpenter, and died the richest man in this richest of all the American settlements. For while the Netherlands in the 17th century was the wealthiest nation in the world, it was interested only in trade, not colonization. Eva's

The 1748 Van Cortlandt House in New York's Van Cortlandt Park.

mother, the former Margaret Hardenbrock, was the widow of the Huguenot Peter deVries when she married Frederick Philipse, proprietor of Philipse Castle at Tarrytown. That Philipse owned a great deal of what is now Westchester County is a matter of record, and gives considerable credibility to the report that fifty servants were kept at the Castle all the time.

Among the tracts of land which Jacobus acquired by inheritance or purchase was a lot of what was then known as Little Yonkers (the name Yonkers coming from the Dutch Yonk Heers or young gentlemen). This land lay north of the Harlem River and below the present big Yonkers, in what is now the Bronx—first settled in 1641 for the West Indies Company by Jonas Bronck, a Dane. Twelve hundred acres of this land that Jacobus bought is now Van Cortlandt Park, the site selected by Jacobus' first son, Frederick, for his house. Frederick's father had already dammed Tibbett's Brook for a mill pond, and had built a sawmill and gristmill to help make this excellent farmland self-sustaining.

By marrying Frances Jay, daughter of the Huguenot Augustus Jay, Frederick brought more Huguenot blood into a family that by the time of his son James' generation already contained, in addition to its basic Dutch, Russian (some of Olaf's forbears, in Holland had been Russian emigrees), Belgian, Bohemian, French, Scotch, Welsh, and, through Philipse, Bohemian, not to mention the English blood that was now beginning to infiltrate.

It is common knowledge that people like Frederick Van Cortlandt either owned or had access to builders' and architectural books of plans, façades, sections, and myriad details. It is also common knowledge that colonial craftsmen were not only capable of performing handwork of astonishingly high quality but had an eye for architecture which could hardly have been more sure of what it wanted to see.

Although no journals or records relative to the building of the house survive, we know that the cornerstone was laid in 1748, and that in August, 1749, when Frederick died, his eldest son James, at twenty-three, inherited the house "as it was finishing."

For the first twenty-five years the social goings-on in this great new handsome house hit an all-time high. They would never be like that again. Here it was, the first important haven of hospitality on the way from New York to the great houses up the Hudson: the Castle, the Manor, the Beekmans, Livingstones, Schuylers. And the last one on the way back to town.

Then in September 1776, James' brother Augustus, who was Clerk of the Common Council in the city arrived with all the irreplaceable city records that weren't in daily use, and hid them

In the delicately detailed drawing room the inlaid mahogany spinet is London 1771, the old violoncello is by William Heims, the richly carved Chippendale table belonged to General Nathaniel Greene, the pair of stools are American Chippendale—18th-century, and the Ispahan rug is 17th-century.

The tiled fireplace and its paneled cupboard wall make it the room's fine architectural feature. The painted Dutch Kas or armoire of painted pine is dated New York 1710. The decoration is in grisaille. The Virginia walnut gateleg table is early 18th-century, as is the soup tureen of Whieldon variegated ware, the side chairs Queen Anne.

In the Washington room the large needlepoint rug is 18th-century European and the fourposter is Massachusetts Chippendale, about 1760, whose linen curtains and bed cover are copied from Hudson 18th-century blue resist pattern. The wing chair is American Chippendale, the tea table Connecticut Queen Anne.

away in the family burial vault on the hill just north of the house. The tin box container is on view in the house today. Then, as an afterthought, thinking of some rare madeira in the cellar, he stored away half a dozen casks in the same safe place. After the war it was known as "Resurrection Madeira."

A year later Lord Howe's army occupied New York City, where it stayed for the next seven years. For nearly five years the British line was held at Kingsbridge on the Harlem River, just south of the house, while the American line was held at Tarrytown. The ten miles between came to be known as the Neutral Ground, with the Van Cortlandt house in the lower part near the British line. This Neutral Ground, from the Hudson to Long Island Sound, was a no man's land.

Life in this no man's land was far from peaceful during these long years. There was a period, in 1777, when the British commander billeted his Hessian mercenaries on the Van Cortlandt lands. And constantly there was skirmishing between foraging parties from both sides as groups from each of the armies strayed from their lines in search of provender. These actions ranged from sniping expeditions to full-fledged battles. In the summer of 1778, the Van Cortlandt woods was the scene of a disastrous engagement which resulted in the massacre of the Stockbridge Indians who were allied with the Americans. Some forty of them were buried on the Van Cortlandt grounds.

Unprotected as the area was, it was also a favorite prowl for the marauding gangs of ne'er-do-wells which so often appear in times of trouble. As the war drew to a close in this disputed area, hardly a family was unaffected in some part by loyalty to the Crown. Even knowing that with an American victory their estates would be confiscated, many held to their loyalty to the King. Colonel James and his brother Frederick were among the Van Cortlandts who remained colonial patriots throughout the ups and downs of the struggle which seemed at times to be centered at James' very house.

It was here at the house on the night of July 23, 1781, that Washington and Rochambeau had dinner with Colonel James, just a few months before James' death. And it was here on November 20, 1783, that Washington spent the night with a party of Continental officers, including General Philip Van Cortlandt, of the Manor at Croton, and Lt. Governor Pierre Van Cortlandt, who had been Acting Governor of the state while General George Clinton was militarily engaged. They were waiting to make their triumphal march into New York City. Finally on the twenty-fifth, the last British soldiers left for Staten Island. The march started from in front of the house the morning of November 21, 1783. Washington made his farewell address on the Wall Street steps where his statue stands today. And that was the end of the Revolutionary War.

THE WILTON STORY

The People

The Marquis de Chastellux, French author and soldier
William Randolph of Turkey Island
Mary Isham, his wife
William Randolph III, builder of Wilton
Peyton Randolph
William Randolph IV
Robert Randolph
Kate Randolph Mayo

the other Randolph masters of Wilton

Five miles from Petersburg, we crossed over the little Randolph River on a stone bridge; and still traveling through a rich and well populated country arrived at a fork in the road, where we of course managed to take exactly the one not leading to Richmond, where we wanted to go. But we had no reason to regret our error, as we went only two miles out of our way, and skirted the James River to a charming place called Warwick. A group of several pretty houses forms a sort of village here; but some really superb ones may be seen in the neighborhood, among others, that of Colonel Cary, on the right bank of the river, and Mr. Randolph's on the opposite shore. When traveling in Virginia, you must be prepared to hear the name of Randolph frequently mentioned. This is one of the first families of the country since a Randolph was among the first settlers, but it is also one of the most numerous and wealthiest. It is divided into seven or eight branches, and I am not afraid of exaggerating when I say that their family possessed an income of upwards of a million."

The Randolph house that Chastellux saw across the James in April 1782 was Wilton, of course, occupied at the time by Peyton Randolph—not the Peyton Randolph of Williamsburg, but his somewhat-less-illustrious cousin. Colonel Cary's house was Ampthill, another famous Virginia mansion. His wife was Mary Randolph, of Curles, on the lower James, a Randolph house long since gone. Long since gone, too, is the "charming place called Warwick" now absorbed into a dismal industrial section of Richmond.

Both Wilton and Ampthill would have been obliterated in the early 1930's if the Virginia Dames had not bought the former and a Cary descendant the latter, both houses then having been marvelously moved to beautiful sites overlooking the James in the well-kept western end of Richmond.

Wilton is not the result of Randolph riches alone, it is even more the result of Randolph style. There wasn't a more stylish Georgian house in the colonies. A touch of Queen Anne austerity in the two principal façades only makes it more so. Inside it is incomparably rich—the only house in the colonies to have been completely paneled, floor to ceiling, in every room, including the closets. Granting that William Randolph III was able to employ the best Williamsburg master builders and craftsmen, the greatness of the house—of any house—derives also a great deal from the taste and intelligence of the owner.

Wilton tells us more about these qualities in the Randolph who built the house than any account available of the man himself. In fact, we know only that he was born about 1719, eldest son of William Randolph II of Chatsworth, (another vanished Randolph house); that he married Ann Harrison, daughter of Benjamin Harrison of Berkeley, father of the Signer who was the greatest of the Harrisons; that he built Wilton about 1753 and died there eight years later in 1761.

Wilton, a superb Georgian house, is unique in that it is paneled throughout. Approaching the great staircase you pass the Simon Willard mahogany grandfather clock and a portrait of Beverley Randolph, brother of William III, on loan from the Virginia Historical Society. On the landing is a mahogany handkerchief table, against the staircase a Sheraton mahogany sofa, and in the foreground a large serpentine front Chippendale table, holding a pair of early altar candlesticks and a Chinese export bowl. As with much of the other hardware in the house, the locks on all the doors are original.

Following general colonial practice in many of the great houses, the masters of Wilton kept their bedroom on the ground floor. It was a good idea. Apart from other conveniences, the mistress of the house could receive family callers and better attend to her household affairs. The bed is Chippendale, the embroidered spread an heirloom. The Chippendale desk is mahogany, as is the barrel-back chair beside it. The card table at the foot of the stairs is Hepplewhite with fingerprint legs, and the stairway, quite naturally, leads to the nursery above.

The nursery at the top of the stairway from the master bedroom is one of the most delightful colonial restorations of its kind. The child-size cherry field bed is Sheraton, the Hepplewhite crib with its canopy top, is mahogany and the cradle is walnut. The bannister-back armchair (early 18th century), with seat made of corn shucks and "sausage" stretchers, is said to have belonged to Washington. The cherry bonnet-top chest-on-chest has all its original handles and finials.

In the dining room the large three piece table is Hepplewhite, around which are six Queen Anne chairs. Beneath the fine Philadelphia Queen Anne mirror the julep table holds a Chinese Export bowl and 16th-century candlesticks. The portrait is of Peyton Randolph of Wilton, son of William III. All of the Randolph portraits hanging at Wilton are on loan from the Virginia Historical Society. The parlor on the right, one of the more glorious rooms in the house, has two portraits attributed to Wollaston. William Randolph III, builder of Wilton, over the fireplace and his daughter Elizabeth over the Chippendale sofa. At the pie-crust tea table are two Philadelphia side chairs. The pianoforte was made by Broadwood & Son of London in 1800.

To get a firmer grasp on the Randolph line, and a better understanding of Wilton's wonders, it is necessary to go back to William III's paternal grandfather, William Randolph of Turkey Island. A remarkable man, he married a remarkable woman. Mary Isham was a descendant of Lady Godiva, who died in 1080 during the reign of William the Conqueror. William of Turkey Island is sometimes called the Immigrant, meaning the first of the family to arrive in America, but as a matter of fact, William's uncle, Henry Randolph, arrived some thirty years earlier. He returned to England on a visit twenty-seven years after he arrived, and in 1672, according to a high Randolph authority, "there is some reason to think that William may have come to Virginia with Uncle Henry."

In any event, in the opinion of the historian Bruce, William became one of the most distinguished men of the colony in his generation. He prospered; he gained political importance and was held by all in high esteem. He was said to be lucky, but if he was, according to Roberta Lee Randolph in *The First Randolphs of Virginia*, winning Mary Isham was the greatest piece of luck in his life. Together they founded one of the truly outstanding families of the whole colonial era.

Their oldest son, William II, inherited the vast Turkey Island holdings on part of which Wilton originally stood. Turkey Island, by the way, was discovered in 1607 by Captain Christopher Newport the year of the Jamestown landing. He and his party were sailing up the James in a shallop, hoping to find "the sea againe the mountynes Apalatai . . . or some other issue." Covered then with thousands of wild turkeys, the island, like a lot of other things in the neighborhood, has long since vanished, leaving its name as an identity for the early great Randolph and the place of his plantation.

The second master of Wilton was the Peyton Randolph who married Lucy Harrison, daughter of Benjamin Harrison, the Signer. Thus Lucy became the daughter-in-law of her Aunt Ann, Peyton's mother. And to complicate the family relationships even further, the Wilton Peyton's cousin, Peyton Randolph of Williamsburg, the statesman, married Elizabeth, another daughter of the Signer. By this time, the strands of the two most distinguished families of the province were inextricably intertwined.

The third master was Peyton's son William, born in 1779, four years before his father's death. The fourth was this William's son Robert; and the fifth was Robert's daughter Kate, the last Randolph to own the famous mansion, which went through six more ownerships before the Virginia Dames bought it in 1933.

No account of the actual building of Wilton has ever come to light; nothing about its builders, nothing about the inspiration for its design. It bears a family resemblance to nearby Ampthill, but Ampthill was built some twenty years before Wilton, and the Carys who built it, and who were experienced builders, were dead some time before Wilton was started.

However, the story of how Wilton was taken down, brick by brick, stone by stone, board by board, and carried to its new site up the river, where it was all put together again, has been told in a five-page, single-spaced, typewritten memorandum prepared by the Richmond construction firm of Claiborne & Taylor, who performed that remarkable feat.

First the house was meticulously measured on its original site, and each dimension so obtained was followed exactly when the same parts and pieces were put together again in the identical places and manner. So the Wilton one sees in its new location on the James is the same structure that was originally erected fourteen miles away, in the middle of the 18th century—the same Wilton that the Marquis de Chastellux remarked upon with such amazement the time he lost his way at Warwick.

THE POTTSGROVE STORY

The People

Thomas Potts, the first emigrant
Martha Keurlis, his wife
John Potts, their son, and builder of Pottsgrove
Ruth Savage, John's wife
Thomas Potts, their first son, inheritor of Pottsgrove
John Potts, Jr., their third son, the Loyalist
Jonathan Potts, their sixth son, the Revolutionary doctor
Isaac Potts, their seventh son, the Quaker ironmaster and preacher

AUTHOR'S NOTE

Because of the varied and noteworthy careers of certain members of the family before and after the Revolution, together with the Revolutionary location of the house, Pottsgrove occupies a pivotal position in this book of houses and people as a connecting link between pre- and post-Revolutionary times. In addition to a distinguished house, the builder of Pottsgrove produced a fascinating family—thirteen children. Of the eight sons, four in particular provide an opportunity to bring Revolutionary feelings and events into focus in a very personal way. Much of the material from contemporary accounts was made accessible in *The Potts Memorial*, by Mrs. Thomas Potts James, privately printed in 1874 and a closely documented history of an important colonial family.

About 1550 the Potts family, as part of a large and continuing emigration, left the German Palatinate for England to escape religious persecution. And it took just a hundred and twenty seven years for persecution to catch up with them in England. For according to a contemporary account of 1677, "On the 18th day of the month called July, the priest of Treseylwys and the priest of Llanidloes in Montgomeryshire, Wales, gave information of a meeting in the house of John Jarman upon which the mayor and constables came thither and arrested seven of the assembly and committed them to prison, and fined several others, who had their cattle seized for their fines" . . . At the head of the list was "John Potts. One cow and six young beasts worth 12s 10d . . ." He lived not far from Colebrook Dale, one of the most important ironworks at that early day in Great Britain.

Thomas Potts, who was born in 1680 in Wales, a close connection of the John Potts who was fined in Llanidloes, came as a small boy to Germantown, was educated as a Quaker, and married a Quaker, Martha Keurlis, in 1699. In 1723 he became engaged in developing the iron mines of Pennsylvania. He called his mines Colebrook Dale, which became the name of the township. The part of the county containing Pottstown, when it was separated from Philadelphia, received the name of Montgomery after the Potts home county in Wales.

John Potts, founder of Pottstown and builder of Pottsgrove, was born in 1710 in Germantown, a town at the time whose name could be taken quite literally, for German, or "High Dutch," as

In Pottsgrove's fine, tawny stonework, the front is in range courses, the rest random.

they called it, was the common language. John's maternal grandparents had emigrated there from Germany with Pastorius. As a very young man, John was taken by his father to the Mana-tawny country, in the Schuylkill valley, where his father, through his wife's family and friends, had already become involved in the iron mines, furnaces, and forges which were being developed in that region, where the ores of iron, lead, and copper abounded—also, according to an old ac-count, "asbestos, magnasites, amethyst, jasper, garnet, schorl, chalcedony, agate, saphrye and beryl."

Thomas Rutter, Samuel Savage, and Samuel Nutt were the men most active in the ironworks, and it was with them and their families and fortunes that the Pottses became inextricably and everlastingly bound in ties of marriage and business and all other concerns, creating a dynasty that reigned throughout the whole ironworking period of forges and furnaces. It was in the house called Coventry built by Samuel Nutt, after whose English ancestral town it was named, eight miles from Pottsgrove, that John Potts in 1734 married Ruth Savage.

Thomas, the first child of John and Ruth Savage Potts, was born May 29, 1735, at Colebrook-dale (as it was now being written) "about half an hour after one in the afternoon." As a young man he soon showed his father's passion for ironmastery, and in 1768, on his father's death, he ac-quired Pottsgrove and its five-hundred-acre plantation for £6,000, having already in 1757 acquired by marriage a large improved landed estate with forges and furnaces, and in 1765, by purchase from his wife's mother, all the rights to the large estate of Coventry. This was described as "the Messuages, Plantations, Lands, Mines, Minerals, Forges, Furnaces, Rents, Tenement, Hereditaments & Real Estate . . . situate in any part of sd. Province of Penn'a, except the estate in Phil. leased to Benjamin Franklin." For all this, including "one negro man named Caesar, one mulatto man named Bill Bonnet, one mulatto boy named Jim, one mulatto boy named Dick, one negro boy named Ben, one negro girl named Sall, one mulatto woman named Betty, and her youngest child named Stephen," he paid his wife's parents, for as long as they lived, an annuity of five-hundred and twenty pounds of "lawful Pensylvania money."

In 1752 John Potts laid out the town, and began building Pottsgrove. A hundred years later the editor of the Pottstown newspaper wrote that "the work, no doubt, occupied a couple of years before completion; for in those days the population was sparse and workmen scarce, expecially builders who could execute work of a character so elegant and substantial as is found in this structure. The edifice is built of sandstone, the front in range courses. The walls are two feet thick, and the partition walls eighteen inches thick; the wainscoting and woodwork inside being very heavy and strong. The first story is eleven and a half feet high; the second, ten feet high, and from the square to the apex of the roof the height is eighteen feet. The hall is ten feet wide. The cellar is divided into five apartments, with strong walls and arched doorways. The roof is pierced with three large dormer-windows, and is surmounted its entire length with a balustrade observatory [a 19th-century addition now removed], from which a splendid view can be had of a portion of Berks, Chester, and Montgomery Counties, laved by the Schuylkill River. The whole building measures about 46 feet by 28 feet. There was formerly a large doorway in the back part of the house, into which it was customary to drive a cart loaded with wood to supply the kitchen fire, but this has been removed. The whole edifice tells plainly of the desire of its founder to combine in this mansion, in which he expected to spend the remainder of his days, comfort, elegance, and durability . . . When the mansion was completed there were few, if any, such residences, as regards size and elegance, in Pennsylvania outside of Philadelphia; and even the city, at that date, could not boast of many superior to it. The settlers looked upon it with wonder and astonishment, and people came from the surrounding country, a distance of thirty or forty miles, to see Potts' big house."

According to Mrs. James: "For many years he continued to be the largest and most successful iron-master in the American Colonies. His comprehensive business mind was devoted to all the improvements of the time, and the severity of the laws and restrictions against the American Colonies by the Lords of Trade and by acts of Parliament appear to have made him a patriot of the Franklin stamp. With the great philosopher he was on terms of intimate friendship, as Mrs. Franklin, in a letter to her husband, calls him 'our Mr. Potts.'

"His landed estate, consisting of nearly four thousand acres in different parts of Pennsylvania, as well as in Virginia, was probably more highly improved than any other in the thirteen Colonies, with mines, forges, furnaces, grist-mills, saw-mills, farms, and tenants of town lots, besides several houses in Philadelphia, one of which, with stores and wharves, was valued at 2,000. He lived in great dignity at his stately house called Pottsgrove, surrounded by his large family of sons and daughters, and connected by birth and marriage with many of the oldest and most important families in Philadelphia."

From the Pennsylvania *Gazette* (Philadelphia) of June 16, 1768, "After a "After a long and tedious illness, died on the 6th instant, at his house at Pottsgrove, John Potts. Esq., a gentleman of unblemished honor and integrity, known, beloved, lamented."

Thomas got the house; and from 1774, and all through the Revolution, Washington was often a guest at Pottsgrove. "The house has sometimes been called his headquarters, and some official letters of the General-in-Chief are dated from this residence. It was a familiar sight in the stately rooms of this old mansion to see Washington, surrounded by his staff, in earnest consultation over maps of the Province, with Baron Steuben, General Knox, Lord Sterling, General Greene, General McIntosh, and Lafayette. It was here, doubtless, that Washington formed the plan to winter his army at Valley Forge on the property of Thomas' brothers and cousins, who seem to have willingly relinquished their houses to accommodate the officers. Valley Forge is situated on the Schuylkill, sixteen miles below Pottsgrove, and during the dark and gloomy winter of 1777 Washington and his wife were often the guests of the different members of Thomas' family. Indeed, the companionship of the wives and daughters of the Messrs. Potts seems to have been the only society of her own sex that Mrs. Washington had during that terrible winter; and many pleasant reminiscences of this friendship are still preserved by the great-grandchildren of the recipients, who treasure with reverential care personal mementos received ty their ancestors from the hands of the General and his wife."

In February of 1776 Thomas Potts was appointed a captain in a Continental regiment of riflemen. In no time, and at his own expense, this patriot had raised, armed, and equipped a battalion, and was commissioned colonel by the Continental Congress.

On July 9 at the State House in Philadelphia he took part in the formation of a new government: "For suppressing all authority in this Province derived from the Crown of Great Britain, and for establishing a government upon the authority of the people only."

Right after the war Colonel Potts performed an act which was not only to revolutionize the iron industry but halt the wholesale destruction of timber (for a single average furnace could consume as much as 6,000 cords of wood a year, or the products of two hundred and forty acres). He discovered the first anthracite in the colonies.

Two years later, on March 22, 1785, while attending the Legislature at Philadelphia "he went home to spend Sunday with his family, and returning on horseback the following day through the muddy roads of the inclement season, his riding-boots became very much splashed, and he dismounted at a pump in High Street to have them washed before entering the House. The effect of the sudden shock to his feet threw the gout to his head, and he expired before morning."

"Though engaged, like the rest of his family, in the iron business, John, Jr., who was born October 15, 1738, had received a superior education in Philadelphia, and was then sent to England to perfect his studies in the law, at the Temple, London. In 1764 he was practising law in Philadelphia, and a partner with his brother Samuel in the Mount Joy Forge. He married Margaret, daughter of Stephen and Anna Carmick, and resided in the city, though he occupied Stowe as a country residence, and built a substantial stone house on the principal street in Pottstown. John became a judge in the Court of Common Pleas, and on the breaking out of hostilities it is known that he inclined to the side of the king. His residence in England and a knowledge of her power led him to view the American cause as hopeless.

"During the occupation of Philadelphia by the British army he obtained a pass to leave the city, and went to Pottstown to look after his affairs, and was for a short time in his own house, there, which was afterwards confiscated. That he was known then to be a Tory by the Continental Congress is proved by the fact that a detachment of soldiers was sent up from Valley Forge to capture him, but just before they reached the house, he escaped by a back window.

"When the Continental army entered Philadelphia, the families of those who had espoused the British cause were ordered to leave the city, and Mrs. Potts, with her children, found a home in the house of her husband's brother, Samuel, at Pottstown. She remained there several months, until General Washington, who was in constant intercourse with the patriotic portion of the family, gave her an escort of dragoons to join her husband in New York, whither he had gone in the train of Lord Howe."

The estate of John, Jr., was confiscated in 1779, and by this act he lost a large and valuable property, which appears never to have been made up to him by the British Government.

The fine house and plantation called Stowe, two miles from Pottstown, "were seized and sold agreeably to law, as the estate late of John Potts, an attainted traitor, to the said Jonathan Potts,

In Pottsgrove's dining room the woodwork is manorial in scale and detailing, expressed also in the flat-arched fireplace and deep window reveals. The chairs and the three-part table are Chippendale, the china is Canton and Ch'ien Lung, the handsome girandole is most unusual, and the dog-wood bough is in an American silver tankard.

Esq., for 20,000 Continental money."

Sabine, in the *History of the Loyalists*, mentions him as one of the "fifty-five petitioners, in July, 1783, from the city of New York, who asked that the same number of acres might be granted them in Nova Scotia as were given to field officers in the army. They represented that their position in society had been very respectable, and that previous to the Revolution they had possessed much influence."

John Potts first settled in Shelburne, a port on the Atlantic side of Nova Scotia. The refugees laid out a handsome town, after the plan of Philadelphia, and at one time the population numbered over twelve thousand. Here the higher class of the Loyalists lived in as much state and elegance as their reduced means would allow, and obtained the *sobriquet* of "the dancing beggars of Shelburne." Between 1783 and 1785 John and his brother Thomas, the Colonel, established a partnership for the sale of stoves in Shelburne, and a clerk from Pottstown came down to attend to the business. Five different kinds of stoves are said to have been sold. Colonel Beverly Robinson took five to St. John, and John took nine to Halifax, for the purpose of introducing them at those places.

In a letter to his brother Samuel, dated Shelburne, 1784, John wrote, "Had not my attachment to our country carried me rather too far, I am fully convinced Lord Howe would have procured me some lucrative office in this Government. [Probably the governorship of Nova Scotia.] It may not yet, perhaps, be too late. It is worth trying. He is a cordial friend . . . I am sincerely averse to office, but my children and family must influence me in these matters."

The corner fireplace paneling in the library bears a family likeness to that in the dining room. As in all the family rooms the woodwork is painted in warm colors; its simplicity a Quaker characteristic. That is a birdcage chess table at which the two Windsor chairs are placed, the armchair signed Ackley. The wing chair is pure Pennsylvania.

If this position was offered to him he declined it; for after living a few years in Nova Scotia he returned to Pennsylvania for a while, and finally went west, where he died.

Jonathan was born April 11, 1745. "Having obtained as good an education as the Colonies then afforded at Ephrata and Philadelphia, he determined to fit himself for the profession of medicine by studying at Edinburgh, then considered the seat of that science. In company with his friend and relative, Benjamin Rush, subsequently distinguished as one of the signers of the Declaration of Independence, he sailed from Philadelphia, August 31, 1766, and after a very stormy passage of fifty days arrived at last safely at Liverpool, having been several times rescued from the very jaws of death."

October 22 from Liverpool he wrote to the family's old friend, Benjamin Franklin, in London:

Worthy Sir:—
You will receive by this post several letters in my favour, of my good friend & relation Mr. Rush from your son the Governor of the Jerseys, who has honored me with a letter to Dr. Alex. Dick of Edinburgh, & also from my father.
Should you think proper to write to any gentlemen in Edinburgh in favour of both Mr. Rush & myself it shall be acknowledged as a particular favour conferred upon
Sir your most obedient & very humble servant
Johathan Potts

With characteristic promptness Franklin replied on November 11, and with characteristic counsel:

Gentlemen:—

With this I send you letters for several of my friends at Edinburg.

It will be a pleasure to me if they prove of use to you.

But you will be your best friend if you apply diligently to your studies, refraining from all idle, useless amusements, that are apt to lessen or withdraw the attention from your main business. This, from the character you bear in the letters you brought me, I am persuaded you will do. Letters of recommendation may serve a stranger for a day or two, but where he is to reside for years, he must depend on his own conduct, which will increase or totally destroy the effect of such letters. I take the freedom, therefore, of counseling you to be circumspect in your behaviour at Edinburg (where people are very shrewd & observing), that you may bring from thence as good a character as you carry thither, & in that respect not be inferior to any American that has been there before you. You have great advantages in going there to study at this time, where there happens to be collected a set of as truly great men, professors of the several branches of knowledge, as have ever appeared in any age or country.

I recommend one thing particularly to you, that, besides the study of medicine, you endeavor to attain a thorough knowledge of natural philosophy in general. You will from thence draw great aids in judging well both of diseases & remedies, & avoid many errors. I mention this because I have observed that a number of physicians here, as well as in America, are miserably deficient in it.

I wish you all happiness & success in your undertaking & remain your friend & humble servant,

B. Franklin

Of the several letters that Franklin enclosed, the one to the head of the medical school is typical of the others:

Sir Alex. Dick.

Dear Sir,—I am heartily glad that the information from my son affords any satisfaction to your friend Mr. Swinton. I beg leave to recommend to your countenance & protection the bearers of this letter, Mr. Rush & Mr. Potts, sons of my friends in Philadelphia, who have come to study in your Medical school. They are strongly recommended to me by many of my acquaintances as young gentlemen of ingenuity & application & excellent morals, & I trust will do honor to their instructors.

Your advice as to the manner of prosecuting their studies & sage councils as to their conduct in other respects must be of great service to them if you favor them therewith, & will highly oblige Dear Sir, Your most obedient & most humble servant,

B. F.

Please to make my respectful compliments acceptable to Lady Dick & the rest of your amiable family.

In one of his first letters home Jonathan wrote:

I have received several letters of recommendation from Dr. Franklin to some of the principal Gentlemen of this place, & also a letter full of good advice, a copy of which I have sent to Papa; these gentlemen to oblige me have sent me frequently tickets to the Plays, Concerts, & Public Dances, but I constantly refused & will always refuse to attend such places, altho' my refusal has offended one or two gentlemen, & lest I should affront them all I was not ashamed to own I was a Quaker, & that I was principled against such entertainments, & that my dress might correspond with my actions, I have taken off my ruffles & untied my hair, & am not ashamed to use the plain language to the greatest Man in Edinburg, not but that it is a great cross to me.

But I shall here conclude after once more intreating my Dr. Brother often to write to me, & begging my dear Gracey to write to me also agreeable to her promise. I have wrote to Papa & Davy twice since Messrs. Neave & Co. protested my bills from John Baynton; I beg I may have both sent me by first opportunity, in the mean time I shall borrow what Money I want from my esteemed friend Benny Rush. Please give my duty to Papa & Mamma & love to all Brothers & Sisters & also to

Uncle & Aunt Morris, Aunt Debby, Sally Morris, Sally Power, Polley Jones, Emlen's family, Uriah Woolman, David Stanton, in particular B. Dorsey & wife, Sarah Zanes, Isaac Zanes if at home, John Pemberton & wife, the three Parishes, Anth. Morris, Brewer, Owen Jones Sen'r, Sam'l Pleasants & wife, Thos. Yorke & wife & to every acquaintance & friend whose names I may have omitted.

With prayers for your prosperity & welfare I subscribe myself
Your much obliged & affectionate Brother,

Jonathan Potts.

The studies of our young Friend were interrupted towards the close of the winter by news from home that his "dearest Grace" was ill and longed to see him. He left for London immediately, and arrived in Philadelphia during the month of April, and they were married in May, 1767. After this he pursued his studies in the College of Philadelphia, and was one of the ten graduates of the Medical School at its first commencement in 1768.

Dr. Potts began the practice of medicine in Reading, eighteen miles from Pottsgrove. In a lengthy exhortation to the citizens of the town on the subject of inoculation for smallpox, published in the local paper, he wrote:

"Suppose there is an Island into which by far the greater part of Mankind are unavoidably forced to enter some time of their life & in their passage to this Island they must pass through a deep & dangerous river in getting over which one in five perish or are drowned.

"But of late there is a convenient Ferry boat built which is always ready & at call, by which they can at any time be rapidly ferried over to the Island & not one in a hundred fall overboard or are drowned, & even should any meet with this accident it is owing to their own mismanagement or carelessness & not to any fault in the boat. Now is there any one whom prejudice has not totally deprived of thinking who would not prefer the passage by the Boat to that of plunging for many days thro' the River struggling for their lives, & into which they are forced without their consent or the least warning, & should they be fortunate enough to get over they come out horribly scarred & disfigured, & perhaps lose one if not both of their eyes."

Early in 1776, as the war came closer, Dr. Potts was very active in raising men and organizing the forces in Reading and the countryside. He had already, in the summer of 1774, been a delegate from Berks County to the provincial meeting of deputies in Philadelphia, and a member of the Provincial Congress held there in January 1775. In April 1776 he petitioned Congress to be appointed Director of the Hospitals in Canada. He received the appointment, and in June 1776 he left New York in company with General Horatio Gates for the north.

During a campaign that was as difficult and full of frustrations for the doctor as it was for the Army itself, his performance was such that General Gates in a letter to John Hancock wrote: "I cannot close without requesting your Excellency to inform Congress of the good care & attention with which Dr. Potts & ye gentlemen of the General Hospital have conducted the business of their department.

"I must beg that some honorary mark of the favor of Congress may be shown to Dr. Potts & his subordinate associates."

A month later he left Army headquarters at Albany with the following letter:

Dr. Jonathan Potts, Director-General of the Hospitals of the Northern Department, having with the greatest care and attention performed the duties of his station and put the hospitals in such a condition as renders his immediate attention unnecessary, has my permission to visit his family in Berks County, State of Pennsylvania, and is to remain there so long as the duties of his office will admit.

Given at Albany this 16th day of November, 1777.

Horatio Gates.

While Dr. Potts was at home, he was appointed by Congress Director-General of the Hospitals in the Middle Department; and the Army being then in winter quarters at Valley Forge, and a large hospital of those wounded at the battle of Brandywine established at Ephrata, he found much to do in his own neighborhood.

Through the long winter when the Continental Army was encamped at Valley Forge his labor must have been great, as at one time no less than eleven hospitals were established there for the sick and suffering soldiers, their insufficient food and clothing rendering them prey of every disease.

Dr. Potts' zeal in the public service had been so unremitting during four years that he was at length prostrated by illness, from which he never recovered, and in October 1781 he died at the early age of thirty-six, at his home in Reading, before the independence of his country, which he so ardently longed for, was achieved.

He was buried in the family graveyard at Pottstown, but without a stone to mark the grave, the Society of Friends disapproving of any monumental marbles.

Isaac was born May 20, 1750, "about eleven o'clock in the forenoon," as his precise biographer puts it. His father died when Isaac was eighteen, and when the son came of age he took a portion of his father's Valley Forge property. He grew up to be a "man of infinite jest and humor, and his social qualities well fitted him for the gay society which he enjoyed."

Then suddenly, when he was attending the burial of one of his slaves across the Schuylkill, "the Spirit moved him to speak words of exhortation and warning." He found himself delivering a funeral sermon. The mourners, knowing him for his gaiety and joviality, were as astounded as he was himself by this performance. "And from this time forth," according to his chronicler, "he became an acceptable Quaker preacher or Public Friend."

Like most of the Quakers, Isaac was decidedly opposed to war—any war. Yet when it became apparent that the American forces were going to occupy his peaceful valley, camp upon the slopes surrounding it, requisition flour from his mills, and make use of his own house as headquarters for the commanding general, he accepted the situation with good Quaker grace. War was wicked, and when Isaac saw the army marching into the valley, many of the men barefooted and bleeding from the rough hard-frozen ground, he saw it as a defeated army, which only made it worse.

It was Isaac who is said to have come upon Washington on his knees at prayer in the snow, and to have told his wife he'd seen a sight he could never forget. "Till now," he told her, "I have thought that a Christian and a soldier were characters incompatible: but if George Washington be not a man of God, I am mistaken, and still more shall I be disappointed if God do not through him perform some great thing for this country."

That was in the winter of 1777-78, when Isaac was twenty-seven. He lived until 1803, and a few weeks before he died he added this last paragraph to his will.

"Life is uncertain, I am in a poor state of health & am to set out on a journey tomorrow, so must apologize for this unmethodical will: but I feel easiest to leave it as it is, with a mind cloathed with the spring & glow of universal love . . . Amen. Farewell."

The dower chest under the window in the children's dining room is early Pennsylvania German. Both the tavern table and the burl bowl on it glow with two centuries of use and care, and the view of the miller's house through the open doorway is a reminder of the days when Pottsgrove was an extensive establishment of farm buildings, gristmill, and housing for the help.

THE WETHERSFIELD STORY

The Houses

The Webb, 1752; the Deane, 1766; the Stevens, 1788

The People

Joseph Webb, Wethersfield merchant
Silas Deane, Revolutionary patriot and diplomat
Mehitabel Nott, Webb's wife, and later Deane's
Elizabeth Saltonstall, Deane's second wife
Isaac Stevens, leatherworker
Sarah Wright, Stevens' wife
Joseph Webb II, inheritor of Webb house
Abigail Chester, Joseph II's wife
Benjamin Franklin
Arthur Lee } *colleagues of Deane at the Court of Versailles*

General Washington
Count de Rochambeau } *conferees at the Webb house*
Chevalier de Chastellux

"Philadelphia, June 22nd, 1775
"My dear,—This will be handed you by his Excellency General Washington, in company with General Lee, and retinue. Should they lodge a night in Wethersfield, you will accommodate their horses, servants, &c, in the best manner at the taverns, and their retinue will likely go on to Hartford.

"We this moment received advice of a battle at Bunker's Hill, but the account is very confused. It is said to have happened on Saturday last, and the news arrived here this morning.

"I have wrote you so lately . . . I have nothing . . . to add . . . May God preserve us!
"I am, my Dear, Yours &c.,

"S. Deane."

As the delegate from Connecticut, Silas Deane was sitting in the Congress which had just appointed Washington Commander-in-Chief of the American military forces, such as they were. It had taken four days for word of Bunker Hill to reach Philadelphia. And now Washington was on his way to "the front" at Boston, carrying the letter for Deane's wife Elizabeth.

Riding along with him was his chief lieutenant, the trouble-making British-born General Charles Lee, who thought he should have been given Washington's job, and who finally became so disobedient and abusive that he had to be cashiered. But then they were two military men together, and together on the evening of June 28 got into New Haven where Washington

From left to right: the Deane, the Webb, the Stevens.

had agreed to review a volunteer company of Yale students and two companies of town volunteers. The next morning they left for Wethersfield.

What happened that night in Wethersfield—or *didn't* happen—is the kind of thing that haunts historians. There is nothing about it in Washington's Diary, and nothing in Deane's letters. Douglas Southall Freeman, the most eminent of the Washington biographers, says he propably did spend the night there, and Freeman's guess is as good as anybody's—better, probably. Anyway, it was from Wethersfield that the General left the next morning for Springfield, then from Springfield for Worcester, and from Worcester to Cambridge, where on arrival he took command of the Continental Army.

Elizabeth was Silas Deane's second wife, the daughter of Gurdon Saltonstall of Norwich, a governor of Connecticut. Deane's first wife had been Mehitabel Webb, widow of the man who built the elegant house next door to Deane's. Not that Deane's house wasn't elegant too; it's rather that its elegance wasn't the conventional kind. When proper Connecticut houses were not wearing porches, Deane's house wore them. When hallways went narrowly down the middle, Deane's hallway was large and square and off to one side. And the great front parlor has in it the only carved brownstone colonial mantel in the state, maybe in all New England. How much of this was due to Deane has never been disclosed. It is only known that he was a man who did things his own way.

Joseph Webb's house next door to the north was built fourteen years before Deane's. While in comparison it could be called a *proper* house, hardly a house in Connecticut can match it for the enchantment of its chaste architectural treatment or the perfection of its furnishings. And certainly not a single house in the state can compare with the place it occupies in Revolutionary history.

The year the Stevens house was built, 1788, the Deane house was attached for debt. Deane

77

was dying in England where he had been living the life of an exile. And the year after, when Isaac Stevens and Sarah Wright were married and moved into their new house, Silas Deane, too ill to make the journey home, was disembarked at Deal, where he died the next day, destitute.

Isaac was thirty-four, is thought to have been a leather worker. Sarah was twenty-three. Isaac was the grandson of Reverend Timothy Stevens, Harvard 1687, the first minister at Glastonbury, while Sarah's grandfather was one of the Proprietors of Wethersfield. Friends of the Webbs next door, they lived long and outwardly uneventful lives. They had a son and a daughter who brought their children into the life of the house. And the home stayed in the Stevens family for one hundred and seventy years. Now charmingly restored, with much of the Stevens furnishings, it also contains a collection of ladies' bonnets and an appropriate display of children's toys and dolls.

Except for the bare records of births and deaths, there is nothing to go on but the house itself. No Stevens letters, diaries or accounts have been uncovered. But what has been uncovered in the house are the original paint colors of the walls; and the decorative scheme disclosed is so subtle, original, and in a way sophisticated, that the young couple almost comes alive.

What they did was to make each room, upstairs and down, a different variation of green, all harmonious; then suddenly, the door of the northeast bedroom opens on a final burst of not another green, but an exuberant blue.

First to come into the area were the Dutch from the New Netherlands settlements around what is now New York City. They were making attempts in the early 1630's to establish trading posts along the Connecticut River, up and down from where Wethersfield is now. But the first people who really came to stay, were colonists from New England.

The first Webb to come to Connecticut was Richard, who emigrated from England before 1626 with his only child Richard Jr. at whose birth in 1611 the mother had died. It was 1635 on the shallop *Blessing of the Bay* that Richard Sr. with the Rev. Thomas Hooker and four others sailed around Cape Cod, into the Sound and up the Connecticut River five miles beyond Wethersfield, founding the settlement of Hartford. And it was Hooker's and Webb's forthright democratic views which were reflected in a frame of government they helped form, and which was first adopted by Hartford, Windsor and Wethersfield.

Just about a hundred years later, the great-great-great-grandson of Richard Webb came with his parents to Wethersfield from Stamford where he was born in 1733. He became one of the most successful merchants of the town and one of its most prominent citizens. In 1748 he married Mehitabel Nott. The next year their first child, Joseph, was born; then Samuel, who became Washington's friend and aide-de-camp in the first part of the Revolutionary War. Then three daughters and another son. Four years later the father built the house that was not only a beauty to begin with, but was to be the scene of one of the momentous occasions in American history.

Less than nine years after the house was finished, in 1761, Joseph Webb died. Two years later, Mehitabel married a bright attractive lawyer, a graduate of Yale, who at twenty-six had just come from New London to practice in Wethersfield. This, of course, was Silas Deane. The next year their son Jesse was born; two years later they built their house next door to the Webb house, which Mehitabel's son Joseph was to inherit, and the year after that Mehitabel died of consumption. Not long after, Silas married Elizabeth Saltonstall.

Both of his marriages were a great help to his social and financial situation, so that in addition to his law practice, Deane was able to buy his way into the mercantile business. He gravitated quite naturally into politics, and was elected in 1772 to the state assembly at Hartford. He was described by a contemporary at about this time as "A man of enterprise, vigor and judgement," and by another as "An accomplished college-bred man of elegant manner and striking appear-

In the Stevens kitchen workability was the watchword, but with it such stylishness: on the paneling around the fireplace and oven, the sliding shutter, the old red dresser, the table and chairs, and all the usable things. Through the door is the dining room with its 1750 Queen Anne table and fine dropleaf table, both Stevens family possessions, as are the silver, glass, and china on the dining table and the gold and white Spode tea set on the dropleaf. The Terry clock is as choice as they come. Note again how the sliding shutters complement the paneling, as they do in all the downstairs rooms. And remember that every room but one is a different shade of green, the wide floor boards left beautifully bare.

In the Webb house a 1750 solid mahogany Connecticut secretary dominates the momentous council room, with its 1730 New England maple drop-leaf table, its two Eliphalet Chapen Chippendale chairs of 1780, its two English Queen Anne chairs, and its 1790 Connecticut Hepplewhite wing chair upholstered in yellow Scalmandre.

ance, accustomed to a showy style of living, equipage and appointment, and a natural diplomat."

In 1774 Deane was sent to Philadelphia as a Connecticut delegate to the first Continental Congress, then the next year to the second, but for some reason the Connecticut Assembly did not reappoint him to the Congress of 1776. Congress, however, kept his services by sending him to France, and that was the last he ever saw of his wife or his home.

He was to serve on two committees: One to sell colonial produce and send supplies needed here by the colonies, the other secretly to buy army clothing, arms, munitions and artillery. He was also to find out if France would receive an American ambassador, and form treaties of alliance and commerce with the colonies.

He was a great success. He formed a close friendship with Beaumarchais, which helped him to send home eight shiploads of military supplies for the Saratoga campaign. He procured many European military officers, among them Lafayette, de Kalb, Steuben, and Pulaski, all of

The stunning feature of the Webb house bedroom in which Washington spent five nights on the occasion of his conference with Rochambeau (held in the council room above) is the French red flock wallpaper. The bedspread is rare rose-color Camlet of 1788.

whom of course became invaluable; but unfortunately many others became a nuisance, and he was criticized for being too taken in by titles and exaggerated claims of prowess. Even so, the good ones outweighed the bad.

Then in September 1776, Deane was joined in Paris by Benjamin Franklin and Arthur Lee. And by February 1778 this commission of three was able to sign two treaties at the Court of Versailles: one for commerce, and one for a military alliance, which must certainly have been the single most effective diplomatic achievement toward the winning of the war. In the midst of the negotiations in 1777, Elizabeth had died back home in Wethersfield.

During the negotiations Lee, who was a member of the powerful Lee family of Virginia, with two brothers in Congress, began sending home criticisms of his colleagues, and complaints that in dealing with the French for war supplies, they, Deane in particular, were plundering the public. Called home, Deane was unable to produce proper vouchers to get the vindication of Congress, and after nearly two years in Philadelphia, returned to France, hoping to speed up the auditing of his accounts. His poor French and careless accountancy made this so difficult that he became deeply depressed to the point of illness. In his bitterness he lost confidence in his country's cause, and was indiscreet enough to confide this in his letters to friends at home. These letters were intercepted, and printed in British-occupied New York. Franklin, Morris, Jay, and many others of his friends kept on speaking in his defense and attacking Lee for his malicious insinuation, but by this time Deane was living in bankrupt misery, first in Ghent, then in London, hardly able to help himself. Finally, he was persuaded to come home, and with the help of friends in London, passage was obtained from Deal on the Boston packet. He was taken there and put on board, but being found too sick to sail, he was carried ashore, where he died. He was buried in Deal in an unmarked grave.

In 1842 Congress paid $37,000 to Deane's heirs on the grounds that the audit made under Arthur Lee's direction was "one-sided, erroneous, and a gross injustice to Silas Deane." His house first went to the Stephen Chesters, then to George Robinson, and then to the E. Hart Fenns who left it by bequest to the Connecticut Dames.

In May of 1781, one month before Deane wrote the pessimistic private letters that laid his patriotism publicly open to suspicion, the most important happening in the life of the house next door to Deane's occurred. For the meeting in the Webb house between Washington and Rochambeau, with all its implications and imponderables, was to result within five months in the surrender at Yorktown. The alliance that Deane had helped so successfully to consummate in France three years before was now about to enter its climactic stage.

On May 6 the French frigate *Concorde* arrived at Boston with the Vicomte de Rochambeau and the Comte de Barras on board; Rochambeau to confer with Washington, and Admiral Barras to assume command of "His Most Christian Majesty's Fleet and sea forces up these Coasts," as Washington expressed it. The French fleet was anchored in the harbor of Newport, Rhode Island, for which the two men and their entourages set off at once. Washington was at his headquarters at New Windsor, just below Newburgh on the west bank of the Hudson, when he received Rochambeau's letter requesting a time and place for their meeting.

Washington to Rochambeau: ". . . As you request me to name the time of the meeting, I appoint Monday the 21st of this month at Weathersfield, which I think is as soon as will be possible for you with convenience. Genl. Knox and Genl. Duportail will accompany me." Then into this dispatch, done in the handwriting of Tench Tightman, the General's able aide-de-camp, Washington inserts, "I will endeavor to be at Wethersfield [the only time he ever spelled it right] on Saturday afternoon myself and have made choice of this town in preference to Hartford because the latter will be occupied by the Assembly of the State which is now sitting." Then again in Tightman's handwriting, "I shall very impatiently wait the pleasure of meeting Your Excellency and the Count de Barras."

A rear view of the Stevens house showing the dark red weatherboarding. A wood-pile and the well house are in their original position. The Webb house is on the right.

From Washington's Diary for May 1781:

"18th . . . Set out this day for the Interview at Weathersfield with the Count de Rochambeau and Admiral Barras. —Reached Morgan's Tavern 43 miles from Fishkill Landing [a ferry ran from Newburgh to the Landing on the east bank of the Hudson] after dining at Colo. Van De bergs [where Washington, Connecticut is now]."

"19th. Breakfasted at Litchfield [thirteen miles]—dined at Farmington [20 miles] and lodged at Weathersfield [15 miles] at the house of Joseph Webb, Esq. the quarters wch. were taken for me and my Suit.—"

From the Journals of General Samuel Blackeley Webb:

"On Saturday the 19th. inst. his excellency General Washington, accompanied by Gen. Knox, Gen. Du Portail, and their respective suites, arrived at Wethersfield; being escorted into town by a number of gentlemen from Hartford and Wethersfield. As he dismounted at his quarters he was saluted by a discharge of thirteen cannon, by the corps of artillery, under the command of Capt. Frederick Bull."

From the diary of (presumably) Baron Cromot du Bourg, an aide of Rochambeau:

"In the afternoon I went to see a charming spot called Weathersfield, four miles from East Hartford. It would be impossible to find prettier houses and a more beautiful view. I went up into the steeple of the church and saw the richest country I have yet seen in America. From this spot you can see for fifty miles around."

Washington was given the bedroom with the famous dark red flock paper. Whether more of Washington's "suit" than General Knox and General Duportail stayed that Saturday night in the Webb house with Washington does not appear in any contemporary chronicle, but Freeman would say, "probably."

"Lord's Day, May twentieth," from Governor Trumbull's diary, "Went with Capt. Fred. Bull in a carriage to Wethersfield—attended divine services with General Washington per tot diem. Mr. Marsh preached. Mat.7.3—blessed are the poor in spirit, for theirs is the Kingdom of Heaven."

82

Washington's Diary says this of the 21st: "Count de Rochambeau, with the Chevalier de Chastellux, arrived about noon. The appearance of the British fleet, under Admiral Arbuthnot, off Block Island, prevented the appearance of the Count de Barras."

Of the 22nd it says, "Fixed with Count de Rochambeau upon plan of Campaign—in substance as follows—That the French Land force should march as soon as Squadron could Sail for Boston [to refit]—[then] to the North [Hudson] River-and there, in conjunction with the American, to commence an operation against New York . . . or to extend our views to the Southward as circumstances and a Naval superiority might render more necessary and eligable..."

From the memoirs of Rochambeau: "General Washington, during this conference, had scarcely another object in view but an expedition against the island of New York, and which he persisted in considering the most capable of striking a deathblow to British domination in America . . . He considered an expedition against Lord Cornwallis, in Chesapeak Bay, as quite a secondary object, to which there was no necessity of diverting our attention until we were quite certain of our inability to accomplish the former. After some slight discussion, it was settled, however, that . . . the French corps should proceed to unite itself to the American army opposite the island of New York, to which the combined army should then approach as near as possible, and there wait until we should hear from M. de Grasse, [commanding the main French fleet in the West Indies] to whom a frigate was to be immediately dispatched.

"General Washington wrote immediately the result of this conference to General Sullivan, a member of Congress. His letters were intercepted; it is believed, and all the papers repeated the report, that he spoke in those letters of the projected attack on the New York islands, with a view only to mislead the enemy's general, and that, consequently, he was very glad that the letters had fallen into the hands of the latter. *There is no need of such fictions to convey the glory of this great man to posterity.* [Author's italics.] His wish was really then to attack New York; and we should have carried the plan into execution if the enemy had continued to draft troops from its garrison, and if the French navy could have been brought to our assistance. But what completely deceived the English general, was a confidential letter written by the Chevalier de Chastelux to the French representative at Congress, wherein he boasted of having artfully succeeded in bringing round my opinion to concur with that of General Washington; stating at the same time that the siege of the island of New York had been at length determined upon, and that our two armies were on the march for that city, and that orders had been sent off to M de Grasse to come with his fleet and force his way over the bar of Sandyhook to the mouth of the harbour of New York. He also complained bitterly, and in rather uncouth language, of the little resource left to a man of his parts [meaning Chastellux] over the imperative disposition of a general [meaning Rochambeau] who was eager of command. The English officer who had charge of every branch of the spying department sent me a copy of the intercepted missive, and, by so doing, his intention had not been most assuredly to set my wits at ease. I sent for the Chevalier de Chatelux; showed him the letter, and then threw it in the fire, and left him a prey to his own remorse. Of course, I did not endeavour to undeceive him, and, *in the sequel, we shall see to what extent this general officer had been made the confident of the real project which I proposed to the Count de Grasse.*" [Author's italics.]

For what happened was this. The French forces from Newport joined the Americans above New York on July 5. Word was received from De Grasse on August 14 that he would sail from the West Indies on August 13 for the Chesapeake, with his entire fleet and 3,000 troops. So Washington at once got ready to march both his and Rochambeau's forces to Virginia.

First, however, the French and American armies made a feint toward Staten Island, not

Almost out of sight in the picture of the three Wethersfield houses on page 77, the Deane house is shown here in a 1964 photograph in process of restoration.

letting on that they were about to head south, which they then did, down through New Jersey and on to the head of the Chesapeake. But before they reached the Bay, De Grasse's fleet appeared August 30 off Yorktown, and the next day he landed his troops.

Then disposing of the British fleet, De Grasse sent his ships up to the head of the Bay and brought back as much of Washington's and Rochambeau's combined armies as the ships could carry . . . The rest is history. On October 19 the English under Cornwallis laid down their arms.

Thus it was that throughout the Wethersfield conference, while the campaign against "New York Island" came to the fore, it was always in the background that the grand fleet of De Grasse, which had already left Brest on its way to the West Indies (from where Washington wondered hopefully if its next move wouldn't be toward the American coast), would in the end be the deciding factor, either at New York or in the Chesapeake. The fact that the end came off Yorktown is a tribute to the rapport between Washington and Rochambeau (despite the scheming Chastellux), which went way beyond immediate moves, and made the Webb house conference one of the greatest military meetings ever held.

Back at the Webb house and that memorable May, Washington wrote on the twenty-third, "Count de Rochambeau set out on his return to Newport, while I prepared and forwarded dispatches to the governors of the four New England States [Vermont was at the time an independent state and didn't enter the Union until 1790, and Maine was still a province of Massachusetts] calling upon them in earnest and pointed terms, to compleat their Continental Battalions for the Campaign...

"24th. Set out on my return to New Windsor—dined at Farmington and lodged at Litchfield.

"25th. Breakfasted at Squire Cogswells—dined at Colo. Vandeburgs, and reached head Quarters about Sunset . . ."

"New Windsor, June 17th, 1781.

"Dear Sir [Joseph Webb]:

Inclosed is my Measure for a pair of draw-Boots [Horseskin] to be made of the Leather Manufactured at your Works–The Measure is exact, and I should be glad to have the Boots well made—neat—and sent to me as soon as possible, with the price in specie, which shall be immediately forwarded to you—

Upon my return from Weathersfield I found Mrs. Washington extremely unwell, she still

The portrait of Silas Deane has been attributed to William Johnston, and that of Elizabeth Saltonstall Deane, Deane's second wife, was painted by Joseph Blackborn in 1762. The portraits are owned by John Webster Buck of Wethersfield, a descendant of the second Mrs. Deane's sister, Sarah Saltonstall Buck.

continues low and weak, but will set out for the Southward as soon as she can bear the fatigue of the journey; she joins me in compliments and best wishes to yourself, Mrs. and Miss Webb—I cannot conclude without assuring you that I have a high sense of your politeness and attention to me while I was at Weathersfield—and that I should at all times be happy to see you at head Qrs.

I am Dr. Sir, Yr. Most Obedt. & Obligd Servt.

Go. WASHINGTON."

Webb's wife, whom he married in 1774, was Abigail Chester, playfully known as the "daughter of kings," seeing that her ancestry goes directly back to British royalty of the tenth century. It was her family who bought Silas Deane's house from his creditors.

Joseph Webb, during the war, was said to have been a prominent purveyor of military materiel and a generous financial contributor to the American cause. One of his two younger brothers, Colonel Samuel Blackeley Webb, is generally supposed to have had something to do with Washington being quartered at the Webb house.

Partly due to the postwar depression and being paid back in paper currency for outlays he had made during the war, Joseph Webb, by 1783, fell into serious financial straits. Some of this misfortune he felt it necessary to blame on poor Silas Deane, who had handled the Webb estate after the father's death, as part of Deane's law practice in Wethersfield. And Deane's letter of October 1783 from London to one of Joseph's brothers in Wethersfield is distressful. "Reflect for one Moment that I spent near Ten Years of the prime of my Life, in the service of Your Family in settling the Accts. in superintending your Education . . . I have met with misfortunes enough from other Quarters without this cutting one of being deemed a Debtor, when I have bestowed the Benefits . . . You must excuse the incorrectness of this letter for I am very weak and scarcely able to set in my Chair while I write."

The senior Webb built the truly stylish house of the three, poor Deane the characterful one, and the Stevenses the most intimate and personal. Together and apart, what a show they put on in the shade of those elm trees; and what stories they have to tell!

The garden side of the fine country mansion begun in 1754 by Charles Carroll, Chyrurgeon, and finished by his son, Charles Carroll, Barrister.

THE MOUNT CLARE STORY

The People

Charles Carroll, Chyrurgeon, who began the house
Charles Carroll, Barrister, his son, who finished it
Margaret Tilghman, the Barrister's wife
James Carroll, né Maccubbin, the Barrister's nephew, the inheritor

Created Lord Baltimore by James I, George Calvert, after visiting Virginia in 1628, persuaded the King to grant him territory north of the Potomac. The charter came through in June 1632, a few months after Baltimore's death. His son Cecilius Calvert became the 2nd Lord Baltimore and proprietor of the colony, which he never visited, governing by deputy, the first governor being his brother, Leonard Calvert.

In 1634, aboard the *Ark* and the *Dove*, about two hundred colonists arrived from England, mostly Catholics like the Calverts; and led by Governor Calvert went ashore in a cove up from the mouth of the Potomac, calling the place St. Mary's City, which became the first capital of Maryland, marked now by a reconstruction of the 1676 capitol building.

The times had been troubled in the colony ever since 1640, when the Long Parliment began in England and the Commons had been established. Boundary disputes, anti-Catholicism, and other dissensions made it a period of upheaval. Then on June 27, 1691, Maryland was made a Royal Province, and when the Church of England was established the following year, order was restored; and in 1695 the capital was moved from Catholic St. Mary's City to Protestant Annapolis.

The Calvert family having become converted in 1715 to the Church of England, the 4th Lord Baltimore was restored as proprietor in May and the charter of 1632 restored as well.

This same year there arrived in Annapolis a medical man from Dublin, now known as Charles Carroll, Chyrurgeon; for there came to be so many Charles Carrolls in Maryland that it was found expedient to designate the different ones, Charles Carroll, Chyrurgeon, Charles Carroll, Barrister, Charles Carroll of Carrollton, and so forth. The Chyrurgeon established himself in medical practice at the capital. "Later," (as related by Lillian Giffen), finding this a very slow way to get rich, "he went into tobacco, built ships, and sent flour and foodstuffs to the sugar islands of the West Indies. But speculation in land, and the development of the iron industry were the principal sources of his ultimate fortune."

In 1723 in Annapolis his first son, Charles Carroll, was born, the Barrister-to-be, in a fine town house the doctor had built, where later the Barrister and his wife spent their winters. The son was taken to Europe for his education, "when he was a child." He later studied at Cambridge, returning home when he was twenty-three, only to go back to England to read law for a while in the Middle Temple. On his first stay he had letters like this from his father: "I hope you will lay out this money in Necessaries for your Person or Endowment of your Mind and not spend in Wine or Riot, Remark that women and wine are the Bane of youth."

1754 is the date that is given for Mount Clare, the great country seat, now so beautifully restored in the heart of Baltimore, which the Barrister inherited on his father's death (along with other vast holdings). This was shortly after his second return from Europe in 1755. The house, started by the father, was finished by the son. It was the Barrister who made the place "the elegant, splendid seat of Mr. Carroll, barrister," which John Adams describes in his diary. "It is a large and elegant house; it stands fronting looking down the river into the harbor; it is one mile from the water;—there is a descent not far from the house;—you have a fine garden, then you descend a few steps and have another fine garden; you go down a few more and have another."

A more breathless account of Mount Clare has been gleaned by Mary-Paulding Martin from the diary of Mary Cary Ambler ("the same fascinator who is said to have turned down George Washington"), written in 1770 on a visit to Baltimore from Jamestown to be inoculated for smallpox.

"About two miles from Baltimore is an exceedingly Handsome Seat called Mount Clare belonging to Mr. Charles Carrel of Annapolis this Seat is within sight of the Baltimore Iron Works & when M Ambler was at the Place the Beauty of Mr. Carrels Seat tempted her to take a nearer view of it & she walked there on Satury Afternoon with Mrs. Brook & took a great deal of Pleasure in looking at the Bowling Green & many Orange & Lemon trees just ready to bear besides which is a new building a Pinery where the Gardr expects to ripen some next Summer, the House where this Gentn & his Lady reside in the Summer stands upon a Very High Hill & has a fine View of Petapsico River, you step out of the Door into the Bwlg Green from which the Garden Falls & when you stand on the top of it there is such a Uniformity of Each side that the whole Plantation seems to be laid out like a Garden there is also a Handsome Court yard on the other side of the House. This Gentn is one of the Propietors of the Baltimore Iron Works. He has no child."

In 1763 the Barrister married Margaret Tilghman, of the eastern shore family, on which occasion the *Maryland Gazette* described her as "a young lady of great Merit, Beauty and Fortune." He was an active force in the affairs of Maryland during the Revolutionary period and was a member of the Committee of Correspondence and the Committee of Safety as well as being presiding officer of several state conventions, including the one that relieved Robert Eden, the last royal Governor, of his office. As one of Maryland's "seven most distinguished patriots," he was the author of that state's Declaration of Rights, proclaimed on July 3, 1776, helped frame her constitution, and served her in Congress. When he died childless in 1783, his widow lived on at Mount Clare, exchanging seeds and plants until her death 34 years later; the estate being willed to a nephew James Maccubbin on condition that he take the Carroll name, which he did. Crowded in by the city and neglected for years, and long since acquired from Carroll descendants by the City of Baltimore, in 1917 it was placed in the custody of the Maryland Dames, who have restored and furnished it with such sensitivity that the house seems to have preserved the living presence of the distinguished Barrister and his charming wife.

In the dining room with its green walls, Adam mantel and portieres of yellow brocade, the Hepplewhite chairs are upholstered to match. The dining table and serving table are Sheraton and the revolving epergne is Waterford. Chairs, tables and epergne were all in Mount Clare with the Carroll family. On the mantelpiece is one of the clocks Lafayette is said to have ordered to honor George Washington, and to have canceled the order when the lines: "First in war, first in piece, and first in the hearts of his countrymen," had "peace" misspelled on the clockcase by the maker.

The Tate House is a rare example of the early raised-roof attic design.

THE TATE HOUSE STORY

The People

George Tate, mast agent, and builder
Mary Tate, his wife

Samuel
William } *their sons*
George
Robert

The single-stick mainmast of a first-line 120 gun man-of-war in the British Navy before the Revolution took a white pine trunk 40 inches in diameter at the butt and 120 feet tall. Such a mast cost the Navy Board £140 F.O.B. Falmouth, Maine, or Portsmouth, New Hampshire, the two principal mast ports in the colonies. A third-rater of 74 guns took a 36-inch trunk 108 feet tall, while a mere frigate of 28 guns took a mast 20 inches by 72 feet, twice the size of a telephone pole. Then there were foremasts, mizzenmasts, and all manner of bowsprits, yards, and spars.

Only one tree in ten or twenty thousand, depending upon the size of the mast, would do. And even then the slightest flaw might condemn it, though that flaw might sometimes remain undiscovered until the giant pole arrived in England. The arrival of a fleet of mast ships from New England in a time of great need, a hundred years before the Revolution, caused Samuel Pepys, (an importer of mast trees, first from the Baltic and then from the colonies) at

The corner cupboard is the jewel of the "best room," and sparkles with its arrangement of Chinese Export porcelain. The whole half-paneled room glows in the afternoon when the sunlight comes through the gold-colored draperies of the western windows.

The gentleman in uniform who adorns the dining room is George Tate's son George, an admiral in the navy of Catherine the Great. The prints are Hogarths, and the furniture and the salt glaze dessert and fruit set are the period of the house.

the time he was secretary to the Admiralty, to jot down in his diary for that day. "thank God!" in exultation.

It goes without saying that the men whose job it was to select the one tree out of ten or twenty thousand which would make a proper mainmast had to be men of uncommon skill. So had the men who supervised the felling. The tree had to fall just right. Huge piles of small trees had to be placed where they would cushion the fall. And snaking the trees out of the woods and "twitching" them in and out of the water; sliding them downhill; or dragging them up with sometimes as many as twenty yoke of oxen: all this was an art and science of a very special order.

Then there was the trimming of the trunks and the loading of the mast ships. These mast ships, by the nature of their cargo, were cumbersome craft, up to a thousand tons displacement, capable of carrying as many as a hundred great masts, with many more hundreds of yards and spars to fill up the interstices.

Two men divided the responsibility for getting the masts to England. One was the King's Surveyor of Woods and Forests. He was appointed by the Crown. It was he who saw that all the suitable pines were blazed with the Broad Axe mark, signifying royal property, and it was he who licensed the colonists who did the cutting.

Responsible for all the rest was the Mast Agent, representing the men who held the great timber contracts with the Navy Board; and by far the most important Mast Agent in Maine was George Tate. He was born in London in 1700, and made a name for himself in the shipyards of England. Then, in time to build his house in 1755, he was sent to Falmouth, now Portland, which, with Portsmouth, furnished practically all of the American masts for the English Navy.

George Tate's chronicler writes that "Tate became 'American' immediately upon arrival ... and when the Revolution broke out ... contributed much aid to the Colonies; but in Church matters he was 'English.'" He married in 1738 and when he and his wife came to the colonies, they had four surviving sons, the last one of whom, Robert, was born in 1751.

Tate's first wife died at sixty in 1770, under very peculiar circumstances that suggest foul play.° Nine years later Captain Tate married Mrs. Coverly, a widow, when he was nearly eighty.

His two older sons, Samuel and William, and Robert, the youngest, all lived near the father. The third son, George, had become an officer in the Russian Navy. In 1775, at twenty-nine, he wrote to Robert from Revel that "Her Majesty [Catherine the Great] has advanced me to Rear Admiral." Nine years later, in another letter to Robert, from Kronstadt, the admiral writes: "Your father informs me, that our present Mother, is turned of Fifty and that she takes great care of him in his Old Age, as he is Eighty Four Years Old." Again from Kronstadt, in 1786, the admiral writes Robert that "the difference between our Father and his wife I have not been informed of as William writes me he supposed you have let me know . . . so pray let me hear."

This is all that is now known of the father's family life, except that in the will he made in 1789 he doesn't mention Mary Coverly. " ... thank God," he wrote, "[I] am of perfect mind and memory." At eighty-six he could read without glasses and was still, it is said, a wonderful penman.

To George, the admiral, he left five shillings, to Samuel five shillings and the interest on a four-hundred pound note, to Robert two seventy-acre lots in Gorham, and to William, who then lived at home with him, all the rest! He died in 1794, and is buried about a block from his house in Stroudwater Cemetery, with his first wife.

It was in Stroudwater, now part of Portland, that George Tate built his house in 1755. It is a house of great style and distinction; a Londoner's house indoors, a New Englander's house outside. A fashionable shipwright, familiar with both sides of the ocean, might have been the builder. William, who lived with his father and inherited the house, made his second marriage the year his father died. Now, if only it were William's letters that had been preserved!

°This involved the son William, who, after pleading guilty to the murder of his mother, was pardoned by the King.

From the land side the first sight of Gunston Hall is unforgettable; each part a delight: the brickwork, the quoins, the windows, the chimneys, all creating a perfect setting for Buckland's beautiful Palladian porch, just as his hexagonal one decorates a similar facade on the river side with its famous great boxwood gardens. The architect is unknown, but one thing is certain, that Buckland, alone, was the composer of the woodworking wonders within, the porches (and maybe more) without. The painting of William Buckland is from a portrait by Charles Willson Peale.

THE GUNSTON HALL STORY

The People

George Mason, the builder and "reluctant statesman"
William Buckland, carpenter and joiner

The builder of Gunston Hall was born in 1725, in what his biographer believes must have been a fairly modest structure on the neck of land that is opposite the present Quantico Marine Base. He was the fourth George Mason of the family in America, the first having come to this country in 1651 at a time when, following the beheading of Charles I in 1649, many Loyalists, were leaving England rather than risk Cromwellian reprisals. Most of them headed for Virginia.

George was ten when his father's small boat overturned in a sudden squall as he was crossing the Potomac from Maryland to Virginia. George inherited his father's entire estate, which comprised several large plantations in Virginia and Maryland; the finest one was in Virginia, and consisted of two thousand acres beautifully located along the Potomac. It was here that he was to build Gunston Hall, named for the family estate in Staffordshire, England, whence his great-grandfather had come following the battle of Worcester.

Until he was twenty-one, George lived with his mother, his sister Mary, and his younger brother Thomson on a family plantation called Chappawamsick, close to one called Marlborough, the home of the children's other guardian, John Mercer. Mercer, a brilliant lawyer, but with a temper so uncontrollable in the courtroom that for a while he was temporarily disbarred, took the education of the Mason children in hand, later giving George Mason a sound background in law. Thomson received his legal training in London and brought Buckland back with him to assist with the construction of Gunston Hall.

In 1746 Mason moved to his Dogue's Neck Plantation, and in 1750 married Ann Eilbeck, only daughter of a merchant of Charles County, Maryland. Portraits of the bride and groom show Ann in a low-cut blue bodice with long auburn hair, full face and lips, and dark eyes; George plump, long-nosed, brown-wigged, with eyes at once quick and contemplative.

Mason was one of the greatest statesmen of his day. Compared with Franklin and Jefferson, he remains a relatively unknown figure, partly because he preferred to work behind the scenes, and partly because for most of the time he lived a life of physical misery due to gout. Famous as the author of the Virginia Declaration of Rights, which gave birth to the Bill of Rights, the first ten amendments of the Constitution, he was not accorded the popular appreciation in history that would have been given to a much lesser figure who kept in the limelight.

The wife he adored died in March, 1773, and was buried in the family burial ground. Years later, in September 1792, Jefferson, on his way from Williamsburg to Philadelphia, stopped at Gunston Hall. "He found Mason hobbling about on a crutch from attacks of gout that were now more frequent and lasting longer. Together the two old friends reviewed the crowded years since the summer of 1776. In spite of the gout and the fevers that had left him 'weak and low' throughout the summer, Mason's memory was good, his manner still impeccably genteel."

A week later George Mason died quietly in his handsome bedroom, with the beauty he had made all around him. He was buried where he had asked to be buried, "close by the side of my dear and ever lamented wife."

It was most likely Mason who determined the basic architectural scheme of Gunston Hall and supervised its construction up to the time it was ready for his joiner to take over. The house itself gives the impression of being a rather modest one in size and manner for its time and place, considering the circumstances of its owner. Within, however, the scale of the rooms and the sumptuousness of the woodwork give the impression of a little palace.

Among all of Mason's many papers there has so far been discovered but one reference to the actual building of his house. But that one clearly indicates his close attention to detail.

"When I built my House I was at pains to measure all the Lime and Sand as my Mortar was made up and always had two Beds, one for outside-work 2/3 Lime and 1/3 Sand, the other equal parts of Lime and Sand for Inside-work ... it is easily measured in any Tub or Barrel, and there is no other way to be sure of having your mortar good without waste, and the different parts of Yr Building equally strong ... If you have any good pit sand, out of your Cellars or well, it will make your mortar much tougher and stronger ... Next to pit sand the River Shoar Sand on fresh water is best and the Sand in the road worst of all; as being very foul and full of Dust.

"I woul'd by no means put any Clay or Loam in any of the Mortar, in the first place the mortar is not near so strong and besides from its being of a more soft and crumbly nature, it is very apt to nourish and harbour those pernicious little vermin the Cockroaches . . . and this I assure you is no slight Consideration; for I have seen some brick Houses so infested with these Devils that a Man had better have lived in a Barne. . ."

The woodwork of the Palladian room is a masterful flight of Buckland exuberance, in the midst of which the delightful Adam mantel, by another craftsman, seems restrained. The portrait of Anne Eilbeck Mason is by Boudet after Hesselius. On the English mahogany piecrust table is one of the silver Denzelow tea sets which Mason gave to each of his daughters. The cups and saucers, the potpourri urns, and the dishes in the cupboards are all Chinese Export porcelain. The chandelier and candelabra are English glass of the 1760's and 1770's, likewise the liqueur set on the Philadelphia lowboy of about 1760.

In the collaboration it was Mason who saw to the soundness of the basic scheme and wall construction, but it was Buckland, when he arrived on the scene from London with his books and tools, who turned the interior into such a tour de force of woodcarving as to outrival any colonial mansion before or since.

On August 14, 1734, William Buckland was born in Oxford. It was an auspicious time for a man of his talents. "Probably at no time in the history of English architecture," a Buckland biography° beautifully sums it up, "has there existed a more perfect knowledge of the technical arts of building than during the first part of the eighteenth century. There was available a trained and highly intelligent school of masons, carpenters and joiners, often men of talent and understanding of the arts and crafts. In the paneling, the delicate adjustment of detail to window and cornice, cupboard and mantelpiece, there is refinement and precision of workmanship. It would be hard to find a more habitable dwelling than the plain red brick house with its white cornice and sash windows that became during the Georgian period the home of the ordinary Englishman both in England and in the colonies of North America. The effectiveness of Georgian architecture owes much to the excellent craftsmanship of the period. The best of the English builders absorbed all that they had learned from other countries and through their own intelligence adapted it to the traditions and needs of their own nation. The ability to assimilate and express their own traditions is a measure of their capacity. It is that which gives to their work the quality of style and lasting value."

In 1748, at the very peak of the period, the 14-year-old boy Buckland was apprenticed for

° *William Buckland,* by Rosemond Randall Bierne and John H. Scarff, F.A.I.A. (The Maryland Historical Society).

The dining room is the first room in America to be done in the Chinese taste that had been made so popular in London by Chippendale. It is still a rare example and by far the finest. Like that of his wife, George Mason's portrait is by Boudet after Hesselius. The slab top (brown marble) side table is English, between 1720 and 1740; the lovely mirror above it, about 1740. The English 'dumb waiter' table holds Ellersware, Whieldon and Queen's ware. The dining table is New York, about 1770; the chairs Massachusetts. The mantel garniture, the punch bowl and dishes are all Chinese Export porcelain.

seven years to his uncle James Buckland, a master joiner in London. In 1755 he was given the equivalent of a degree. In the same year Thomson Mason, who was completing his legal training in London as a member of the Middle Temple, received a letter from his brother George asking Thomson to find him in London a well-trained joiner to help finish his new house on the Potomac. By a stroke of great fortune, Thomson found William Buckland and made an agreement with him, quoted here in part.

INDENTURE OF SERVICE, BUCKLAND TO MASON

This Indenture, Made the Fourth Day of August in the Twenty ninth Year of the Reign of our Sovereign Lord George Second King of Great-Britain, Etc., And in the Year of our Lord One Thousand Seven Hundred and fifty five—Between William Buckland of Oxford Carpenter & Joiner of the one Part and Thomson Mason of London Esqr.—of the other Part, Witnesseth ... That He the said William Buckland shall and will, as a faithful Covenant Servant, well and truly serve the said Thomson Mason, his Executors or Assigns in the Plantation of Virginia beyond the Seas, for the Space of Four Years, next ensuing his Arrival in the said Plantation, in the Employment of a Carpenter & Joiner. And the said Willm Buckland doth hereby Covenant and Declare himself, now to be the Age of Twenty two years and Single and no Covenant or Contracted Servant to any other Person or Persons, And the said Thomson Mason for himself his Executors or Assigns, in Consideration thereof, doth hereby Covenant, Promise and Agree to and with the said Willm Buckland his Executors, and Assigns, that He the said Thomson Mason his ... Executors or Assigns, shall and will at his or their own proper Costs and Charges, with what convenient Speed they may, carry and convey or cause to be carried and conveyed over unto the said Plantation, the said Wm Buckland and from henceforth, and during the said Voyage, and also during the said Term shall and will at the like Costs and Charges, provide for and allow the said Wm Buckland all necessary Meat, Drink, Washing, Lodging, fit and convenient for him as Covenant Servants in such Cases are usually provided for and allowed and pay and allow the said William Buckland Wages or Salary at the Rate of Twenty Pounds Sterling per Annum Payable Quarterly.

Four years later, at the end of his indenture, George Mason inscribed the following on the back of the document:

The within named William Buckland came into Virginia with my Brother Thomson Mason who engaged him in London and had a very good Character of him there; during the time he lived with me he had the entire Direction of the Carpenters & Joiners Work of a large House; & having behaved very faithfully in my Service, I can with great Justice recommend him to any Gentleman that may have occasion to employ him, as an honest sober diligent Man, & I think a complete Master of the Carpenter's & Joiner's Business both in Theory & Practice.

G. Mason
8th Novr., 1759

[Notation in Buckland's hand:]
WBuckland was born
Augt ye 14th 1734   1773
                         1734
                         ——
                          39

At or near the end of his service with Mason, Buckland married a girl named Mary Moore he had been courting in the neighborhood. After his marriage, and after he had completed eight other commissions in Virginia, Buckland then went on to Maryland to complete thirteen more, mostly in and around Annapolis, of which his outstanding triumph was the Hammond-Harwood house, ranking in many peoples' opinion right along with Gunston Hall. Then suddenly, in 1774, he died, presumably in Annapolis, though "the *Gazette* did not give his death a single line."

For nearly a century and a half Buckland remained in oblivion. Now, thanks to the restoration of Gunston Hall and the Hammond-Harwood house and to the publication in 1958 of his biography, everyone who has admired his work is able to know a great deal more about the man who performed it.

As was customary in Colonial Virginia mansions, the Mason bed chamber shared the ground floor with drawing room, dining room and sitting room; served as headquarters for the household. The cupboard on the left held Anne Mason's clothes, the one on the right, medical supplies, surgical instruments, sugar, spices, and rare herbs. The furniture is largely American Chippendale.

THE JOEL LANE HOUSE STORY

The People

Joel Lane, pioneer, patriot and politician, builder of the house
Martha Hinton, his first wife
Mary Hinton, his second wife, Martha's sister
William Tryon, Royal Governor of North Carolina
Edmund Fanning, Tryon's son-in-law, the Loyalist

In October 1859, David Lowry Swain—a former Governor of North Carolina, but then President of the University of North Carolina and State Agent for the Collection of Historical Material—wrote a letter from Chapel Hill. Though the letter concerned General Joseph Lane of Mexican War fame, it gives a little summary of the Lane family in which Joel Lane becomes the central figure.

"There is probably no family," he writes, "whose authentic history can be more clearly traced through every period of the annals of North Carolina." Then surely setting a record for backhanded compliments, he goes on to say that "In proportion to their numbers, comparatively few of its members have aspired to or obtained political distinction, or indeed distinction of any kind. On the other hand there are probably few that have enjoyed greater average respectability." In speaking of the Joseph Lane who died near Halifax on the *Roanoke* in 1776, he said, "His three sons—Joel, Joseph and Jesse—were pioneer settlers in the neighborhood of Raleigh, in 1741. Of these, Colonel Joel was the wealthiest and most conspicuous. He conveyed to the State 640 acres of land [it was really something over a thousand], the site of the present city of Raleigh. His dwelling house, at the period of its erection the best within a hundred miles. . . . All three were Whigs during the Revolution, and Colonel Joel and Jesse did service in the army, the latter as a private."

Joel's forebears came from England by way of Jamestown, as with many another North Carolinian. Joel's house, too, architecturally, had many Tidewater Virginia antecedents. When Joel built his house at Wake Cross Roads, now right in Raleigh, this was all open country. That it would someday be a city and the capital of the state was an idea that probably hadn't occurred to anyone —except possibly to Joel.

As Colonel Lane's house was the only one of any importance anywhere near the crossroads "he was often inconvenienced," according to Marshall DeLancey Haywood, his chronicler, "by the number of travelers who claimed his hospitality. To get rid of those who were not his personal friends, he caused to be erected a small ordinary . . . afterward turned into a schoolhouse." It was said to resemble somewhat the architecture of Wakefield, the name by which for many years his house was known.

Joel Lane was an officer in the militia, but whether he took part in the Battle of Alamance Creek in 1771 is not known for sure. "He probably did," his chronicler says. In any event, his father-in-law, Colonel Hinton, commanded the county militia called out by Governor Tryon, and the soldiers made their rendezvous at Wake Cross Road, right where Joel Lane lived.

The purpose of this military performance was to destroy the Regulator movement, a purely local North Carolina rebellion of the little Piedmont farmers against the one-sided rule of the rich Tidewater aristocracy. At first it took the form of more or less peaceful demonstrations, but at the nearby Hillsboro courthouse, when Edmund Fanning, the Governor's son-in-law, who had been convicted of extortion, was allowed to go unpunished, violence broke out and the movement became an open rebellion, simpler to subdue by force than by correcting the causes.

A close-up of the scene at the courthouse is provided by the judge himself, Richard Henderson, in a report to the Governor.

"On Monday last being the second day of Hillsborough Superior Court, early in the morning the Town was filled with a great number of the people shouting, hallooing & making a considerable tumult in the streets. At about 11 o'clock the Court was opened, and immediately the House filled as close as one man could stand by another, some with clubs others with whips and switches, few or none without some weapon. When the House had become so crowded that no more could well get in, one of them (whose name I think is called Fields) came forward and told me he had something to say before I proceeded to business. The accounts I had previously received together with the manner and appearance of these men and the abruptness of their address rendered my situation extremely uneasy . . . Thus I found myself under a necessity of attempting to soften and turn away the fury of this mad people, in the best manner in my power, and as much as could well be, pacifie their rage and at the same time preserve the little remaining dignity of the Court.

"The little hopes of peace derived from this piece of behaviour were very transient, for in a few minutes Mr. Williams an Attorney of that Court was coming in and had advanced near the door when they fell on him in a most furious manner with Clubs and sticks of enormous size and it was with great difficulty he saved his life by taking shelter in a neighbouring Store House. Mr. Fanning was next the object of their fury, him they seized and took with a degree of violence not to be described from off the bench were he had retired for protection and assistance and with hideous shouts of barbarian cruelty dragged him by the heels out of doors, while others engaged in dealing out blows with such violence that I made no doubt his life would instantly become a sacrifice to their rage and madness. However Mr. Fanning by a manly exertion miraculously broke holt and fortunately jumped into a door that saved him from immediate dissolution. During the uproar several of them told me with oaths of great bitterness that my turn should be next. I will not deny that in this frightful affair my thoughts were much engaged on my own protection, but it was not long before James Hunter and some other of their Chieftains came and told me not to be uneasy for that no man should hurt me on proviso I would set and hold Court to the end of the term."

Governor Tryon, whose recently reconstructed palace at New Bern is one of the sights of that charming old colonial capital, set up his headquarters in the Theophilus Hunter house on the Fayetteville road, and while waiting for reinforcements he had his army cut a road through the wood in the direction of "Regulator country." The actual fighting he left in the hands of Joel Lane's father-in-law.

It was all over within a month, and when Tryon returned to his palace he found orders to take over at once the Royal Governorship of New York, which was the last he saw of his palace. He took Fanning along as his secretary, who in 1775 "raised a Loyalist regiment which fought in partisan

Like Joel Lane himself, his house in North Carolina had Tidewater Virginia antecedents. Lane built it in about 1770, out in the wide open country of Wake County. It is now the oldest house in Raleigh, in the center of the city that has grown up all around it.

In this room in 1788 Raleigh became the capital city of North Carolina. The secretary is an early Wake County piece made by Negro slave cabinetmakers. The chair belonged to Joel Lane. The portrait is of Philip Ludwell, the first deputy governor of North Carolina, which became a Royal Colony in 1729.

actions about New York and was notorious for ruthless cruelty," according to the Columbia Encyclopedia, which also tells that in the Revolution Tryon led Tory raids into Connecticut.

Before and during the Revolutionary War and after, the capital of North Carolina was located, as a rule, wherever the Governor happened to reside. But in 1788 the General Assembly was instructed to fix a permanent spot, "provided it should be within ten miles of Isaac Hunter's plantation in Wake County." Commissioners were appointed to purchase a site. They had seventeen tracts from which to choose, and the meetings were held in Joel Lane's house. On the first ballot, the tract offered by Lane received only two out of six votes cast. It had to get a majority, and the board adjourned until the next day.

As the next day's session was related by Kemp P. Battle, LL.D., in his 1892 Centennial Address in Raleigh, "Lane himself was a man of influence, who had served the state in the Colonial Congress and as Senator for ten years in succession. Very probably he offered new inducements as to price." It was his own property to price as he wished; but for whatever reason, Lane's crossroads site got five votes out of six. And Battle went on to say that: "Possibly Lane was adversely criticized for his tactics in winning the contest. There was abundant room for unpleasant talk on account of his entertaining the commissioners at his house. They were acting as judges, and were certainly, notwithstanding their high character, liable to criticism that they ate the bread of one of the litigants. I cannot find their accounts of expenses, but" [in extenuation,] "it is altogether probable that they paid for their entertainment."

On at least two occasions during the Revolutionary War, for a week at the beginning and a week toward the close, the house was used for State legislative purposes, as being the most commodious building in the vicinity, though the largest room is less than 16 feet square. For the use of the house and for stabling, feed, and pasturage, Lane who put in a bill for a hundred pounds sterling, received instead 15,000 pounds, or 30,000 dollars. They had paid the poor fellow in practically worthless postwar paper money.

THE FOURTH HOUSE STORY

The People

Brother Charles Holder, saddler ⎰
Brother Gottlieb Caulder, potter ⎱ *early occupants of the house*

M oravians from Bethlehem and Nazareth in 1753 began migrating from Pennsylvania to North Carolina, settling there on a 100,000-acre tract of land called Wachovia, all around what is now Winston-Salem. Salem was founded in 1766, Winston in 1849, and the two were joined in 1913 to become the largest tobacco-manufacturing city in the world. But the old Salem restoration is the thing to see.

The Moravians came down in caravans of horseback riders and great high-wheeled wagons drawn generally by six horses. The going at times was very rough indeed. Crossing the wide Susquehanna on flatboat ferries cost from fifty to ninety dollars for the wagon trains and eight dollars for each horse and rider. The route was usually by way of Lititz and York, Pennsylvania, Frederick, Maryland, and Leesburg, Virginia. Twenty miles a day was a good average and, when there weren't too many breakdowns, twenty-four days was fair for the trip.

Of the forty or so original buildings still standing within the scope of the restoration, the 1767 Fourth House, the fourth to be built, is the earliest. Back in the thirties it was bought by the North Carolina Dames to save it from demolition, and is now leased to Old Salem, Inc., which is in the process of restoring it as this is being written.

Brother Charles Holder, a saddler, lived in it from the time of his marriage in 1772 to 1808, when he died a widower. All properties were enclosed, and it was "against the orders of the community to have a door in the fence," which explains why it was noted in 1789 that "Brother Charles Holder has a little hole through which he can get into the yard of Brother Praetzel, which must not be tolerated." Late in 1810 Brother Gottlieb and his wife moved in. He was not only a potter by trade, but a forester by profession, and it was he who supervised the cutting of the Congregation's timber.

These people were all skilled craftsmen, educated, musical. They were good builders, potters, leather-workers, gunsmiths, silversmiths and clock-makers. Town life was communal: all property and principal businesses were owned by the Congregation and administered by an election board of officials. As George Washington said when he addressed them in May 1791, "From a Society whose governing principles are industry and the love of order, much may be expected toward the improvement and prosperity of the country in which their Settlements are formed."

THE MOFFAT-LADD HOUSE STORY

The People

Captain John Moffatt, builder of the house
Catherine Cutt, the Captain's wife
Samuel Moffatt, their only son
Catherine Moffatt, their only daughter
William Whipple, Catherine's husband, the Signer
Sarah Catherine Mason, Samuel's wife
Robert Cutt Moffatt, son of the Samuel Moffatts
Mary Tufton Moffatt, called Polly,
    daughter of the Samuel Moffatts
Dr. Nathaneal Haven, husband of Mary
Maria Haven, daughter of the Havens
Alexander Ladd, Maria's husband
Alexander Hamilton Ladd, their son

John Moffatt, painted about 1751 by John Greenwood.

At his marriage to Catherine Cutt in 1723, as recorded in the New England Historical and Genealogical Register of 1870, Captain John Moffatt gave his ancestral home as "Dunster in the county of Summerset." Admittedly, where the Captain came from in England matters less than that on his first trip to America. On his trim flagship, in command of a fleet of those clumsy-looking barge-like mast carriers, he came to Portsmouth (which was a natural place to come to for masts) and, while he was there waiting for his return cargo to be carried aboard, he made up his mind to stay.

He became one of the richest men in town and built one of the most beautiful houses in the colonies. He seems to have been a man who made up his mind in a hurry. Within a few days he met Catherine Cutt, the Kittery shipbuilder's daughter, and it wasn't long before they were married.

As for his English background, there is a letter dated August 1963, from Mr. Gordon Moody, Hon. Sec. of the East Hertfordshire Archeological Society which says, "I find that /a/ John Moffatt was a free tenant of the Manor of Dunster, his heir (unnamed) appears in the lists until 1721, but is missing from the 1723 list." That was the right year. Elsewhere Mr. Moody says, "The only instance of the name Moffat in Herts that I know of is in connection with the property known as *Moffats* at Brookman's Park (North Myrmms), which takes its name from a family of that name recorded there in 1563. The owner then was Dr. Moffat (also spelled Muffet, Monflett, etc.) who wrote a book on silkworms that has led to the association of the Miss Muffet nursery rhyme with the house."

As the genealogical research is still proceeding, the Moffatt story here will have to start with the year the Captain came to Portsmouth, 1723, the same year he married Catherine Cutt. A man of action, according to one chronicler he at once "set about dealing extensively in anchors, duck, lumber, nails and paints, rum, rope and rigging in Portsmouth and upriver Piscataqua towns. He got out masts and spars for local builders and for export to England, and by 1759 was one of the largest owners of Piscataqua merchantmen sailing for Bristol and Bordeaux, Liverpool, Grandterre, 'Affrica,' and Cork."

In 1732 his only daughter Catherine was born, and in 1738 Samuel, his only son, who graduated from Harvard in 1758 and became actively engaged as a shipowner and importer, traveling back and forth with considerable frequency between Portsmouth and London. On one of his visits to England he became engaged to a girl named Sarah Catherine Mason, which was a kind of coincidence, for the girl was a great-great-great-granddaughter of the John Mason who back in 1630 was sole proprietor of New Hampshire, another of those Crown grants so vast and vague—"all the land between the Merrimac and the Piscataqua, bounded on the northwest by the Great Lakes and the St. Lawrence."

As a matter of fact, Sarah's father, John Tufton Mason, a colonel in the British marines, had been the last of the Mason family to claim his inheritance of the territory. Born in Boston, he had come as a young man to Portsmouth, hoping to sell his principality to the Provincial Assembly, which refused to take his claim seriously. Whereupon he joined up with the colonial troops as a captain under Sir William Pepperell of Kittery in the attack on the French Fortress of Louisburg. And so taken were his fellow officers by the young captain's gallantry and good spirits, that they organized a company to buy the captain's claim, which languished on for years through the courts almost to the time Samuel began courting the captain's daughter. Nothing ever came of it.

A sweep of balustrade, supported by a succession of turned, twisted and fluted balusters, carries the eye upward to a richly ornamented soffit. The wallpaper is Dufour's Vues d'Italie of 1815–1820. The gateleg table served the Provincial Council at Governor Wentworth's house. Before it became the dining room, the room at the left was General Whipple's office. Especially noteworthy is the elaborately pierced and carved border on the crossetted panel above the fireplace. The arched niche and the fireplace came along later during the early Ladd occupancy.

103

It was an early American custom that a father might build a house as a wedding present for a bride and groom. Washington did it with Woodlawn Plantation when his foster daughter Nelly Custis married his nephew Laurence Lewis, and Captain Moffatt did it forty years earlier with this extremely stylish Portsmouth mansion for Samuel and Sarah. Colonel Mason came over for the wedding, and the young couple moved in on the first of February 1764.

For Samuel and Sarah it was too good to be true. But by 1768 Samuel's money affairs got out of hand, so that even with his father's help he found himself over his head in debt. As one old-timer put it, Samuel's "college education and fashionable life, as might be supposed, had not qualified him for strict and prudent application to business." It was a choice between flight and debtor's prison, that abysmal feature of the British judicial system which still prevailed in the colonies.

Samuel's escape was certainly a planned one. Sarah was pregnant, so she remained at home with the two small boys in the wedding-present house. And down the river in Pepperrell's Cove the brig *Diana* and her Captain William Whipple waited, ready to set sail for the West Indies. Whipple's interest was due to the fact that he was in love with Samuel's sister Catherine. Catherine was thirty-six, William was thirty-eight, and the courtship had been going on for quite a while.

Samuel's destination was Demerara, now British Guiana, where he set up as a planter and lived the rest of his life. Shortly after her daughter was born Sarah left the baby at Portsmouth and joined her husband. The two boys came along ten years later. The daughter, Polly, never saw her father, and didn't see her mother again until after Samuel's death in the West Indies, when the mother returned to Portsmouth.

When Whipple got back to Portsmouth, Captain Moffatt's wife had died and the Captain and Catherine were living in the big house, which Moffatt had bought back from the creditors who had seized Samuel's estate. At this point, William finally married Catherine and moved in with his wife and father-in-law.

William Whipple was just about to embark on his Revolutionary career as a patriot-soldier-statesman. Born across the Piscataqua at Kittery, he was commanding his own vessels before he was twenty. Then after ten or so years at sea, doing very well for himself in the African slave trade, he dropped all that and became a Portsmouth merchant, at which he did even better. When the Marquis de Chastellux came to Portsmouth with the French fleet in 1782 and visited the Whipples, he said about Mrs. Whipple that she was "neither young nor handsome, but of good understanding and gayety."

As Revolutionary sentiment mounted, Whipple's own Revolutionary sympathies caused him to be chosen a member of the Provincial Congress, to which he was reelected in 1776, becoming a signer of the Declaration of Independence. He made his name as a soldier, too. He commanded the New Hampshire troops at the Battle of Saratoga, ending his military career as a major general, and ending his days as a judge on the State's superior court.

William was the first of the three to die, in 1785 and childless; the Captain a year later at ninety-four. Catherine lived until 1823, dying when she was ninety-one.

Captain Moffatt in his will had passed over Samuel's older son John because John had joined the English Navy. Instead, he left his estate to the younger grandson Robert at the boy's coming-of-age, sixteen years thence. In the meanwhile the Captain's daughter was to have the house and all the income from the estate. There was a lot of litigation, and it was ten years on top of the sixteen before the courts decided in Robert's favor—Robert who didn't care about the house; only wishing to sell it, he turned out the aging Mrs. Whipple.

This extremely handsome house in a town of distinguished houses is by an architect unknown. It look out over the Piscatauqua where Captain Moffatt's wharves and warehouses were. His counting house wa inside the doorway on the right.

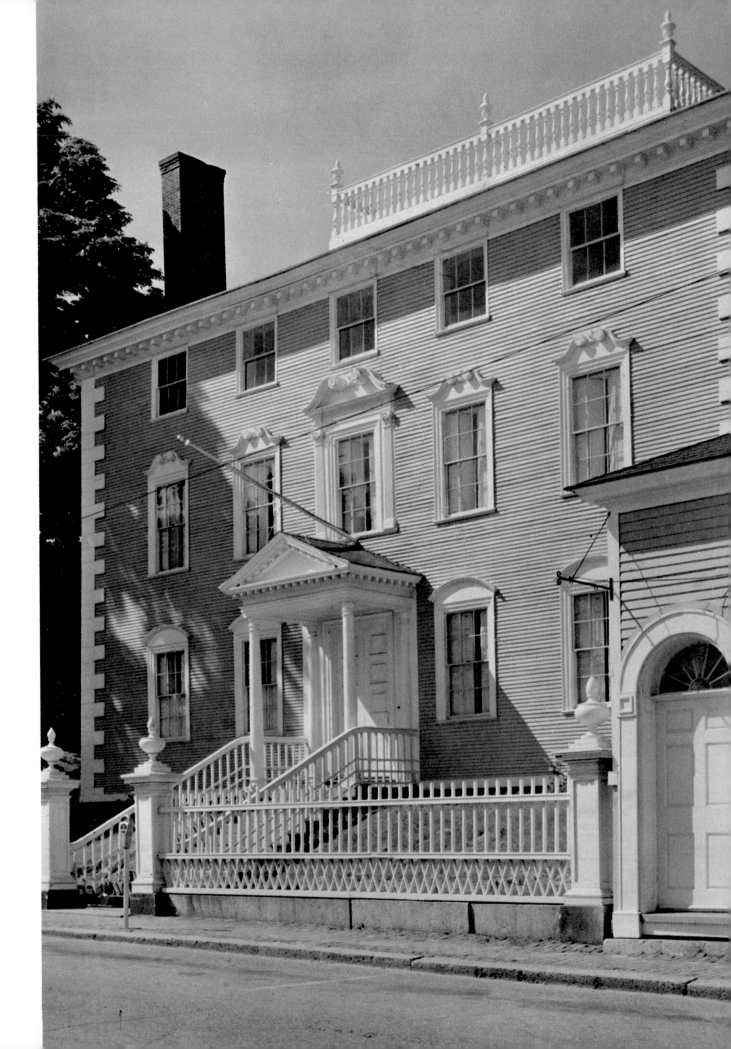

The Counting House on the left is a separate little building built about 1831 or 1832 by Alexander Ladd. It is outfitted with a notable collection of office furniture of the period. The first floor kitchen, recently restored under the direction of Mr. William Perry to its 1763 period by the generosity of New Hampshire Dames and their friends, is directly above a second, brick-floored kitchen in the cellar. The shutters are original as is the dresser base and the scalloped edge of the shelving.

Robert's sister Mary in 1786, the year the Captain died, eloped with Nathaneal Haven, a promising Portsmouth doctor, and when their daughter Maria was about to marry Alexander Ladd of Exeter in 1807, the Havens, by giving Robert $14,000 for the house, made it again a wedding gift for the family bride and groom.

When the Ladd's son, Alexander Hamilton Ladd, inherited the house, he became the last member of the family to pass his whole life in it, devoting his days to his gardens until he died in 1912. The heirs the following year, for the lifetime protection of the house, leased it to the New Hampshire Dames. Its restoration is one of the Society's masterpieces.

THE BURGWIN-WRIGHT HOUSE AND ST. PHILIP'S CHURCH STORY

The People

Maurice Moore, founder of Brunswick Town

John Ashe ⎫
⎬ *leaders of the colonial armed resistance*
Hugh Waddell ⎭

William Tryon, Royal Governor

John Burgwin, Loyalist builder of the house

Lord Cornwallis, commander of the British forces and temporary tenant

General Nathaniel Greene, commander of the Revolutionary forces

In spite of the moccasins and mosquitos, when Colonel Maurice Moore, soldier, adventurer, entrepreneur, came riding down the west side of the Cape Fear River in 1725 with his entourage, he was so taken with the river lands that he arranged a grant of fifteen thousand acres from the Lords Proprietor of North Carolina Province, laid out the town he called Brunswick, and began selling lots to his friends and their friends, creating a community of refined and cultured people."

Long before, in 1660, a London group had formed the Cape Fear Company and sent settlers from New England to the same river region. But by 1663 the several attempts that had been made at settlement were abandoned, due mostly to the marauding of Indians and Spaniards, who remained a menace even after Brunswick had become established.

A few years after Brunswick Town began building, another settlement was started fifteen miles farther up the river; it was first called New Liverpool, inheriting from Liverpool in England the names of its early streets. The settlers were of several minds about the name, for there were some who called it New Carthage and others who named it New Town; but New Liverpool stuck, at least until 1740 when the name Wilmington was formally adopted out of deference to the Provincial Governor's patron, the Earl of Wilmington.

In the meanwhile, houses were going up all over the place in Brunswick Town. The town's life was to be a short one, but a busy one. It was a town where things happened. For one thing, as an aftermath of the War of Jenkins's Ear, Brunswick was captured and held for three days by Spanish marines from three warships that suddenly appeared off the town. Highly irritated by this intrusion the townspeople counterattacked with such fury that they not only killed or captured most of the marines but by a lucky shot from shore exploded the main powder magazine on one of the ships and sent the other two scurrying away. Furthermore, the money they got from the goods and slaves they salvaged from the sinking ship went a long way toward building St. Philip's Church, whose roofless ruins today have a haunting beauty all their own.

The church took twenty-three years to build, and in 1776, only two years after it was finished, it was gutted by fire when the whole town was burned and battered down by bombardment from British gunboats. But nobody was there at the time; everybody had left this unprotected town, most of them having moved up the river to Wilmington for protection. A few families moved back after the war, rebuilding their homes after a fashion, but it was a town no longer, and by 1830 it was abandoned.

Outlasting the town itself is its fame as being the scene of the first armed resistance to the Stamp Act. Resistance to the Act in 1765 took various forms throughout the colonies, but here in Brunswick and Wilmington the colonial militia took matters into their own hands. Under Ashe and Waddell they presented themselves at the residence of the Royal Governor at Brunswick and made it clear to Governor William Tryon that they were prepared by force of arms to prevent the landing of the stamps from the British sloop *Patience*. The Governor could see from his window the futility of pursuing this royal design any further, and so reported to his King. Stamps were never issued in North Carolina.

In Wilmington, six years after this occurrence, a man named John Burgwin, a former treasurer of the colony, built a mansion which is the finest early house in the city, if not the earliest house still standing in the town. Burgwin lived in it for only a few years, because shortly before the Revolution he took off with other Loyalists for England, where he conveniently "broke his leg," the customary excuse at the time for not returning. The house was then bought by Judge Joshua Wright, who was living in it when in April 1781 a Major Craig of Cornwallis' staff "requested" the house as headquarters for the British commander, who was on his way to Wilmington with his army from his encounter with General Greene's forces at Guilford Courthouse.

Charles Cornwallis (later First Marquis) was born in England in 1738. Educated at Eton, he was commissioned an ensign at eighteen and saw service in Europe in the Seven Years War. It is interesting that as a member of Parliament he heartily opposed the tax measures that helped to bring on the Revolution. As general he was sent over in 1776, served successfully under Howe on Long Island, in the New Jersey campaigns, and at the Battle of the Brandywine. In 1778 he became second in command to Clinton, the British commander. 1780 began the fateful Carolina campaign which led to the Yorktown defeat and the end of fighting. For those at home he was not held responsible, and in 1786 he was made Governor General of India. And the same year, on the way up the Ganges with his troops to suppress anti-British forces, he died at Ghazipur, where he is buried.

Nathaniel Greene, the Revolutionary General, was born on August 7, 1742, at Warwick, Rhode Island. In 1775 he commanded three Rhode Island regiments, and at the outbreak of the war was made a brigadier general in the Continental Army, commanding the army that occupied Boston after the siege. He was under Washington at Trenton, Germantown and Valley Forge. After the defeat of Gates at Camden, South Carolina, Washington in 1780 put Greene in command of the southern campaign, whose success caused the weakening of Cornwallis and the beginning of the end for the British.

Under Greene the Revolutionary forces began a series of harassing raids and counter-raids and other engagements in which the British, while not broken, were baffled by American frontier rifleman-raiders. This led to the battle at Guilford Courthouse. While the battle was technically not an American victory, it did cause Cornwallis to fall back on British-held Wilmington, and after resting and refitting his troops, make his way to Yorktown.

Judge Wright and his family remained in the house during Cornwallis' stay. After all, he was there for only a few weeks; long enough, however, for his young officers to find Judge Wright's daughters very attractive hostesses at teatime. In fact, many years later, in the 1890's, on a ship returning from Europe, a Wilmington descendant of the Wrights was told by an Englishman on board that one of his ancestors had been an officer on Cornwallis' staff; the officer and one of the daughters had fallen so in love that they had cut their initials together on a window in the house (which turned out to be true).

The house has been handsomely restored and furnished by the North Carolina Dames, who use it as their headquarters and maintain it for the interest and pleasure of the public.

Specialists attribute the design to a masterbuilder with a Philadelphia background. The structure is as sound as it was the year it was built; if anything, it has grown more beautiful with age. Closely associated with the history of was St. Philip's Church, a short distance down the Cape Fear River, whose ruins amid the remnants of Brunswick Town have a poetry of their own. In the Burgin-Wright drawing room the woodwork is all original. The wing chair was owned by Fielding Lewis of Fredericksburg fame, the tripod table is Chippendale, the settee Adam, the paste garniture on the mantel is early Chinese, and the tea set is pink lustre.

109

THE BOLDUC HOUSE STORY

The People

Louis Bolduc, habitant, *merchant, builder of the house*
Agathe Groveau, Louis' first wife
Marie Courtois, his second wife

Long before Marquette (1637), La Salle (1643), and Joliet (1645), were born, English, French, and Portuguese fishermen—their eyes bulging—were pulling salmon, cod, and halibut from the Gulf of St. Lawrence as fast as they could fill and empty their nets and baskets. It was literally true what John Cabot told the King in 1497, that these waters were simply "swarming with fish."

And as the fishermen set up shore bases to sun-dry their catch before carrying it on the long voyage home (a month at least), fishing led to fur trading with the Indians. For this the French had a real knack, and the hatters of Paris provided an insatiable market, particularly for the pelts of beavers, leading to a scarcity of these creatures along the coast, and causing the French fur traders to strike deeper and deeper inland. It followed, of course, that in addition to the traders, French explorers and missionaries soon were cutting and canoeing their way far into the vast American wilderness.

Settlements that became great cities like Quebec and Montreal served as home bases for the expeditions, and the Indians' birchbark canoe became the means of conveyance which made the French penetration possible. In 1615 Champlain got as far as Georgian Bay, in 1634 Nicolet got as far as Wisconsin, and in 1673 Joliet and Marquette, by way of Green Bay, the Fox, and the Wisconsin, reached the Mississippi, paddling down as far as the Arkansas before poling back against the current. Then finally, on January 4, 1682, La Salle made rendezvous with his lieutenant, the Sieur de Tonti, where the Chicago flowed into Lake Michigan. The river was frozen solid as far as it went, and past the portage the Illinois was frozen too, as was the Mississippi as far down as Fort Crevecoeur, now Peoria. But De Tonti had the foresight to have sleighs made by his Indians, and at the fort built two years before, where La Salle had found everything in order, the expedition was able to launch its canoes. It was quite a party. Twenty-three Frenchmen, eighteen Indian men, ten Indian women, taken at the Indian men's insistence, and three Indian children in cradles.

By the 14th of February they were passing the site of Ste. Genevieve, Missouri, where Louis Bolduc would be building his first house in about 1770, and on the 9th of April La Salle and his party went ashore at the mouth of the Mississippi, where with great ceremony the famous land-grabber claimed the whole vast river valley for the King of France, calling it in his honor Louisiana.

In a census taken the year La Salle left Quebec to organize his expedition, a man named Louis Bolduc was listed as a tax collector for the same King Louis XIV. The tax collector Louis had a son of twelve, also Louis, who could as easily as not have become the grandfather of the Louis Bolduc who was born near Quebec in December 1734. In any event, it was this last Louis who at some point came with his wife Agathe to Kaskaskia, where he did well enough to be able, by 1770, to build a house across the Mississippi at Ste. Genevieve.

In 1763 the rule of France in North America was ended, and towns like Kaskaskia and Ste. Genevieve, as they grew, grew more and more American. Actually, while Kaskaskia prospered during

The restoration undertaken by the Missouri Dames makes the Bolduc house the showpiece among American French Colonial preservations. The garden and the grounds also have been given an authentic French Colonial flavor. The stone outbuilding is a reconstruction of the cook and bake house, used as such until the existing kitchen was built into the *galerie*. In the main all-purpose room at (right) the floor is of the original boards, sound as when new. The French rush-seated child's chair is about 1775, the diamond-pan cupboard of 1790 has its original glass, as does the French gilt mirror which has been in Ste. Genevieve since 1785. The iron ratchet, from which hangs an old wire 14 light chandelier, 18th-century, was brought from France to Ste. Genevieve about 1790, the same date as the fine old French buffet.

the dozen years from 1809 when it was first the capital of Illinois Territory and then of the State, its days were numbered due to the ever-flooding Mississippi, which finally in 1895 finished off the town once and for all. As the other French towns of the Illinois country have by now lost all their French identity, Ste. Genevieve, with a great deal of French colonial character, remains the only residuum of New France north of New Orleans, with Louis Bolduc's second house, of 1785, now faithfully restored by the Missouri Dames, as the town's most notable survival.

The first Bolduc house, hardly half the size of the present one, was built down by the river, where Ste. Genevieve was originally settled. The town was the shipping point for the lead that was packed there on muleback from the mines back in the Ozarks. And the produce of its rich bottom lands, also shipped down the river to New Orleans, likewise contributed to the town's prosperity. So it was worth the town's while, after the Mississippi floods of the 1780's, to move up to the top of the hill rather than move away entirely.

Down below was where the three Bolduc children were born—Elizabeth, Louis, and Etienne—and down below was where Agathe died while Louis was away on a business trip to New Orleans. It was also where Louis remarried, this time a French girl from New Orleans, Marie Courtois.

It was Louis and Marie who built the new house in the new town on the hill. Whatever they could salvage from the first house they probably made use of in the second, as it was discovered during the restoration that some of the lumber had been used before. However, the first house was not only half the size of the second: it was almost certainly of the lighter construction followed in the French *habitation* represented by the Dames' exhibit in the Chicago Historical Society, shown later in this book.

The larger, later house as it stands is a fascinating achievement. Louis and Marie followed plenty of precedent. Reputedly the peculiar half timber wall construction had its origin in Normandy (though why there, where wood is so scarce and stone so plentiful poses a question). It could just as well have begun as a kind of Canadian log cabin, with vertical timbers instead of horizontal.

Where this Mississippi Valley style picked up the surrounding porch, or *galerie*, with its more flatly pitched roof (making such a charming effect and providing such a livable feature) is a question easy to answer, for it was so obviously from the West Indies, where Haiti was a French colonial island and full of houses exhibiting this architectural fashion. As a device, the covered *galerie* was not only ideal for the hot summers of the valley but as well for the weather protection it gave the clay-filled vertical timber walls.

The planning of the grounds, as it has been reconstructed here, is beautifully in keeping with that of the house itself. The immediate yard, with its packed-clay surface, has a clean-swept appearance that could only be French. And the spike-topped stockade fence is a vestige of a time when a house really needed protection against intrusion.

The house is Louis Bolduc's greatest, if not his only, claim to fame, though it is said that in 1780 he advanced $275 to the gallant George Rogers Clark, who had just driven the British from Kaskaskia, Cahokia, and Vincennes. He must have been rich, though it is said he never learned to write his name. There is a story of a friend of Bolduc who sat one day in Louis' house boasting that he had more money than Louis, and was about to lay a bet on it, but when he saw Louis start out of the room with a big basket to get his gold, he lost his nerve, or so it is said. It is probable enough that Bolduc built not only the best house in Ste. Genevieve, but the best of its kind and era still standing in the whole Mississippi Valley.

THE EVANSVIEW STORY

The People

Don José Bontura, tavern keeper
Fanny Combs, Bontura's wife
Captain Thomas P. Leathers, steamboat owner

T he fort of Natchez," according to Diron d'Artaguette in 1723, when he came there as de Bienville's inspector general, "is a rather sorry fort of piles the size of a leg . . . It is situated at the top of the hill, which is nearly four hundred feet high. In the country around the fort, which is all hills and valleys, several good farmers cultivate maize, beans and other vegetables in quantity . . . The Natchez Indians are scattered along in little villages to a distance of two leagues from the fort . . . They adore the sun from which they claim their chief is descended."

Everybody who came along admired the situation. First the high bluff above the river from where Evansview, with one of the best views in town, has looked out upon the Mississippi since 1790. Begun during the Spanish occupation, it was added onto in 1830, but it was always mostly American in character, as are the rest of the Natchez houses. The Spanish accents that still persist in Evansview and the others come from the ironwork trimmings. Now and then a flaring double-pitch roof indicates a carry-over from the French colonial farmhouses that lie along the Mississippi Valley from Illinois to Louisiana. But that is all.

If the early history of Evansview was ever written down, the records have been lost or mislaid. It is not known for sure who built it, who lived in it from 1790 to 1860, or who made the additions to it in the 1830's. But because it has always been a town house, facing on what was once the public park, and because it has a large, five-arched coach house in the courtyard and a ballroom opening on to the courtyard—all the appurtenances of an important residence—it could have once been the official domicile of a "Spanish Grandee," as is sometimes stated.

Then, after the Spaniards left, it could have been for a while the home of Sir William Dunbar, a Britisher who was official surveyor to the Spanish Government, which granted him the land for his services just before the Spaniards left—a grant which the United States refused to recognize. Then after Dunbar died, it could have been lived in by the English family of Dart who ran the famous Tattersall Stables over on Canal Street. However, all this history lies in the cloudland of conjecture, from whose romantic mists much of the Natchez' past emerges.

But in 1860, a year before the War, when Don José Bontura, a Portuguese-American who had made a fortune at his tavern in Natchez-Under-the-Hill, married Miss Fanny Combs of Pleasureville, Kentucky, and bought the house, the clouds of conjecture can be said to have cleared away, but only momentarily. The marriage and the purchase are matters of record. Don José also did actually buy the Tattersall Stables, from which he continued to furnish planters with fine horses and mules from Kentucky, and to provide townspeople with livery service, both On-the-Hill and Under-the-Hill.

This was the beginning of the Bontura period—the name by which the house was known until it was presented to the Mississippi Dames by Mr. and Mrs. Hugh Evans in 1961. In the early Bontura days, it has been claimed, the Bonturas were on various occasions hosts to Mark Twain,

Known before 1963 as Bontura, the large main part of Evansview is thought to have been built during the last French occupation, the earlier galleried and colonnaded wing beyond the courtyard just before the Spanish left. The ornamental ironwork is a typical adornment of the Natchez scene. In one of the parlors the unauthenticated portrait of George Washington as a Virginia colonel, like the one of Martha Washington in the parlor adjoining, is known to have been in Natchez since 1840. The pair of French Colonial rosewood armchairs were brought from Mexico and are stuffed with Spanish moss.

114

Stephen Foster, and Captain Thomas P. Leathers. Twain might well have been a visitor, though he never mentioned it in print. He began his river career in 1847, the year after the Bonturas were married, and finished it the year after theBonturas bought the house, the year the War began, when Twain went west to become a reporter.

However, when it comes to Captain Leathers, the most widely known Natchezian of his day, it is inconceivable that the famous steamboat captain wasn't a frequent guest of the hospitable Bonturas, both at the tavern and at the house on the hill—unless he held a grudge against them.

From first to last, Leathers owned and commanded six different steamboats named *Natchez*, all carrying his gilded figurehead of a Natchez chieftain. He also owned the speedy *Princess*, with which he set a record from New Orleans to Natchez, a record that stood for many years, during which time he kept the elk horns that had been her figurehead displayed on his wharf, where they were mounted on a polished block of wood with the inscription, "Why Don't You Take the Horns Princess' time to Natchez, 17 hours and thirty minutes."

Then on June 30, 1870, came the famous race between the fastest *Natchez* that Leathers had ever owned and his swiftest competitor, Captain John W. Cannon's *Robt. E. Lee*. The Civil War had come and gone. The Bonturas' house had been grazed by a shell from the Federal gunboat *Essex*. And now the latest *Natchez* had been built in 1869, marking Captain Leathers' postwar comeback. Already she was a fierce rival of the *Lee* for the river business. No boat had ever carried more cotton than the *Natchez*.

Captain Cannon had stripped his boat down to the bone: he had only a handful of passengers for the race. Except for lack of freight, Leathers was running as usual. They had left New Orleans at five in the afternoon. The boat that would beat the record of the *Princess* would have to be at Natchez by a little after ten in the morning. By nine the bluff was crawling with people; every riverside window at the Bonturas' was filled with faces straining to see as far down the river as possible.

Then a boat came around the bend. But it was the *Robt. E. Lee*. However, the *Natchez* was right on her heels, six minutes behind. Seeing that his boat had beaten the old *Princess* record by nineteen minutes, Captain Cannon pulled the *Robt. E. Lee* into the Leathers wharf where the wharf master was ready to deliver the elk horns to the deck officer. Then the *Lee* picked up two coal barges and turned upstream, with hardly a pause, emptying the coal on board and turning the barges loose, just as the *Natchez* swept in to let off and take on passengers, lash on *her* coal barges, pull out and proceed.

Soon both boats were out of sight again, even from the windows of the Bontura house. And as the telegraph messages clacked over the wires into Natchez from up the river, the news grew worse as the *Natchez* fell further and further behind. She was making her regular stops, while the *Robt. E. Lee* was strictly running a race, and won it. She made the 1,218 miles from New Orleans to St. Louis in three days, 21 hours, and 57 minutes. The *Natchez* tore in three hours and 43 minutes later. And a lot of money changed hands at the Bonturas'—On-the-Hill and Under-the-Hill.

Don José died in 1875. Fanny remarried, and she and her heirs after her kept the house in more or less good shape until the Evanses came along and bought it in 1941. They lived in it off and on for twenty years, putting it back into splendid pre-Bontura condition; then they gave it to the Mississippi Dames, renaming it Evansview because of all the sights you can see from the windows. Tankers ten times the size of the *Natchez*; the Trace, along which Jackson led his troops to New Orleans in 1812, now a super-highway; the sun-loving Indians long since eliminated. . . . But one thing will always be the same. The "more exalted and splendid scenes of life" are there to stay. Glamor in Natchez will never be allowed to leave.

THE LIBERTY HALL STORY

The People

John Brown, the Senator, builder of Liberty Hall
Margaretta Mason, his wife
Mason Brown, first son, inheritor of Liberty Hall
Orlando Brown, second son
Thomas Jefferson, General Lafayette, George Wythe, President Monroe, General Andrew
Jackson, Major Zachary Taylor, and John's brother James

John Brown was the oldest of four brothers. He and his next brother James became United States Senators. Both Samuel and Prentice W. Brown, the younger two, became doctors. All four had careers of outstanding distinction.

All four were born in the Shenandoah Valley of Virginia (John in 1757), and all began their education at their father's grammar school called Liberty Hall—a good name for a school, and good name for a house, too, the Senator decided.

John went on to Princeton, which he left suddenly one day in December 1777 to join Washington's Army in retreating across New Jersey with Cornwallis at its heels. Retiring into Penn-

In Margaretta's parlor, the portrait over the mantel is by Gilbert Stuart (on wood) of Margaretta Mason Brown's brother, the Reverend John Mitchel Mason of New York City. A warm friend of Alexander Hamilton's, Mason was called to Hamilton's bedside after the duel with Burr, and gave the funeral oration before the Society of Cincinnati. The very effective coloring in this room is pale water blue and coral. The furniture is Chippendale, Sheraton and Hepplewhite, mostly American.

The Kentucky painter Matthew Jouett's portrait of Dr. Samuel Brown, the Senator's brother, is over the mantel, the cherry Kentucky secretary belonged to the builder of the house, as did the wing chair at the right of the fireplace, and the early wire fender and andirons. In this room were entertained presidents, generals and hosts of other celebrities, including Lafayette, who with his son and suite quite unexpectedly paid a courtesy call on Margaretta Brown during the town's celebration in his honor.

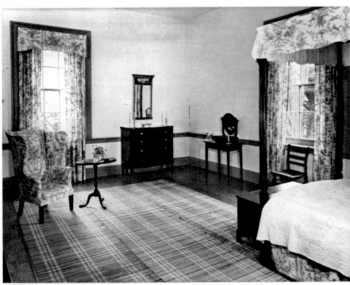

In January, 1796 Senator Brown bought a whole square in the newly plotted town of Frankfort and proceeded to build his house of bricks and timber prepared on the place. In the Gray Lady room named for an aunt of Mrs. Brown, who died in it, the cherry blanket chest, the Browns' own swell front chest and the cherry candlestand are all Virginia pieces. The bed is American of the Chippendale period, and the shaving mirror spent four generations in an old Kentucky home.

117

sylvania, Washington returned the night after Christmas, crossing the Delaware through the ice and routing the Hessians billeted at the Trenton Barracks; John's first action took place on that celebrated occasion.

After serving for a time as an aide-de-camp on the staff of General LaFayette, John broke off his military career near his twenty-first birthday to enter William and Mary College. In a letter from Williamsburg to his uncle he described the "very considerable Revolution" the college had undergone. "The Visitors met on the 4th instant & formed it into a University. . . annuld the old Statutes, abolished the grammar school continued Mr. Madison President & Professor of Mathematics Appointed Mr. Wyth Professor of Law, D. McClung of Physick Mr. Andrews of Moral Philosophy, & Monjr. Beline of Modern languages. Each of these Professors have an Annuity of eight Hogsheads of Tobacco," which at the time in Virginia was used as legal tender, just as whiskey was to be in Kentucky.

He had a chance to do secretarial work for one of the Randolphs (he doesn't say which), but that would have meant moving to Richmond. "& if I should," he wrote, "I am unaquainted with the place & uncertain how I am to be provided for & as he is a Gentln of great delicacy perhaps it might be improper to quit him & attend Mr. Wyth's Lectures."

John did right, and stayed on to study with George Wythe, the teacher of John Marshall, Thomas Jefferson, James Monroe, and Henry Clay, and owner of the finest house in Williamsburg.

In a letter of July 6, 1780, to William Preston, the uncle, he goes into great detail about his work with his distinguished teacher (note that now he is spelling Wythe's name correctly).

"Mr. Wythe ever attentive to the improvement of his Pupils founded two Institutions for that purpose, the first is a Moot Court, held monthly or oftener in the place formerly occupied by the Genl Court in the Capitol. Mr. Wythe & the other professors sit as Judges, our Audience consists of the most respectable of the Citizens, before whom we plead Causes given out by Mr. Wythe Lawyer like I assure you. He has also form'd us into a Legislative Body, consisting of about 40 Members Mr Wythe is Speaker to the House, & takes all possible pains to instruct us in the Rules of Parliament. We meet every Saturday & take under our consideration those Bills drawn up by the Comtee appointed to revise the laws, then we debate & alter (I will not say amend) with the greatest freedom I take an active part in both these Instructions & hope thereby to rub off that natural Bashfulness which at present is extremely prejudicial to me. These Exersises serve not only as the best amusement after severer studies, but are very usefull & attended with many important advantages . . ."

A year after William and Mary, John had a chance to read law at Monticello under Jefferson, "who had freely proposed to give me every assistance in his Power." He proceeded to Charlottesville and found himself board and lodging less than a mile from Monticello with a Colonel Lewis.

"Col° Jefferson supplies me with all necessary books & proper Instructions, & when any difficulty in reading arises I can attend him for assistance with ease the distance being so small."

About 1782 John came to Kentucky, which was still a district of Virginia, and two years later he was elected from the district to the Virginia Senate, where he worked for the separation of Kentucky, for some accommodation with Spain for free navigation of the Mississippi, and for protection from the Indians, which just about describes the situation at the time. By the role he played in the negotiations with the Spanish government at New Orleans he opened himself to considerable criticism at the time.

Elected to Congress in 1789 and 1791, he resigned in 1792 to become one of the two first United States Senators from the newly formed state of Kentucky. He served in the Senate until 1805, when he retired at forty-eight to private life.

In January 1796 he bought a whole square in the new town of Frankfort and began to build his house. Three years later, in New York City, he married Margaretta Mason. On November 10 Mason was born in Philadelphia, and by 1801 the Browns had moved into Liberty Hall, where Orlando was born that same year on September 26.

On July 1, 1819 Margarette Brown wrote from Liberty Hall to her son Orlando at Princeton, " . . . THE President [Monroe] has arrived—and departed— He was received with due public honors (as the papers will inform you) yesterday Morning he breakfasted with *us* in company with Genl Jackson; and that *Hero* (whose cool, determined, and successful courage, has never been rivalled in antient or modern times,) who so bravely defended Fort Harrison; Major Z. Taylor . . . Your Father presided at the public dinner, and has been much distinguished by the President."

John's brother James, who had served in the United States Senate since 1812, resigned in 1823 to become President Monroe's Minister to France.It was he who delivered not only the Monroe Doctrine to the French Government, but to General Lafayette a letter from President Monroe, informing the marquis that by a resolution of Congress he had been invited to visit the United States, and that a frigate would be sent to carry him to America, where Lafayette in 1824 and 1825 made his triumphal tour.

Margaretta wrote to her step-mother in July, 1825, in New York " . . . the arrival of General LaFayette occasioned as much bustle (in proportion to the population) here as at New York, and I must relate a **circumstance** which I know will give you pleasure, as it was the cause of great gratification to me. There was a splended Ball to be given in the evening, but as there were many Ladies who did not attend Balls, and yet wished to see the General, they were introduced to him at his Markee, I was one of the number and had such a hearty and long-continued shake of the hand as to occasion the envy of many an impatient expectant. In the evening twelve or fourteen of my particular friends took tea with me and urged me to go to the Ball in order to have another interview with the General. I told them my objections, that I had not frequented any place a public amusement for many years, and that although I might spend a few minutes in a Ball room without contamination, yet I thought it inconsistent with the profession I had made. Several of my friends replied that they were church members as well as myself and that though they would not go at any other time, yet as such an occasion would never come again they thought themselves justified to attend. Thus we parted, they all paraded off to the Ball, except Elizabeth Humphrey's and myself, but they had not been gone more than 20 minutes when who should arrive here but General LaFayette, his son and suite. The General spent nearly an hour with us in most delightful conversation, while those who went to the Ball did not exchange a sylable with him. Had I not a triumph?

"The General was introduced to Mason at Lexington. He told him politely that he was indebted to his family for all the honor and pleasure he had received since his arrival in America for that if his uncle James Brown (our Minister at the Court of France) had not become Security for his return, he would never have been permitted to leave France. He paid but one other visit in town, and that was to Mrs. Todd, a sister of Mrs. Madison."

Senator John Brown died on August 29, 1837, at Liberty Hall, and his widow on May 28 the following year, their older son Mason inheriting the house. "To keep the inheritance even," the Senator gave a house, finished just before the Senator died (and described later in this book), on the same property to the younger son Orlando.

For more than 140 years this grand old house was in the possession of Kentucky's first United States Senator and his descendants. Then in 1937 it was deeded to Liberty Hall, Incorporated, "to be maintained for all time as an open, semi-public property." Now in the custody of the Kentucky Dames, beautifully restored and furnished, it faithfully reflects the finest taste and culture of early Kentucky.

THE TRAVELER'S REST STORY

The People

John Overton, jurist, land speculator, builder of the house
Andrew Jackson, seventh President of the United States
Rachel Donelson Robards, Jackson's wife

Among the "maidens" who came to Jamestown in the early days of the settlement to make wives for the colonists was one named Mary Waters from St. Sepulchre's Parish in London. The colonist she married was a man named William Overton. It was their grandson James who married Mary Waller, daughter of Colonel and Mrs. John Waller of the Louisa County, Virginia, gentry. According to a family chronicler, the Overtons always had a way of "marrying well," which was the case here.

The youngest of the eight children of this excellent marriage was John Overton, who became a public figure of importance in Tennessee, the maker of a fortune in Tennessee lands, and the builder of Travelers' Rest, but who is best remembered as the political adviser and intimate friend of Andrew Jackson.

John Overton was born in 1766 and lived in Louisa County until he was twenty, when he followed an older brother to Kentucky. There he stayed for two years, during which time he got to know Rachel Donelson, who was then married to a Louisa County man named Robards. Rachel, who was wretchedly unhappy with Robards, described with such devotion the Cumberland settlement, where Nashville is now and where Rachel's widowed mother lived, that in 1788 John, who had been studying law, went to Nashville to practice. He found a boarding place there with Rachel's mother, and there at the Widow Donelson's he met the tall redheaded Irish-American lawyer who had just come out from North Carolina, also to practice here.

Andrew Jackson was just a year younger than John—twenty-one to John's twenty-two. They shared one of the two cabins on the place, "and slept in the same bed," Overton recounted thirty years later when Jackson was running for President. The Robardses took the other cabin on their return from Kentucky.

Robards' outlandish jealousy became fastened on Jackson, who soon was aware of Rachel's wretchedness as well as her attractions. One of Rachel's friends described her as "the gay and lively Mrs. Robards, the best story-teller, the best dancer, the sprightliest companion, the most dashing horse-woman in the western country."

Actually, although the Donelsons were part of the well-born frontier aristocracy, Rachel, for all her charm and accomplishments, and the fact that she was "better family" than Jackson, was almost illiterate. The fact of Robards' jealousy "gave Jackson great uneasiness," Overton wrote, and Jackson moved from the Donelson cabin. But the separation of the Robardses was bound to take place, and this was followed by a divorce that did not become final for two years. In the meanwhile, Rachel and Jackson, through a misunderstanding of the divorce terms, were married. And even though they went through a second marriage ceremony later, the incident was to plague Jackson politically throughout his whole public career, with Overton a constant and scrupulous defender. "I have been intimate," he wrote "with the mutual and uninterrupted happiness of the General and Mrs. Jackson, which I have at all times witnessed with pleasure." Rachel died seventeen years before her husband and was buried in the garden of the Hermitage, where he joined her on his death.

The 1743 fruitwood-satinwood spinet in the parlor was made by George Astor of London where the ancestors of the John Jacob Astor family were instrument makers. The wing chair is also English 18th-century. Engravings of Overton and Jackson are over the spinet, and over the mantel are portraits of Overton and Mary McConnell White, his wife, who used to say about her husband's height that he could walk under her outstretched arm.

Although no longer part of a 5,000-acre plantation, Travelers' Rest is still set off by its park-like surroundings. In the dining room the inlaid banquet table is Hepplewhite, the chairs English Sheraton, and the unusual early American walnut inlaid corner cupboard has its original brasses. Over the mantel, with his sword above him, is the famous Confederate cavalry general, Nathan Bedford Forrest, who woke up here to find a Union soldier in the next bed.

Those early times in Tennessee were feverish with speculation in land, and both young lawyers joined in the fray. In 1894 Overton and Jackson, together with a man named Winchester, bought five thousand acres where the city of Memphis stands today. Starting off with three hundred acres, where he began building Travelers' Rest six miles south of Nashville in 1799, Overton kept adding to it until he had a nice twelve-hundred-acre farm.

Jackson was as financially unlucky as his friend was fortunate. He lost his part of the "Memphis" tract, but managed to hold on to the Hermitage, which today is a historic shrine about ten miles from Travelers' Rest.

Overton never took an outwardly prominent part in politics. His power lay in the parts he could perform behind the scenes, and during Jackson's campaigns for the presidency in 1828 and 1832 Overton's skill as a strategist contributed mightily to Jackson's successes. After he had served as judge on the Superior Court of Tennessee from 1804 to 1816, he declined every offer to take a political post, preferring to devote himself to his farm.

In Clayton's *History of Davidson County, Tennessee*, Overton's importance in the history of Tennessee land litigation techniques is clearly established. "The litigation then was chiefly concerning the titles to real estate, and old lawyers, as well in Kentucky as Tennessee, will remember that there was a good deal of it, and very profitable it was too. A good land-lawyer was the highest eminence of the profession. Judge Overton at once obtained a full practice, and by his industry and attention to business kept it till he was transferred to the bench. A system of law, based upon the acts of 1777 and 1783 of the North Carolina Legislature, disposing of lands in the Territory of Tennessee, had to be built up by the bar and bench of Tennessee, and Overton, as lawyer and judge, exercised considerable influence in moulding the system to suit the wants and necessities of the new community. The English law-books failed to afford a precedent for settling the titles to boundaries of adjacent wild lands, involving the questions of special entries, younger grants, elder entries, the ages of marks on trees, the authority of plats to control the calls in grants, and various other points springing from the peculiar system adopted by North Carolina; and hence the difficulty of the task which had to be encountered by our earlier judges. The constructions of our land-laws, as ruled whilst Overton was on the bench, became established law, and the points are not now controverted in the courts. He was conscientious in the discharge of his duties, giving to every case, no matter how small the amount involved, a patient attention, and *studying it* before he delivered an opinion."

He was a passionate gardener and grower, and was once honored by a visit from the famous French arborist François André Michaux, when Michaux was here gathering material for his book on American forest trees. Overton's peach orchard was notable for the brandy he distilled from the fruit. "He was a good liver," one of his descendants writes," but there is no record of his ever having been affected by anything he drank, although he wrote a great deal about the condition of his stomach." He liked his toddy, with breakfast as well as with other meals, a taste he shared with his best friend. Among his papers was a receipted bill he probably paid for Jackson.

Genl A. Jackson
18/12

		Mr. Chuaup D	
March	10th	Supper Harse & Lodging	87 1/2
"	11	Breakfast. 11h 1qt Glap Gin To ay 3/.	75
"	11	1 qt. G. Gin To ay 3 /. Supper Horse & Lodging	1.37 1/2
"	12	Gin 11h. Breakfast 11h	50
"	"	Supper Harse & Lodging ------	87 1/2
"	13	Breakfast 11h	25

$4.62 1/2

Overton built his house in three stages. The first, in 1795, was the bachelor stage; the second, in 1799, some afterthoughts; and the third—the four-room addition he made in 1820—was of course the married stage, done right after his wedding at fifty-four, to the daughter of General James White of Knoxville, a widow with five children. He "married well"; his wife bore him three children, and brought him happiness for his final thirteen years.

But the crowning triumph of his life came in 1828 when Andrew Jackson was elected President. The two old friends kept constantly in touch; this letter from the White House set the tone of their correspondence.

Judge Overton's brick law office was faithfully reproduced after a fire had burned it down in the 1930's. The beams and lumber used throughout are old, the brick handmade by the old process, and brick courses counted and laid exactly as in the old building, and foundations measured exactly. The books seen on the shelves are the Statutes of North Carolina on which Judge Overton based much of Tennessee's code, especially the land laws which he, more than any other person, was responsible for writing.

My Dr. friend.

I lift my pen merely at present to acknowledge the receipt of your kind letter of the 25th & to say to you how much pleasure it afforded me whilst reading.

My son will set out in a few days for home & will see you shortly after this letter reaches you to whom I refer you for the news of this place—all things however are going on smoothly . . .

I fondly cherish the hope to see you here. I am sure it would add to my health & length of days—no happiness on this earth can excell the pleasure of the meeting of old friends after a long absence, & particularly at an advanced age . . . It is *this* that makes life now tolerable to me. The duty I owe my country, the cheering idea of meeting my Dr wife beyond, & you on this side the grave, alone buoys up my depressed & troubled mind. . .

We are still very busily employed. Our ministers to England & France will sail in a few days, and I have reasons to believe we will be able to accommodate our difference with England on the basis of a just reciprocity.

My son will be directed to call on & communicate to you freely.

Present me affectionately to yr

Lady & family & believe me yr friend

Andrew Jackson

The honble
John Overton

Whenever Jackson came to Tennessee, the Overtons drove over to visit him at the Hermitage. On one of these visits they met the young Henry P. Wise, then an ardent Jacksonian, later to be Governor of Virginia and one of Lee's major generals. Wise subsequently described Overton as an extremely able politician, "but not pious." Wise went on to say: "His head was perfectly bald, a finely shaped head, covered by a bandana handkerchief; his face very sharply cut at angles. He had a pleasing chin, but he had lost his teeth and swallowed his lips."

Late in the summer of 1832, the year before he died, Overton spent some time in Washington with Jackson discussing the strategy for the second presidential campaign in the race with Henry Clay. A month after his old friend's second inaugural in March 1833, Overton died at Travelers' Rest. He left his widow, who outlived him by thirty years, the house and all twelve hundred acres of the land, all the furnishings, all the farm equipment, and all of his 51 slaves.

According to Clayton, discussing the time before Overton's death, "Political excitement was then at the highest pitch, and the war between Jackson and the Bank was raging. He [Overton] reflected that, after his death, many of those letters, intended for his own eye, might fall into the hands of his friend's enemies, and garbled extracts find their way to the public,—such a thing had happened and might happen again,—few would be living who could explain the circumstances under which they were written, time and the events of life might have induced a change of opinion concerning men and things, and with a singular prudence he committed the correspondence to the flames, remarking that, living or dead, he would not betray the confidence of a friend."

Poor posterity!

The house always maintained its reputation for hospitality, often fairly bulging with visitors, even during the Civil War. For a while it was right in the middle of the Battle of Nashville, when once at dinner General John B. Hood and seven other Confederate generals, all at one time, were sitting around the table. And once, at night, when Travelers' Rest was under Union guard, the wily Confederate cavalryman General Nathan B. Forrest slipped into the house, went to bed in the dark, and woke at dawn to find a Union soldier in the next bed, still sound asleep.

Travelers' Rest remained in the family until 1946, when the Tennessee Dames acquired it to preserve it as it was in the Overton-Jackson days.

124

THE XIMENEZ FATIO HOUSE STORY

The People

Juan Ponce de León, Spanish explorer and discoverer of Florida
Pedro Menéndez de Avilés, Spanish naval officer and founder of St. Augustine
Andres Ximenez, builder of the house

Ponce de León, a veteran of Columbus' second voyage, sailed from Puerto Rico in March, 1513, and landed on the southern promontory of the North American continent in April at the time of the Easter feast, *Pascua Florida*. He claimed it for Spain and named it La Florida, believing it to be one of the "fabled" Bimini islands, where the fountain of youth was supposed to gush. Failing to find a spring that answered this description, he departed, still under the impression that he had landed on an island.

Nothing much of any consequence occurred in La Florida until 1564, when René de Laudonnière with a company of French Huguenots established a settlement called Fort Caroline near the mouth of the St. Johns River. When Philip II of Spain heard about this he ordered his brilliant young captain general of the Indies fleet to destroy the French fort and set up a Spanish colony on the coast. It was August 28, 1565, when the Menéndez fleet of eleven vessels, with 500 colonists aboard, entered the harbor where Ponce de León had landed half a century before. Naming the place after St. Augustine, whose name day it was, and disembarking the colonists, Menéndez sailed north to Fort Caroline, where he failed to bring Admiral Jean Ribaut's fleet into combat. Returning to St. Augustine, he began building a fort. In the meanwhile Ribaut set out to catch him by surprise, only to have his fleet destroyed in a hurricane south of St. Augustine. Menéndez meanwhile marched overland to Fort Caroline and slaughtered nearly all the French, who had been left practically defenseless. Then returning he encountered remnants of Ribaut's crews who, washed ashore, were on their way back to Fort Caroline, and slaughtered them. These massacres were fittingly revenged three years later by French forces under Dominique de Gourgues

The bloodbath which St. Augustine had undergone recurred when Drake bombarded, burned, and sacked the settlement in 1586, again when some British corsairs under Captain John Davis in 1665 did the same, and still twice more in 1702 when it was bitterly besieged by forces from South Carolina and in 1740 when Oglethorpe made his vicious attack from Georgia.

The Castillo de San Marcos, started in 1672, the first masonry fort in America, was a help, but it was mainly by old-time Spanish tenacity that the town remained in Spain's possession until, in 1763, it passed peacefully by the Treaty of Paris to England. For hordes of Tories from the colonies it became a haven during the Revolutionary War, its English period lasting until 1783, when England gave Florida back to Spain in return for the Bahamas. The English moved over to the islands and St. Augustine was Spanish again until 1821, when Spain, under some unorthodox pressure by the unorthodox Andrew Jackson, reluctantly ceded Florida to the United States.

It was during the comparatively peaceful second Spanish occupation that Andres Ximenez, a merchant of the city and a native of Ronda in the Kingdom of Granada, in 1798 built his house. In his house, as he declared in his will, "I have a grocery store and a billiard table with everything pertaining to it."

He had bought the lot the year before, and on it he also built a kitchen, a wooden privy, and a woodshed. Across from his house on Aviles Street he had another lot on which he had a kitchen and what he rightly described as a "little house," seven by eight by seven feet high. This he rented to a mulatto named Marcelino Espinosa, who purchased some of the merchandise from the estate after Andres died.

Ximenez had been born in 1753 in Ronda. He married Juana Teresa Pellicer in St. Augustine in 1791 when he was thirty-eight and Juana fifteen. She had five children before she died in 1802. the two oldest survived the father, who died in 1806 requesting that the three children be outfitted in black for the period of mourning and that he himself be "shrouded in the robes of our Seraphic Father St. Francis." Juana's family took care of the children and the heirs occupied the house for the next thirty-three years.

For twenty years, until 1875, the house was run as an inn by Miss Louisa Fatio, granddaughter of Francis Philip Fatio I, a famous name in St. Augustine, and a name made well known all over the East by Miss Louisa's Fatio House, where many distinguished writers and painters were guests.

The house is typical of its period, built flush on the street with an overhanging balcony and the proverbial outside stairway in the rear. The walls are made of the native soft, whitish natural limestone, of broken shells and corals, called coquina; these masonry walls were then cemented over to keep out the moisture. In the rear is the separate old kitchen containing the original built-in bake oven.

The living room downstairs in the Ximenez Fatio house is furnished in keeping with the second Spanish occupation of St. Augustine.

THE DUMBARTON HOUSE STORY

The People

Samuel Jackson, beginning builder of the house
Joseph Nourse, Federal officeholder, finishing builder
Robert Mills, architect, friend of Nourse
Charles Carroll, owner after Nourse
Benjamin Latrobe, architect, friend of Carroll

F iske Kimball called it "one of the very finest and most beautiful houses in the United States." And Kimball, who was one of the foremost American authorities on art and architecture, knew every early house in the country worth knowing. But even Kimball couldn't say for sure who was principally responsible for the style and distinction of the house as it stands today. However, he and the architect of the restoration believed the mansion was at least begun by a man named Samuel Jackson in 1799.

That was the year Jackson bought the property, which had changed hands six times in the preceding three years; a reflection of the wildly fluctuating prices caused by the frenzy of land speculation in the newly created federal capital called Washington City. But now the property was to stay put for nearly five years; and the fact that Jackson almost at once took out a mortgage for twice what the property cost him, and then another, was what led Kimball and his colleague to their conclusion. Also, there was the matter of the 1800 penny discovered in the west wall of the hall during the restoration in 1931.

How far Jackson got with the house no one knows. But the fact that in 1804 the mortgages were foreclosed on him made it seem that he couldn't have finished it. If he had brought it anywhere close to completion, he could most certainly have raised the mortgage. At any rate, it went at public auction, for an unknown amount, to Gabriel Duvall, then Comptroller of the Currency, and later for many years on the Supreme Court, who bought it "in behalf of the public." Duvall turned right around and sold it for $8,581.67 to a man named Joseph Nourse, pronounced "nurse."

Nothing at all is known about Jackson, but a great deal is known about Nourse. Born 1754 in London, he was fifteen when he came to Virginia with his family, who soon acquired a plantation in what is now West Virginia, across the road from Harewood, the Samuel Washington place, where James Madison married Dolly Payne Todd.

In the Revolution, Nourse started off in March 1776 as military secretary and aide-de-camp to General Charles Lee, commanding the Southern Department of the Continental Army. In December he was made Assistant Clerk of the Board of War; in 1777 Deputy Secretary at $780 a year; then in 1778 Secretary of Ordinance and Paymaster at $90 a month, a post he resigned that September to become Assistant Auditor General at $10,000 a year.

According to *Joseph Nourse and His Descendants*, compiled by Maria Catharine Nourse Lyle, Nourse in September 1781 was "elected the first Register of the Treasury, a post he held until May 31, 1829, when he was removed by President Jackson whose avowed intention was to "sweep out the nursery," meaning the Register's office where five Nourses then held positions.

In the formal library, the Sheraton side chairs, two of a set of six, belonged to Judge Daniel Newcomb of New Hampshire, whose father-in-law rode with Paul Revere. Surmounting the 1790 English mirror is a liver bird, emblem of the city of Liverpool. The 1795 card table is Baltimore Hepplewhite, the Wedgwood bust of Keats, black basalt. The desk, 1775, is probably a Charleston piece, likewise the Sheraton reading chair, 1815. The Chippendale bracket clock is by Garland of London, late 18th-century. The garden facade of Dumbarton is dominated by the beautiful curving bays. The street side is shown on the frontispiece.

128

In 1784 Nourse married a Philadelphia girl named Maria Louisa Bull, and during the brief time that New York City was the federal capital in 1789 and 1790, the Nourses lived in New York. They then followed the Congress to Philadelphia, where they lived for the ten years that city served as the seat of government.

In 1797 John Adams succeeded George Washington as President of the United States. In 1799 Washington died, and in 1800 the Congress moved to William Thornton's still-unfinished Capitol in Washington City, and John and Abigail Adams moved into James Hoban's not-yet-completed Presidents' House, or Presidents' Palace, as it was also called before it became known as the White House.

Washington City was a mess. As John Dos Passos wrote in *Prospects of a Golden Age,* "The streets were a morass. At high tide the creeks backed up into the low lying lots. Clumps of unfinished buildings moldered in the scrubby undergrowth." As Abigail Adams tartly remarked in a letter home, "If the twelve years, in which this place has been considered as the future seat of government, had been improved, as they would have been if in New England, very many of the present inconveniences would have been removed." She was drying her clothes in the great unfinished audience room. "The principal stairs are not up, and will not be this winter . . . To assist us in this great castle, and render less attendance necessary, bells are wholly wanting, not a single one being hung through the whole house, and promises are all you can obtain. This is so great an inconvenience, that I know not what to do, or how to do it."

When Congress moved to the new Capitol, it was the task of Joseph Nourse to move all the Treasury Department records over from Philadelphia. A contemporary commentator called him "an efficient cooperator under the immortal Hamilton in arranging the details of the Treasury Department and setting in motion and perfecting the system of our finances."

While the Adamses were getting settled, and later while Jefferson, after 1801, was first getting settled too, Samuel Jackson was up there in Georgetown beginning to build the house now called

The dining room fits into the right hand bay on the garden front, as the curving wall suggests. The dining table was made in Deerfield about 1795, its French plateau from the Van Rensselaer Manor, the ten Sheraton side chairs were probably made in Salem about 1795, while the Chinese Export porcelain plates belonged to Eliza Custis Law, Martha Washington's granddaughter. The painting by Charles Willson Peale is of the children of Benjamin Stoddert, first Secretary of the Navy.

In the library chamber the blue and white Chinese bowl is on an American shaving stand of about 1800. The bandbox beside it is early 19th-century by N.B. Brower, N.Y. In the corner is a Hepplewhite bureau in mahogany and maple New England about 1795, the same as the field bed, with its puffed quilted counterpane, as are the Sheraton side chairs. The rug is an Aubusson.

Dumbarton. If it was a question of getting architectural help, there was plenty of it around. Hoban, Thornton, and Benjamin Latrobe had offices, with highly competent draftsmen who could have helped. Thornton did Tudor Place in Georgetown and Woodlawn for Nellie Custis and Lawrence Lewis near Mount Vernon, both with a somewhat Dumbarton feeling. And as far as that goes, there were many gifted master builders here at work who could have started Dumbarton for Jackson and finished it for Nourse.

As a matter of fact, Robert Mills, one of the best architects of his time, was working in Latrobe's Washington office from 1803 to 1808, while the Nourses had Dumbarton. What is more, he was such a friend of the Nourse family that he not only lived in the house, but met their god-daughter there, when she was 16, and married her when she was twenty-five. In his diary Mills states that he paid for "very good board the sum of $2.50 per week."

It was Mills, of course, who was the architect of the Washington Monument; and although the design was not completed until 1833, and the execution begun in 1848, Joseph Nourse in May, 1829 was off on a fund-raising trip for the scheme on the very day that President Jackson decided to "sweep out the nursery."

In 1813 Joseph Nourse sold the house to Charles Carroll (a cousin of the Signer, Charles Carroll of Carrollton), who called it Bellevue, thus making himself Charles Carroll of Bellevue. And one of the first things that Carroll did was to get Latrobe to design a classic portico for the front of the house. He then lived on there until 1820, when he rented it and moved to Genesee, New York.

On August 24, 1814, President Madison and members of his Cabinet and military staff had ridden off to reconnoiter. The British were rapidly advancing on Washington with the intention of destroying the new Capitol and capturing the President. The Federal defenses were in considerable confusion. Dolly Madison was running from one window to another with her spyglass. The gunfire was getting closer and closer as Dolly finished a letter to her sister: "Will you believe it, my sister? We have had a battle . . . and here I am still, within sound of the cannon. Mr. Madison comes not. May God protect us! . . . At this late hour a wagon has been procured, and I have had it filled with plate and the most valuable portable articles, belonging to the house . . . Our kind friend, Mr. Carroll, has come to hasten my departure, and is in very bad humor with me, because I insist on waiting until the large picture of General Washington is secured . . ."

It has been said that Dolly found a haven at Carroll's house, but the truth is that she and her servants rode off ahead of the British and spent the night in an Army tent, making a rendezvous with the President the next morning. In the meanwhile, both the White House and the Capitol were sacked and burned.

A hundred years later, when Q Street, which had been dead-ended before the house, couldn't wait any longer to keep on going to Dumbarton Bridge, the owner of the house, John L. Newbold, had it gently moved out of the way a distance of a hundred yards. The wings, having no cellars, had to be taken down, brick by brick, and brick by brick rebuilt. But the main body of the house, shored up on great timbers, jacked up onto huge rollers, and hooked onto a windlass, was inched across to its fine new site by a single white horse, according to Charles M. Mackall, of Greenwich, who was a boy of 12 at the time, and rode the horse.

In 1928, after prolonged negotiations, the old Bellevue of Charles Carroll, built before him by Nourse and Samuel Jackson, and witness of the founding days of the Federal City, was bought by the Dames to be the headquarters of the National Society. Three years later, renamed Dumbarton House, it was restored to the early Federal period by Horace W. Peaslee, A.I.A., with the late Fiske Kimball as consultant. And in 1932 it was opened to the public as a dignified residence of the young Republic; Federal without, and all wonderful Sheraton and Hepplewhite within.

Here behind the windows of the other curving bay is the music room with the harp by Erat of Wardour Street, London, after 1810, the piano by G. Astor & Co., London, between 1796 and 1815, and in the foreground a set of musical glasses, about 1800. The portrait that doesn't quite fit into the photograph is of George Washington's brother Samuel's children Harriot and probably Lawrence Augustine. The English Sheraton armchair of 1800 is the "Martha Washington" type. The Pembroke tea table is Baltimore Hepplewhite, 1795, its silver tea service by William G. Forbes of New York City, 1773-1809. The console table is Louis XVI, about 1775, and the pair of English mirrors Hepplewhite, about 1800. The three Sheraton side chairs, about 1795, belonged to Christopher Lowndes of Bladensburg, whose daughter Rebekah married Benjamin Stoddert, parents of the children in Peale's portrait in the dining room. Through the right hand window on the terrace can be seen an Adam terra cotta urn by Wade of Lambeth, about 1790.

In the library furnished by the Louisiana Dames the portrait is of James Pirrie, the owner when Audubon lived here. The mahogany slant-front secretary is Hepplewhite, about 1795. On the Hepplewhite handkerchief gaming table the chessboard with its red and white ivory chessmen is the original Oakley set. The Sheraton barometer is by Rouchette & Co., Liverpool, about 1795. The draperies are gold silk damask. The charming house and its romantic setting speak for themselves.

THE OAKLEY STORY

The People

John James Audubon, artist and ornithologist
Lucy Bakewell, his wife
Mrs. James Pirrie, owner of Oakley and employer of Audubon
Eliza, her daughter and Audubon's pupil

What might well have been left a plain colonial dwelling anywhere in the North has here in the climate of the South been given the glamor of tall double-tiered porches on both long façades. These have been veiled with louvered blinds combining sharp stripes of shadow with caverns of cooling shade, and have further been trimmed with stairways and railings. To catch the air the whole house has been set up floatingly a semistory above the ground but resting on a raised recessed basement almost hidden in the shadow beneath.

Thus a basic shell of the barest architecture, as so often in the South, has become a kind of fairy princess whose palace, as again so often in the South, is a grove of great live oaks hung with silvery Spanish moss. And as a final touch the air all around Oakley is always alive with the flutter of warblers and filled with the music of the mockingbirds and the fragrance of mingled perfumes.

Not *quite* the final touch: the house and the whole countryside around it have been given a special aura by the fact that for a mere five months in 1821 Audubon lived here at Oakley, teaching the daughter of the house to dance and draw, and going off into the woods, where he painted thirty-two of his finest pictures of birds.

The house was built in 1799 by a man from Natchez named Ruffin Gray, who died before the house was finished. His widow married a Scotsman, James Pirrie. The Pirries had three children, of whom only one daughter, Eliza, survived. "My lovely Miss Pirrie," Audubon called her.

Although at various times Audubon would give New Orleans as his birthplace, he was actually born in 1785 in Haiti, the natural son of a French sea captain, trader, and planter and his Creole mistress. When the boy was four his father took him to France, where he lived with his father and his father's lawful wife, went to school, began a collection of French bird drawings, and studied drawing with David in Paris. In 1803 he came to this country. In 1808 he married Lucy Bakewell, and together they spent most of the next twelve years in Kentucky, where Audubon and a friend from France tried keeping store, and Lucy taught school. The painting of birds occupied too much of Audubon's attention; storekeeping failed, and Audubon went to New Orleans, where Mrs. Pirrie found him and engaged him to tutor Eliza. He was to get sixty dollars a month and have room and board at Oakley for himself and his thirteen-year-old protege, John Mason, whom Audubon was training to paint backgrounds for his birds.

"We arrived at the landing . . . on a hot sultry day," Audubon in May wrote in his journal, "Bid adieu to our fellow passengers, and climbed the hill to St. Francisville . . .

"The aspect of the country was entirely new to me," he continued, "and distracted my mind from those objects which are the occupation of my life. The rich magnolias covered with fragrant blossoms, the holly, the beech, the tall yellow poplar, the hilly ground, and even the red clay, all excited my imagination. Such an entire change in the face of nature in so short a time seems almost supernatural; and surrounded once more by numberless warblers and thrushes . . . The five miles we walked appeared short, and we arrived and met Mr. Pirrie at his home . . . we were kindly received."

In an essay called *Audubon's Happy Land*, Katherine Anne Porter writes about a visit she made to St. Francisville and the West Feliciana countryside. "The town's most treasured inhabitant was Audubon, and its happiest memory. This is no afterthought, based on his later reputation," she continues. "And it is the more interesting when we consider what kind of reputation Audubon's was, almost to the end; nothing at all that a really materialistic society would take seriously. He was an artist, but not a fashionable one, never successful by any worldly standards; but the people of St. Francisville loved him, recognized him, took him to themselves when he was unknown and almost in despair. And now in every house, they will show you some small souvenir of him, some record that he was once a guest there. The Pirries, of New Orleans and Oakley, near St. Francisville, captured him in New Orleans at the moment when he was heading East, disheartened, and brought him to Oakley for the pleasant employment of teaching their young daughter, Miss Eliza, to dance and draw, of mornings. His afternoons, and some of his evenings, he spent in the Feliciana woods, and we know what he found there."

Audubon returned in October to New Orleans, where Lucy came to meet him before he left for the North, and before she went to teach in West Feliciana. It was quite a while before he came back, with portfolios bulging. Birds from New England, New York, New Jersey, Pennsylvania, the Carolinas. And he writes of landing after dark, going first on foot to the little town where a friend would lend him a horse. Not a light in the town. No answer to his knocking. Opening the door he was met by the smell of death, and realized it was the yellow fever. The town was deserted.

He walked on to the house of another friend, far out of town. There he got a horse and rode madly through the night, losing his way in the woods, and finally after daylight found his way to St. Francisville, then on to the house where Lucy was living. He went in and heard the sound of a piano, and there was Lucy giving a lesson. She looked up and came to him and "we embraced," he wrote, "and wept with love and relief."

Audubon stayed on to teach the children of the rich Feliciana planters, dancing especially. "The dancing speculation," he wrote, "fetched two thousand dollars; and with this capital and my wife's savings I . . . foresee a successful issue to my great ornithological work." He left in 1826 for London, leaving Lucy behind in Louisiana. He wrote her for the next five years of the preparation and completion of the priceless plates. When he returned to her in 1831 he brought with him not only the first great elegant folios of the Birds of America, but finally, too, the real beginning of his fame.

The Kemper Log House, now in the Cincinnati Zoo.

THE KEMPER LOG HOUSE STORY

The People

*James Kemper, frontier teacher
and preacher
Judith Hathaway, his wife
Reverend David Rice, Kemper's
theological preceptor*

auquier County was Virginia log-cabin country when James Kemper was born there in 1753. Not far from the Kempers' cabin lived the family of Captain John Hathaway, whose daughter Judith became James Kemper's bride and the mother of their fifteen children.

While the Revolutionary War was going on, John was the schoolteacher of the locality, sharing the farm work with Judith after school hours, and studying theology at night under the guidance of the Reverend David Rice. Then for a while after the war he made some extra money on a surveying expedition along the borders of North Carolina and Tennessee. But it was in 1785 that the Kempers' adventures began.

The Reverend Rice had "projected" a school in Lincoln County, Kentucky, not far from Danville, which he called the Transylvania Seminary (also to be known as Rice's School), and had asked John to come out and be the first master of its grammar school.

By selling everything he owned except his two horses and wagon and a few household effects (even Judith's loom), Kemper was able to pay his debts and start off for Kentucky with his wife and six small children.

After six years of teaching at the school and simultaneously completing his theological studies with Father Rice, during which time his wife produced four more children, John Kemper received his license to preach and was appointed to "supply" the church at Cincinnati, then a tiny frontier settlement on the Ohio in the Miami Purchase.

The Kempers' first house was in the village proper, but within two years or so they had moved out to the Walnut Hills section in the country, where for ten years they occupied what came to be known as the Kemper blockhouse, finally moving into their newly built log house on June 4, 1804, where, the very first night, Charles, their fifteenth and last child, was born.

The Reverend Kemper made his mark as an educator and preacher in the early days of Cincinnati, and his log house is the oldest house still standing in the town, remaining much as it was when the Kempers lived there. Authentic Kemper furnishings are used throughout the four rooms, and many of the Reverend Kemper's books and personal belongings are there.

John died there at eighty-one, Judith at eighty-eight. It was lived in by their children, grandchildren, and great-grandchildren for more than sixty years after Judith died. It is, therefore, not surprising that numbers of direct descendants of the Kempers still live in Cincinnati, where for many years they have been active in the ministry, teaching, the arts, and business. Threatened with demolition in 1912, no longer occupied by the family, the house was saved by a committee of preservation-minded citizens, who had it moved to the Zoological Gardens. In 1953 the house was given by this committee to the Ohio Dames, who with great care and ingenuity have brought out the essence of the Kemper period in its furnishings and restoration.

135

55 Beacon Street is the left-hand half of the double house designed by Asher Benjamin and built in 1808 by young James Colburn, the precocious Boston merchant.

THE 55 BEACON STREET STORY

The People

James Smith Colburn, the builder (1808)
William H. Prescott, the fourth owner (1845)
Asher Benjamin, the architect
Susan Lorimer, Colburn's first wife
Benedict Arnold
Bonaparte   } *European contacts*
Talleyrand
Madame Recamier
Sarah Prince, Colburn's second wife

About the year 1807 I purchased a lot of land of Jonathan Mason, Esq., in Beacon Street, enough for two houses, and had two beautiful houses built thereon. One I intended for myself and the other for my sister. They were planned by myself and the work executed by A. Benjamin, Architect."

Like countless clients before and since, James Colburn felt himself to be the architect, and the architect someone who merely carried out the client's design. At any rate, he was right when he said "They are two superb houses with (their) two bowfronts, circular dining rooms, and drawing rooms over, with folding doors." It is a further tribute to the architect that they were finished within a year.

Asher Benjamin, at thirty-three, had quite a few handsome houses to his credit when he came to Boston and designed this pair on Beacon Street. But more than from his actual commissions, like this one here, his reputation was going to be made from his books—books that had a lot to do with the looks of northeastern houses in the first half of the 19th century.

About Benjamin's early Boston years, Juliette Tomlinson found out for her sketch in the *Connecticut Antiquarian* that "they were criss-crossed with lawsuits, business was hard to find, and the little that materialized was slow on payment. From 1806 through the 1820's, his name appears often in the court records. Sometimes judgements went against him, but more often in his favor. In spite of these difficulties, he managed to publish several books on buildings, bury one wife, acquire another, and add substantially to his growing family." He died in 1845 at seventy-two.

At a time when the Massachusetts Dames, who were restoring it as their headquarters, were trying to determine whether the architect had been Benjamin or Bulfinch, a lady from Georgia rang the Beacon Street bell to ask if she could look at the house. It had been built, she said, by her great-great-grandfather. Not only that, but at her home in Augusta, she said, she had James Colburn's memoirs in manuscript, from which, through her generosity, the Dames were able to make the copies that are now in their possession.

In his journal, Colburn comes right out and says that he was born to be something of a mercantile genius. He worked in stores from the time he was 12. At barely 17 he had formed a partnership with a young friend who was something of a mercantile prodigy himself. But the boy wonder of the two was James. He was bitten by the idea that, if he could only get to England, with his peculiar talents he could make all the right contacts with British manufacturers and send back goods to his partner which would sell in Boston at handsome profits.

His powers of persuasion were certainly impressive. "I went to Benjamin Bussey, Esq., an old and respectable merchant and importer in Boston," the boy writes, "who was under some obligation to me for some accidental services I had done him. He took a friendly liking to me, and although a very cautious, shrewd and careful man, he invited me to his house in Summer Street where I used to go once or twice a week. During one of these visits I observed that I was going into business with Mr. Otis, and was going to England and should feel extremely thankful for any little aid he could afford me. He threw cold water on my project, saying I was too young and too inexperienced for such an undertaking and I combated him in argument and it seemed I had the advantage, for he was rather astonished at my views and wished to know where I had obtained them. I told him I wanted a little of his assistance. He frankly asked what and how much. I told him I wanted him to loan me a thousand dollars by a letter of credit on his Bankers in London payable in one year. I wished him to say in the letter of credit anything about me, or my firm, that he could consistently say of our integrity and respectability. To all of this he acquiesced, and I left him with a joyful heart and communicated the result of my visit to Mr. Otis, which was as agreeable to him as to me."

Within two months, by "selling some goods at auction, which we had purchased on credit, we were able to purchase a Bill on London for one thousand dollars and pay my passage of $200 in money. This, with Mr. Bussey's letter of credit of $1000, was every cent I started with for London . . . seventeen years of age, with no clothes but those I had on, and no friends."

Arriving in London, "I went to a tailor and got a complete suit of clothes and rigged myself according to the fashion of London from head to foot, and in a way suitable for a London merchant."

His progress from the head of one manufacturing house to another was truly astounding. It was clear that these great solid Britishers had never encountered quite that kind of cocksureness before. At seventeen he rose to meet them at their own level, and that is where in the end they accepted him.

After staying on for a few days at the Croskeys Inn, James heard of a place run by a woman in Bride Court where he could have his breakfast and a room with trundle bed for half a guinea a week, and dine wherever he chose. "As economy and saving were my objects," these were the lodgings he took, having only his dinners to get, "which I always took care to get cheap." He had been there for two months, when one morning the junior partner of the banking house that carried his letter of credit came to call with some papers. Looking about him in the entry where they were standing, the banker asked Colburn how he came to be living there. "I told him a Leicester man at the 'Croskeys Inn' introduced me. He said I had got into the wrong house, a bad house where girls were kept as mistresses, and that I must move at once." The banker told him of an inexpensive boarding house on St. Swithin's Lane, near the Lord Mayor's house, where many clerks and merchants from the Continent resided ". . . Here I lived," Colburn concludes, "until I got married, which was I believe in May 1799, and I was only eighteen years of age."

His bride was Susan Lorimer, "a pretty, lively, sensible and well educated woman," according to Colburn, "then about fifteen years of age." He'd been introduced to the Lorimers, a Scotsfamily in the wool-dyeing trade, by two Graham brothers from Vermont, both colonels and descendants of the Duke of Montrose. The brothers had married Susan's two older sisters.

It was Colonel Burr Graham who took him about this time to meet Benedict Arnold at his house in Baker Street. They were "ushered into a splendid drawing room by a servant in livery, who said the General would wait upon us in a few minutes. I must confess my heart beat quickly," Colburn recalls.

"In a few moments in came a small decrepit old man with a cork heel, lively in his manners, walked quick and shook hands with the Colonel very cordially, and then says the Colonel, 'I have brought a young friend with me from Boston whom I beg leave to introduce to you.' The General shook my hand most warmly and said he was delighted to see anyone from America, although they had treated him ungratefully and immediately observed that his reward for gaining the victory [at Saratoga] was his cork heel (holding it up), and that General Gates got all the honor . . . I departed with the Colonel perfectly delighted with my visit, and which I shall never forget. I would rather have made that visit than to the King of England, for let me ever so much condemn the Traitor, I was glad to see a man that had been so conspicuous and so brave a General. He did not live long after this interview.''

Susan and James were married in May at St. Mary LeStrand's. At the door were ''a number of fishwives.'' Someone in the crowd asked what was going on. ''Only a boy and a girl going to be tied together,'' the fishwives screamed. James remarks, ''I felt mortified that we should be taken for boy and girl, as I felt myself old enough, big enough and as capable as judging for myself as anyone, and the end proved the correctness.''

''In less than a year our first child was born, a son, whom I named James Bussey Colburn, the middle name out of compliment to my friend Benjamin Bussey of Boston.''

Leaving his wife and baby, James then made a business trip to Holland, Belgium, Germany, and France, meeting celebrities by the score and making mercantile arrangements wherever he felt he and his partner could end up with sufficient profit. Later, on more of a pleasure trip to Paris with Susan, James went well equipped with letters of introduction which gave the young couple opportunities to meet everybody who was anybody in Paris at the time. They talked with Madame Recamier, with Talleyrand, and a host of other notables, were entertained at balls, the opera, even at court. If they had wanted to, they could have reached right out and touched Napoleon and Josephine. In September 1802, James decided to take Susan on a visit to Boston, his first trip home. Leaving the baby with its grandparents they sailed with their manservant John and their maidservant Ann on the *Sampson* from Gravesend on September 12. All went well until the 19th when James's diary reports ''Mrs. C. is very sick . . . from the effects of seasickness.''

On the 23rd, ''Mrs. C. continues quite ill. I was never better and can eat my allowance, which is lucky as I have to be nurse.''

By October 2, ''My dear wife is growing worse and nearly distracts me. She will hardly let me leave her for a moment, she has no rest and continually talks about dying. Her fever continues.'' And so the distracted diary goes on, getting more and more distracted every day, as Susan goes through this siege of violent illness, until October 24, when she dies.

James could not bear to have her buried at sea, and the captain agreed to have her body encased in tarred canvas and laid in a well-salted coffin, the coffin being lashed securely in the longboat on deck. A week later they landed at Boston, and the day after Susan's funeral took place from James's father's home in Concord.

James stayed on in Boston; bought out Thomas Otis; and when a man named William Gill, who had been working for the firm, married James's sister, he made William the European partner. On their return from their first preliminary English visit, the Gills brought back James' son, who in due course married, moved to California, had many children, and was a lifetime comfort to his father.

Just as James's house was finished he ''became attached to Sarah Prince and became engaged and was married on October 18, 1808, by Rev. Dr. Lowell at Mrs. Prince's, and it was quite a large wedding for those times. We went immediately to my new house in Beacon Street, which I had furnished with new and elegant furniture, where I continued to reside as long as I lived in Boston. The house was well calculated for company and we saw a great deal of both dinner company and dinner parties and gave several splendid balls there. We lived in a great deal of fashionable style, as I could well afford it, for I was then worth one half a million dollars. I kept the handsomest carriage and the most beautiful pair of dapple gray horses ever seen in Boston, with a coachman named Miller, well known, with a footman, all in livery, and two leopard dogs, one before and the other behind, that always followed the carriage. It was the most splendid turnout that was ever seen in Boston in those days. It was so conspicuous that I never liked it to be sent for me and hardly could ever ride it to church or anywhere else, I got it to please my wife and for her convenience and was willing she should enjoy it, as I could well afford it."

In 1819 the Colburns moved for his health to Charleston, South Carolina, where for the next forty years until he died he had his ups and downs with various mercantile enterprises, the downs having to do with the machinations of the sons he had by Sarah.

Until 1937 the house on Beacon Street had the good luck to be occupied by owners with the will and means to live in it the way it was meant to be lived in. But in 1937 it started downhill as a hackwork hive of kitchenette apartments, until in 1944 the Massachusetts Dames came to its rescue in the nick of time.

It will always be an honor to the house that the third owner after James Colburn should have been the great historian William H. Prescott. The first thing he did was to build an addition to house, install on the second floor the most valuable private library in the country, and set up a secluded study on the floor above in which he finished *The Conquest of Peru* and worked on his *Philip II*. An early Encyclopaedia Britannica, in describing Prescott's 55 Beacon Street home, calls it "a spacious house commanding a fine view of land and water" (the view is gone since the area has been built up), then goes on to mention that "to the back of this abode, Prescott added a noble room to contain his library." According to Samuel Morison, the historian, the large glass panes in the windows of the house, which were the first of that size in Boston, were put in by the partially blinded Prescott in order to get more interior light.

Over the westerly bay window of this library Prescott hung two crossed swords, one of which had been carried by his grandfather Colonel Prescott (called by Washington "Prescott the Brave") at the Battle of Bunker Hill; the other in the same battle by the grandfather of Mrs. Prescott, Captain Linzee, who commanded the British sloop *Falcon*, which lay off Charlestown in that same battle.

It was when Thackeray saw the swords in 1852, while staying at the Prescotts, that he got the idea of writing *The Virginians*, his novel of two brothers on opposite sides in the Revolution, which opens with these words: "On the library walls of one of the most famous writers of America there hang two crossed swords which his relatives wore in the great War of Independence. The one sword was gallantly drawn in the service of the King, the other was the weapon of a brave and honoured republican soldier. The possessor of the harmless trophy has earned for himself a name alike honoured in his ancestor's country, and his own, where genius such as his always has a peaceful welcome. The ensuing history reminds me of yonder swords in the historian's study at Boston."

He wasn't at all an old man when he died—sixty-two. His semi-blindness came from being hit by a crust in a college dining-hall fracas. But there was plenty of family money to ease at least certain aspects of his disability. Being a rheumatic and dyspeptic seemed to bother him more than the damage to his eyesight, but he was always a gay person, with a keen sense of humor, and a peculiarly charming personality. His eyes always looked perfectly normal.

He had had a mild stroke in 1858, but not severe enough to interfere to any great extent with his work. Then on January 29, 1859, after Mrs. Prescott had read to him as usual from the morning paper, and left him for the morning with his secretary, he walked about noon into his library, where his secretary found him unconscious. In an hour he was dead. On the 31st he was placed in the Prescott family vault under St. Paul's Church in Boston. It was in that same year that James Colburn died in South Carolina.

In the lovely drawing room on the second floor, stretching the full width of the house and facing Boston Common, is a Federal marble chimney piece carved in the Adam style. It was put in at the time the house was built. The rug is a fine Aubusson. Among the objects in the treasure table are two snuff boxes used by Hancock and Washington and the latter's egg cup.

Asher Benjamin designed this full elliptical room on the first floor to take advantage of his rounded Federal bay. Originally the dining room, it is now redecorated by Mrs. Henry Tudor in memory of her mother, a distinguished Massachusetts Dame, using early Empire furnishings and French wallpaper. Framed letters by Prescott, Holmes and other are on the curving bookcase.

The dining room on the second floor rear was Prescott's library during the years he occupied the house. The four pedestal dining table has a small matching table to add when a longer table is needed. The 18th-century longcase clock was made by Isaac Rogers of London. The large convex mirror, one of a pair, is 19th-century as is the crystal chandelier. The fine white marble chimney piece from Salem is carved with flower-filled cornucopias with Flora in between and caryatids.

141

THE HARMONIST HOUSE STORY

The People

George Rapp, Harmonist leader
Frederick Rapp, the leader's adopted son and chief lieutenant

Beginning in the early part of the 19th century, a scattering of communal settlements took root in this country, flourished for a while, then began to go to seed. While they flourished, all property and means of production in the settlements were held in common ownership. The people were largely from south Germany, separatists from the dogmatism of the Lutheran church. They were pietists; they believed in the religion of the heart; and, while in some of their communities the custom of celibacy was accepted as one of their creeds, a certain latitude was allowed in its observance.

Only in this country could communities of that kind have been safe from the interference of either church or state. Still, they were doomed in time to fail. No closed community could withstand the forces of infiltration from without and defection from within, no matter how peaceful. But these communities had their periods of prosperity, and the towns and villages that have been in part preserved provide a fascinating record of the way these people lived, and of their often remarkable achievements.

Probably the most fascinating record was that provided by the followers of George Rapp, for under his leadership they first created in 1805 a very successful settlement in western Pennsylvania, which they sold to their great advantage nine years later, migrating to the banks of the Wabash in Indiana, where they created an even more successful settlement. After ten years they sold that too, moving to a better location back in Pennsylvania to create their third and final settlement, which did very well indeed until Rapp's death in 1847. After that the movement began gradually to lose its original identity bit by bit, and by 1906 had lost it altogether.

George Rapp was born in 1757 in the Württemberg village of Iptingen, where his father was a farmer and grapegrower. By the time he was forty, he had long since become prominent as a preacher whose concept of Christianity recognized the right of the individual to interpret the teachings of Jesus for himself, with the power to communicate directly with God. His group of followers was growing, along with the strength of his leadership. He had enormous energy, both of mind and body, and he had the courage to stand up against the authority of the established church, whose interference, however, finally became so intolerable to him and his group of followers that in 1803 it was decided to emigrate to America.

He sailed ahead with his son John and another member of the group. In Philadelphia he made arrangements to buy some three thousand acres twenty-five miles north of Pittsburgh. By 1805 seven hundred of his followers had made their way from Württemberg to western Pennsylvania, where they built the first Rappite community and called it Harmonie. The Harmonie Society was formed, under whose laws all the property and possessions of the members became the common property of the community, and all the labor of the members was performed in the common cause. Should a member wish to withdraw from the Society, he would be entitled to nothing but his original contribution.

Thanks to Rapp's remarkable management and the esteem in which he was held, Harmonie soon became a thriving town of "one hundred and fifty dwellings, six large brick houses, an inn, a store, a weaving shop, a dye plant, a woolen factory, a spacious meetinghouse, a four-story granary, a variety of mills, a brewery, and shops for various trades. There were also barns and stables, and a large warehouse built away from the town on the banks of the Ohio."

But in ten years' time the need for more space, easier access to water transportation, a milder climate, and a soil more suitable for grapegrowing caused Rapp to set out in search of a new location. With a few leading members of the community, including the son Frederick he had adopted, and who was to become his right-hand man, Rapp and his party journeyed by boat down the Ohio until they reached the southeastern corner of Indiana where the Wabash flows into the larger river. It was not far from here that they found what they were looking for. The site was fifty miles up the winding Wabash, but from the town of Mount Vernon on the Ohio it was only fifteen. There they bought 25,000 acres of the beautiful fertile valley for $61,000, with an option on 30,000 more acres adjoining, which they took up a little later.

After selling the Pennsylvania property for $100,000, they laid out the new place (also called Harmonie) on a larger scale than the one before, and in June 1814 brought down 100 of their best builders to get it ready for the others, who arrived in separate batches during that fall and the following spring.

Within ten years the Harmonists had built:

82 one-story houses	2 ice houses
34 two-story houses	2 greenhouses
4 large family rooming houses	several smaller granaries
2 churches, the first frame, and the second brick	1 steam gristmill
	several smaller gristmills
2 schools	1 building for flour storage
1 granary or "fort"	several wine presses
several cider presses	1 packing house
numerous farm buildings	1 tannery and curriery
2 distilleries	1 light leather manufactory
2 breweries	1 shoemaker's shop
1 cotton gin	1 soap factory
1 weaving and fulling shop	1 saddler's shop
1 dye works	1 blacksmith's shop
1 tailor shop	1 watchmaker's shop
1 store	1 wagon maker's shop
1 hotel	1 carpentry shop
1 library	1 cooper's shop
1 doctor's office	1 lime kiln
1 apothecary shop	1 brick kiln
1 hospital	several pottery ovens
several wash houses	1 rope walk
several dry houses	rollers for extracting oil from flax and other seeds
several food-processing plants	

"Serene and confident, they lived modest and uncomplicated lives surrounded with ease and good taste. Their ability to create comfort and graciousness in the middle of the wilderness, with only the most basic tools and materials, was the constant wonder of their visitors and their neighbors. The great church which dominated the town, the well-designed and comfortable houses, the pleasant inn, and the well-stocked store amazed the traveler who had found

The great brick chimney is used here entirely for heating the living room. On its opposite side, in the kitchen, is an oven as well as an iron cooking surface designed with typical Harmonist ingenuity and practicality. The brick-filled timber construction is clearly indicated. Two child's Shaker chairs are hanging from pegs on the wall. The basket and the child's rocker on the hearth are Harmonist, as are the braided runners, the pewter plates and four-legged stool. This authentic Harmonist dwelling has been faithfully restored by the Indiana Dames to show as accurately as possible the building methods, ways of life and even some of the philosophies of the followers of George Rapp.

his refuge in drafty cabins as he made his way about the frontier. Here he could rest comfortably, eat well, and make purchases ranging from good whiskey to fine linen and silk handkerchiefs. The Harmonie store did not stock its shelves with homespun and saltpork merchandise."

Don Blair, the Harmonist authority, goes on to describe, in his excellent monograph called *Harmonist Construction* (Indiana Historical Society, Indianapolis, 1964, $1), the methods and materials employed by the Harmonists in their buildings, particularly in the two-story frame houses which are among their most outstanding technological triumphs, and of which the Indiana Dames' Harmonist House is the most finely preserved example still to be seen in the town.

By using mass production of standardized parts they anticipated modern prefabrication by more than a century. All structural timbers were fully prepared in the shop, the mortise joints made, the pegs and peg-holders cut, all parts numbered and ready to be taken to the building site at the proper time and fixed into their proper places—all at a minimum of wasteful and cumbersome site labor.

As the building scheme for, say, twenty two-story frame houses was identical, it was possible over the winter, in a heated shop, to mass-produce twenty identical sets of parts and pieces, ready to be assembled quickly and expeditiously in the spring. The ingenuity and engineering skill which went into the way the various timbers were arranged and joined are borne out out in the extraordinary durability of these houses. They are as sound and strong and straight today as they were when they were built. None has ever burned down. Because of the way the heating arrangements—the stoves and fireplaces and chimneys—were designed, it was almost impossible for a room to catch on fire. But if it should, then, because of the way the walls and floors were constructed, it would be almost impossible for the fire to spread.

Both inside and outside walls were brick-filled, and, because of the understanding that went into their design and construction, they provided such a high degree of heat and sound insulation that their comfort and quietness by present-day standards are astonishing. The same is true of the insulation in the first-and second-floor ceilings. Here the Harmonists contrived an insulation panel called a Dutch biscuit, made by wrapping a piece of wood one by four by eighteen inches with almost two inches of mud-filled straw; the ends of the board were tapered to slide into grooves cut in the ceiling rafters, the lower faces of the biscuits flush with the lower edges of the rafters, thus providing a perfect binding surface for plastering.

In addition to all these more-or-less-invisible virtues, the Harmonist houses make up in their fine proportions for any lack of extraneous ornamentation they may exhibit. This virtue of simplicity they share with the houses of the Shakers, the somewhat similarly communistic and celibate sect famous for its furniture.

Even in their celibacy, the Harmonists showed the same high sense of organization which went into the building of their houses, for there were regulations that permitted augmentation of the population at stated intervals, so arranged that, when the children came, they came "in little flocks, all within the same month perhaps like farmers' lambs."

In 1824 the Harmonists decided to move again. They wanted to get closer to the eastern markets, and away from the vexing western currency; and, besides, while all was harmony within, their relations with outsiders were not as wholly harmonious as the Harmonists would have liked. Also they had a chance to sell the property. Robert Owen, the British social reformer, a pioneer in the cooperative movement, wanted to buy it.

So Rapp led his flock back to Pennsylvania, this time right onto the banks of the Ohio, eighteen miles above Pittsburgh and about twenty-five miles away from the first Harmonie (now named Wurtemburg). They called the new community Economy—now the city of Ambridge. Just as it was with the first Harmonie, the architecture of the Harmonists here did not achieve the organic identity it reached in Indiana. Here in Economy, using a lot of outside labor, a great deal of that identity was lost. In Indiana it was the real thing.

THE NOLAND HOUSE STORY

The People

Lieutenant C. F. M. Noland, lawyer, journalist, sportsman, courier
Major William Noland, Federal officeholder, father of the lieutenant

Arkansas Territory was created by Congress in March 1819, with Arkansas Post, founded by the French in 1686, as the capital—but only for the first few years. The capital was then shifted a hundred miles up the Arkansas River to a much newer and more accessible settlement called Little Rock. There during the next twelve years, until 1836, when Arkansas became a state, a cluster of remarkably nice houses grew up in the center of the town. All of them were still standing, miraculously, in 1939, by then in the center of a large modern city, when it was happily decided to restore them.

One of the houses served as a meeting place for the Territorial Legislature, and the whole group of thirteen restored buildings now goes under the name of the Arkansas Territorial Capitol Restoration. It is one of the freshest and most utterly beguiling little restorations in the United States. Besides the house in which the Territorial Legislature met, there is the house of the founder of the Arkansas *Gazette*, who moved up with his paper from Arkansas Post when the capital was changed. Behind his house is the old print shop of the *Gazette* (still being published in Little Rock).

Another house in the group was the residence of an Arkansas Governor, Elias N. Conway, with the usual separated kitchen, and with a milkhouse and a stable. Then in the center of the group there is a house that is in a way the best of all—the one once occupied by Lieutenant Noland, his wife Lucretia, and his son Berk (short for Berkeley). It is here that the Arkansas Dames have done their delightful bedroom.

Noland's family were Virginia gentry related to the Berkeleys. For a short time Noland's father was a member of the State Legislature, where he became known as the introducer of a bill against duelling which in 1809 became Virginia law. Noland was born there in Loudoun County in about 1808, and in 1823 went to West Point, from where he was dismissed in 1825 for deficiency in drawing and mathematics. He had a reputation for not taking anything too seriously. Later in life an old friend said of him, "He believed to be sad was sinful."

While he was at West Point his father was appointed by President Monroe to be Receiver of the United States Law Office, and was stationed in the Ozarks at Batesville, Arkansas, where the ex-cadet turned up shortly after leaving the military academy. At Batesville the father promptly put the son to studying law under Judge James Woodson Bates, father and son living together in the judge's house.

In 1827 the father finished his tour of duty in the Territory and went back home to Virginia, leaving Fent, as the boy was called (for Fenton, the second of his Christian names), in Batesville studying law. But journalism became his primary career. It began with the letters he wrote about Arkansas to his Virginia relatives, letters (now in the Berkeley Papers at the University of Virginia) which led him to become a contributor to various newspapers and magazines, mostly to the New York *Spirit of the Times*, a publication devoted to racing, hunting, fishing, and the theater.

The showpiece of the Arkansas Territorial Capitol Restoration in Little Rock is the group composed of Lieutenant Noland's house, his law office on the left, and the detached kitchen on the right, which form a courtyard containing the well house and a charming, old-fashioned garden. In the bedroom maintained by the Arkansas Dames the leather trunk at the foot of the sleigh bed was used by Lieutenant Noland's father when he was sent by the Land Department in Washington to "collect the monies of the Territory." Attached to it is still the wooden tag with his initials. The boot at the right of the original mantel belonged to the lieutenant. Its mate was discovered, in the fall of 1964, in the Valentine Museum in Richmond and donated to the Noland House, too late for this picture.

147

Fent had an affinity for the first three of these subjects in particular, and through the frontiersmen he learned the ways of the Arkansas woods and streams and wrote about them in two widely different manners: first as a keen, accurate reporter, and second as a wild exaggerator. Always famous as the home of the tall tale, Arkansas grew more and more famous as Fent's fictions grew taller and taller.

Noland became not only a fine horseman but one of the popular racing reporters of his day, visiting the tracks at Louisville, Lexington, St. Louis, and New Orleans, and sending out his colorful accounts to English as well as American periodicals. His unfailing humor and ready wit made friends wherever he went, and among politicians as much as the men of the woods.

Just when Noland went to live in the house that now bears his name in the Territorial Restoration is not known, but the chances are he was living there when the legislature was preparing the State Constitution that had to be sent to Congress for affirmation before Arkansas could be admitted as a state. At any rate, he was the man chosen to be the messenger. He was to get $500 for his service.

Noland left Little Rock with the document on Friday morning, February 5, 1836. This is a matter of record. It is also a matter of record that he arrived at the Capitol in Washington on March 8. There are two versions of how he made the journey. One is that he went by horseback, the other that he went by steamboat and stage. There is no explanation of why it took him so long. None of his many letters describes the journey. According to the established rates of travel for 1830, it should have taken two weeks instead of four and a half.

In fact, while Ambrose Sevier, the Arkansas representative in Congress was waiting impatiently for Noland, a copy of the Arkansas *Gazette* arrived on February 29 with the Constitution printed as a supplement. And to save time it was this newspaper copy of the Constitution which was laid before the House of Representatives, the original being substituted when Noland finally turned up. Once in Washington, "he held a reunion with his father and was presented by him to all the distinguished men of the nation, including 'Old Hickory,' who twitted him for abandoning the Democracy for Whiggery."

For a while during the 'thirties he was a political writer on the Arkansas *Advocate* in Little Rock, rival of the *Gazette*. Noland's paper was against the Governor at the time, a man named Pope, whose nephew became so enraged at a particularly taunting attack on his uncle, written by Noland, that he challenged Noland to a duel, to take place at some distance from town. Noland's first shot struck young Pope in the leg. Though Pope died as a result of the duel, his death was due as much to the exposure he suffered on the long trip back to Little Rock as to the bullet wound itself.

After a fifteen-year fight with tuberculosis, Noland died in Little Rock in June 1858 in the house of a friend. It was in the last year of his life that he was called upon by a correspondent of the New Orleans *Picayune*, who wrote, "I have him to thank for a half hour of as hearty laughter as could be desired, though he himself was interrupted every few minutes by that premium cough of his." He never complained about his cough. In fact, he made fun of it. He only complained that in the woods it interfered with his stalking of game.

Wheatland is just as it was when Buchanan lived here.

THE WHEATLAND STORY

The People

James Buchanan, third owner of Wheatland and 15th President of the United States
Ann Coleman, his fiancée
Esther Parker (Miss Hetty), his housekeeper
Harriet Lane, his niece and hostess
Czar Nicholas, Queen Victoria, and Abraham Lincoln

Described by his biographer as one of the least known American statesmen, James Buchanan was born April 23, 1791, in a log cabin at Stony Batter, near Chambersburg, Pennsylvania. His family moved a few years later to Mercersburg nearby, where Buchanan's father had both a farm in the country and a store in the town. There James went to the old Stone Academy until he was fifteen, then to Dickinson College in Carlisle. He studied his law in Lancaster, which was to be home for him the rest of his life.

In 1814 he held his first elective office in the Pennsylvania Legislature, and in 1820 was elected to Congress. President Jackson appointed him Minister to Russia in 1832, where he was appalled by the splendor and pomp of the St. Petersburg court, but from where he warned his correspondents in America that "they are not very delicate about opening letters here."

Returning home he was elected to the United States Senate in 1834 and in 1845 was appointed Secretary of State by President Polk. He was made Minister to Great Britain in 1853 by President Pierce, and on March 4, 1857, he became the 15th President of the United States. During the mounting crisis of the four years that followed he retained the conservatism and moderation which characterized his whole political life. It is possible that he was one of the most conscientious and least inspired public figures of importance in American history.

Yet cheering crowds were always on hand to greet him at railroad stations. They called him Old Buck, and it cannot be denied that in two respects he stands alone: he is still the only President ever to be elected from Pennsylvania, and the only bachelor ever to be put in the White House.

As a young lawyer he fell in love with Ann Coleman, the daughter of a self-made millionaire ironmaster living in Lancaster. The course of his courtship and its tragic end can best be told by contemporary letters, uncovered by Philip S. Klein in his biography.

For Buchanan, business came first, and for two months in the fall of 1819, when he was twenty-eight and Ann twenty-two, his law office was buried in an avalanche of work, and, as one of Ann's friends wrote to another, Ann had begun to feel "that Mr. Buchanan did not treat her with that affection that she expected from the man she would marry, and in consequence of his coolness she wrote him a note telling him that she thought it was not regard for her that was his object, but her riches."

Another friend describes how "Mr. Buchanan was obliged to go out of town on a business trip. He returned in a few days and casually dropped in to see . . . Mrs. William Jenkins, with whose husband he was on terms of intimate friendship. With her was staying her sister, Miss Grace Hubley, . . . a pretty and charming young lady. From this innocent call the whole trouble arose. A young lady told Miss Coleman of it and thereby excited her jealousy. She was indignant that he should visit anyone before coming to her. On the spur of the moment she penned an angry note and released him from his engagement. The note was handed to him while he was in the courthouse. Persons who saw him receive it remarked afterward that they noticed him turn pale when he read it. Mr. Buchanan was a proud man. The large fortune of his lady was to him only another barrier to his trying to persuade her to reconsider her rejection of himself."

Shortly thereafter Ann Coleman died of a sudden illness thought to have been brought on by grief. Buchanan never married.

In 1849, when he retired as Secretary of State, Buchanan returned to Lancaster where he bought the country house called Wheatland, which had been built twenty years before by his old banking friend William Jenkins. Jenkins had sold it some years since to another old friend of Buchanan's, William Morris Meredith, who was about to be President Taylor's Secretary of the Treasury. It was therefore a house that Buchanan knew well, and from all the things he said about it, up to the day he died there twenty years later, he loved it more than any other place (or perhaps even any person) in the world.

His young niece Harriet Lane came to live with him, as did Miss Hetty, his housekeeper. From all the evidence it is safe to say that practically everyone who met Harriet was enchanted with her.

While he was Minister to Great Britain, she came to visit him in London and became the rage of the Court. When Buchanan and Tennyson were receiving honorary degrees at Oxford, the biographer describes how the students paid only polite attention to the dignitaries, but went wild about Harriet, whistling and shouting their approval; and at Buchanan's farewell dinner with the Queen, most of her conversation, he said, was about "dear Miss Lane."

This was the young woman who at twenty-seven went with President Buchanan to Washington to be his hostess at the White House. Miss Hetty went, too, as housekeeper, but there was some friction between the two, and Buchanan sent Miss Hetty back to Wheatland.

Four years later she wrote, "I receive so many evidences of kindness and good feeling, and so many regrets at my leaving that it makes me feel very sad." When Lincoln paid his first call at the White House she wrote, "The glimpse I caught of him was the image of . . . our tall, awkward Irishman who waits on the door . . . they say Mrs. L. is awfully *western*, loud & unrefined."

On their way to the capital for the Inauguration, Buchanan turned to Lincoln and said, "My dear sir, if you are as happy in entering the White House as I shall feel on returning to Wheatland, you are a happy man indeed." "Mr. President," Lincoln replied, "I cannot say that I shall enter it with much pleasure, but I assure you that I shall do what I can to maintain the high standards set by my illustrious predecessors who have occupied it."

Two years later in the summer of 1863 there were rumors at Lancaster of 35,000 Confederate troops at York, twenty miles away across the Susquehanna. Mr. Klein writes about Buchanan's reaction. "With the first news of Lee's advance into Pennsylvania, he had packed Harriet off to Philadelphia and shipped away his most important papers. He had tried to make Miss Hetty leave, but she said firmly that she would stay if he did. He had told friends who urged him to get out of the invasion area that he would remain at Wheatland if it should be surrounded by a hundred thousand rebels. He and Miss Hetty would see it through together." The "rebels" got no closer than Gettysburg, a good sixty miles from Lancaster.

In the bedroom occupied by Buchanan's charming
niece, Harriet Lane, who was his hostess here at Wheatland, as well as at the White House, and in London
when he was ambassador there, the carved fourposter
is of West Indian mahogany. The prayer bench and
prayer books belonged to Harriet. The chair is Belter.
Above the drawing room black and white marble mantel the big gilt mirror is 1810. Beyond the marble top
table is a red velvet conversation sofa. The portraits
are of Queen Victoria and the Prince of Wales, presented to Buchanan by the royal family along with
one of Prince Albert. The Chickering piano was bought
by Buchanan for Harriet Lane.

The Old Indian Agency House was built in 1832 by the U.S. government near Fort Winnebago, for the use of the Indian Agent's family—at that time the Kinzies. The Kinzies loved their house, with its simple New England lines, but left it in eight months when Kinzie despaired of advancement in the Indian service. In 1932 the Wisconsin Dames bought it and restored it true to the times when the Kinzies lived in it so briefly.

THE OLD INDIAN AGENCY HOUSE STORY

The People

John H. Kinzie, Indian agent
Juliette Magill, John's wife
Dr. Alexander Wolcott, Juliette's uncle and husband of John's sister
Lewis Cass, Governor of Michigan Territory (1813-31) and Secretary of War (1831-36)

Born in 1803 in Campbell, Canada, where his father had a trading post, John Kinzie was still a baby when he was brought by his family to Fort Dearborn, where the Chicago River then flowed into Lake Michigan (it now flows out). Here Kinzie *père*, who is usually called the Father of Chicago, took over the trading post established a few years before by Jean Baptiste Point du Sable, a San Domingan Negro, and settled his little frontier family in what is now one of the busiest business blocks in the world.

When John was nine the War of 1812 was beginning, and, fearful of an Indian uprising inspired by the British, the fort was abandoned on orders from General William Hull, who had just surrendered to the British at Detroit. The general's baggage had been captured a few days before with all his papers and plans, and he panicked, with the result that the Fort Dearborn people were set upon by Indians on the Lake Michigan dunes and most of the men, women, and children massacred. Hull was sentenced to death by courtmartial for cowardice but was saved by his Revolutionary record, and his name merely dropped from the Army roll.

Fortunately for the Kinzies, they had been spirited away in time by some friendly Indians to Detroit. The fort was rebuilt four years later; the Kinzies returned, and around the fort and the trading posts of Kinzie and others the city of Chicago began to grow. When young John was 15 he was apprenticed to Robert Stuart, agent of the American Fur Company at Mackinac, and was sent there to learn the fur trade.

He had been at Mackinac for two years when Governor Cass stopped by one day on a territorial trip with a party that included his secretary Robert Forsyth, who happened to be John's uncle, and Doctor Wolcott, who happened to be the uncle of John's future wife. Not only that—having just been appointed Indian agent at Chicago, the doctor was destined to meet John's sister Ellen, whom he married in 1823.

The next time John met the Governor was on the Mississippi at Prairie du Chien, to which John had been transferred by the fur company. This was at the time of the Indian treaty of 1825, and John's ability in Indian languages impressed the Governor so much that he asked John to come to Detroit and be his secretary. Then when Fort Winnebago had been built at the portage between the Fox and Wisconsin rivers, and it seemed desirable to establish an Indian agency there, the Governor recommended John for the job, and in 1829 John was appointed.

The Indians, for the most part, had felt friendly toward the French; then gradually they became allies of the British conquerors of the French. But the American conquerors of the British were different. They were coming in to stay, and the Indians didn't like the idea of moving on beyond the Mississippi, as the Americans had made up their minds the Indians would have to do. More and more, hostile activities of the Indians had to be subdued by force of arms, and the methods and mores of combat on the part of the Americans were often no more civilized than those of the Indians.

The first year at Fort Winnebago John familiarized himself with the situation there and made plans for the agency. He always had a way with the Indians, spoke their languages, understood their habits, and sympathized with their predicament. As agent they addressed him as Father.

The piano in the living room is a Nunns and Clark of 1830, the same make as the one the Kinzies carried out and back through the Wisconsin wilderness. The stool is an 1810-20 piece in the Sheraton style. The mantel is a memorial to Juliette Gordon Low, granddaughter of the Kinzies, and founder of the Girl Scouts, from the Girl Scouts of the Great Lakes Region.

He saw to their needs and disbursed the annuities they received from the Government for the lands they relinquished. When a mediator was called for, he became the mediator.

Before he had a chance to begin actual work on the agency itself John was persuaded by the Wolcotts to come with them on a trip to New England. In Boston he met Wolcott's niece Juliette Magill; they fell in love, and on August 9, 1827, were married.

Juliette's mother was a Wolcott from Middletown, Connecticut, where Juliette had been born in 1806, making her three years younger than John. She had gone to Emma Willard's school at Troy, New York, then the most advanced school for girls in the country. Her landscape sketches were quite unusual; she played the piano, and she wrote with wit and grace, in the romatic manner so popular at the time. Her novel, *Walter Ogilby*, was published in 1869, and the book of her experiences in Wisconsin, called *Wau-Bun* (Ojibwa for "the break of day"), first published in 1856, has gone through seven editions.

Wau-Bun begins with the Kinzies' departure September, 1830 from Detroit on Juliette's first journey with her husband to what is now Portage, their agency home, and Fort Winnebago. Mrs. Kinzie seldom uses dates, so it can only be surmised that it took the steamer *Henry Clay* several days at least to get to Green Bay. Here they left the *Henry Clay* and made their way up the Fox River in small boats rowed by *voyageurs*, who sang all the way in rhythm to their rowing. There were stretches in shallow water, or in water choked with wild rice, where their French-Canadian boatmen had to break rhythm, or use paddles, in which case they couldn't sing, but would swear wonderfully in French. The going was very slow at times, and, although again there is no true indication of the time it took, but it must have been about a week (it is now a three-hour drive).

For how the Kinzies lived at Portage, and how they got the Indian Agency House built, Louise Phelps Kellogg provides the best possible account, from which the following excerpts are taken.

"They occupied for the first months of their stay one of the officers' quarters, there being no house prepared especially for the agent and his family. . . . The agency quarters were [to be] across Fox River on a knoll opposite Fort Winnebago. Mr. Kinzie had already made application in his report of Agency affairs, December 31, 1830, for an appropriation of $1,500 for a house for the agent and $400 for a blacksmith's house and shop. The only building then at the Agency was an old log barracks, part of the earlier temporary quarters at the fort, which had been removed and put up again on the Agency hill. For the convenience of the Kinzies logs were cut in the

In the dining room the two-pedestal table is attributed to Duncan Phyfe. The chairs are Hitchcock type, the tea set gold and white Ridgeway porcelain. The clock is by Aaron Willard, Jr., Boston, 1825-30. The 1812 picture of silver rock melon, printed in color and finished by hand, is by George Brookshaw. The sideboard is mahogany, late Sheraton of about 1815.

neighboring tamarack swamp and a dairy, stable, and smoke house were added to the barracks. To this makeshift Agency House, the Kinzies removed in the summer of 1831 and arranged their fine furniture and made for the time and place a delightful home. 'It was surprising,' wrote Mrs. Kinzie, 'how soon a comfortable, homelike air was given to the old dilapidated rooms, by a few Indian mats spread upon the floor, the piano and other furniture ranged in their appropriate places, and even a few pictures hung against the logs. The latter, alas! had soon to be displaced, for with the first heavy shower the rain found entrance through sundry crevices, and we saw ourselves obliged to put aside, carefully, everything that could be injured by moisture.' The mistress of the house found her roof so leaky that she wore her bonnet around the house to protect her hair.

"With the first appropriation of $1,000 went the recommendation that the commanding officer at Fort Winnebago should assign soldiers from the garrison to build the house for the agent. August 11, 1831 Kenzie wrote that the commandant, Captain Plympton could not detail soldiers for this purpose, since the fort needed more barracks and all the soldiers that could be spared were required for that purpose. Kinzie feared that this would delay his home for several years; he therefore asked Cass, then Secretary of War, to obtain for him an appropriation of a second thousand dollars, stating that his family was much crowded in the blacksmith's house. 'I shall not make any preparation for building,' he concluded, 'until I hear from you, which I hope will be soon.' He must have received encouragement from Cass for in his report at the close of 1831 he placed an estimate for $1,200, which would be necessary 'for the completion of the house which is in progress for the Agent, and from the difficulty of obtaining materials and mechanics will require at least that sum.'

"This was the summer of the Black Hawk War and Kinzie was not able to secure any assistance whatever from the garrison which was constantly out on duty. The frame of the house had been raised before the war became acute around Fort Winnebago. It was thought at first it would be confined to northern Illinois; even after the hostiles had pushed into what is now Wisconsin and the pursuing troops under General Henry Atkinson had built Fort Atkinson on Rock River, Fort Winnebago seemed many miles from the scene of the conflict. Kinzie himself rode out often to the south, seventy miles or more, to quiet the Winnebago Indians on Rock River, while the women of the Agency every evening crossed the small bridge leading to the fort and passed the night within its protecting walls. Finally in July it was found necessary to send the women and children to Fort Howard for safety. This flight suspended all building operations until the close of the war. This last battle was fought August 2 and soon all again was security at the Portage.

"The Winnebago, for whom the Agency was established, were forced to sell in the autumn of 1832 all their lands south of the Fox-Wisconsin waterway and to remove north of that boundary. They intend to make their villages, for their future homes, on the west bank of the Wisconsin, from 20 to 30 miles below this place, at Prairie des Sacs, and some of them will make their villages on the Barribault River, where there are now 4 large villages, between 8 and 20 miles from here. The Indians of Fox River, Winnebago and Green Lakes will remove to the Barribault.' All these changes made Kinzie believe that the Agency would be the center of the largest Indian population in the Northwest, except Chicago, and that it would be raised from a sub-Agency to a full Agency. His house he thought would be adequate for many years.

"Notwithstanding the Indian disturbance," Mrs. Kinzie wrote, 'the new Agency House had been going steadily on, and soon after the departure of the Governor and his party, we took possession of it to our no small satisfaction.'

"Governor Porter was very much pleased with Kinzie's efficiency and with the way he built the house. He wrote March 25, 1833, that the agent 'deserves the thanks of the government for expending their money judiciously, economically and well. The buildings are now worth more than they cost.'

"The Kinzies lived in their new home only about eight months after its completion but they were months fraught with tragedy for their Indian wards. Having planted no fields during 1832 and now having sold their lands, and promised to evacuate them by June 1, 1833, the Winnebago were in great straits for food. They crowded around the doors and windows of the new house, peering in anxiously. 'We were soon obliged to keep both doors and windows fast, to shut out the sight of misery we could not relieve . . . It was in vain that we screened the lower portion of our windows with curtains. They would climb up on the outside, and tier upon tier of gaunt, wretched faces would peer in above to watch us, and see if indeed we were as ill provided as we represented ourselves to be.' At last the boats came with the promised corn and the lawn in front of the house was a scene of wild hilarity. 'We could scarcely refrain from laughing, to see old Wild-Cat, who had somewhat fallen off in his huge amount of flesh, seize "the Washington Woman" in his arms and hug and dance with her in the ecstacy of his delight.'

"The Kinzies now decided that the time had come for them to leave the Agency and vacate the new house. The government refused to raise the sub-Agency to a full Agency or to increase the agent's salary. Kinzie saw himself reduced to a round of routine duties, with an ever increasing horde of Indians to guard and satisfy. Moreover, his old home beckoned him, Chicago was growing fast and promised a great future. Kinzie determined to throw in his lot with the new metropolis; he resigned his Agency to take effect July 1, 1833. The last paragraphs of *Wau-Bun* recount the farewells of the agent and his wife and the regret they felt to leave their Indian children and their Agency home.

"After the removal of the Winnebago Indians, we have no record of the occupancy of the house for several years. Fort Winnebago was evacuated in 1845 and left in charge of a single soldier until in 1853, the property was sold by order of the then Secretary of War, Jefferson Davis [who as a lieutenant fresh out of West Point had been stationed at the Fort. When the Kinzies first arrived, Mrs. K. was much amused by the monumental furniture Davis had designed.] The next year the land on which the Agency House stood was patented to James Martin who after three years sold to George C. Tallman. From Tallman the land, now become a farm, passed into the hands of the family of James B. Wells, by whom it was sold in 1878 to Edmond S. Baker, whose home it became until his death October 3, 1928."

Now owned by the Wisconsin Dames, the house has been restored in a way that would have delighted the Kinzies and made this kindly, enlightened couple feel completely at home.

Orlando Brown's House in Frankfort, Kentucky,
by Gideon Shryock.

THE ORLANDO BROWN HOUSE STORY

The People

Orlando Brown, the owner
Gideon Shryock, the architect
Mary Watts Brown, Orlando's first wife, his cousin

Readers of the Liberty Hall story a little earlier in the book will recall that Senator Brown gave a house to his younger son Orlando "to keep the inheritance even."

This is it. And like Liberty Hall, in the same block, it is one of the architectural prides of Frankfort—of all Kentucky, in fact. It has an architectural tie with another building in the town—the Old State Capitol—one of the most appealing public buildings in the country, both Orlando's house and the Capitol being the work of a gifted young Kentucky architect named Gideon Shryock.

Gideon's father lived in Lexington, where he was an unusually able builder, with a good library of architectural books; and, by the time Gideon was twenty-one, the boy not only was experienced in all the building trades but was able to do some designing. At this point he had the choice of following in his father's footsteps or of preparing himself further to practice as a professional architect. Deciding on the latter, he set out in 1823 on horseback for Philadelphia to work and study there in the office of William Strickland. A student of Latrobe, Strickland was an outstanding exponent of the Greek Revival style, which was the overwhelming taste of the times. No wonder, then, that Shryock became known as a Greek Revivalist too. But while he could turn out a strictly copybook classical design with the best of them, most of his work has a strong personality of its own. Certainly the Old State Capitol in Frankfort, which Shryock did when he was barely twenty-four, is a personality building first and Greek Revival second; and it is only the porch of Orlando's house which makes any reference to the fashion that was all the rage in 1835.

"I have been waiting the return of Mr Shryock," Orlando in April, 1835 wrote his wife, who was visiting relatives in Nashville, "who only got back on yesterday and this afternoon we talked over a plan—from which he is to make a drawing of the house—an estimate of the cost—the proportions etc . . . When I get Shryock's plan I will write you again . . . We have agreed already as to the front which is to be taken from a plan of a country house in England which we selected from one of his books on architecture."

As was apparent in the case of the Liberty Hall people, the Browns were not only given to letter-writing on a great scale, but to letter-saving of a kind most helpful to the historian. For, in the case of Orlando's house, the chronicler again has access to a rich accumulation of letters, letters that now tell not only how the house became built, but how it became furnished.

True to his word, Orlando wrote to his wife twelve days later, as soon as Shryock had brought around the plans. ". . . the front is very handsome, having a portier extending . . . from the wall and supported on four columns"—the Greek Revival touch. There were to be four big rooms on each floor, the front ones somewhat larger than the rear, and wide hallways between. "Immediately adjoining your room, and situated somewhat as our pantry is, there is to be—what do you think! why a neat little room in which pegs can be attached to the walls—shelves put up, and anything else done there that you may fancy."

There is a good deal about the preparations being made behind the scenes, by the carpenter, the stonemason, the bricklayer (the bricks were going to be made on the place). Orlando preparing his wife for the fact that "When you get home you will probably not see anything done on the lot," yet. "I have no doubt that we will be able to occupy it before cold weather sets in." Which gives a familiar ring to these words in a letter Orlando's mother wrote to Orlando's wife that December: "Orlando is building on the same lot upon which we reside [in Liberty Hall], but his house will not be ready before next summer."

For a glimpse at the furnishing problems, here are some lines from a letter to Orlando from his mother in New York, the "next summer," where she was shopping for a piano to go in the new house.

"I do not think that Mary W. will like the style of the framework—It is all clumsy in the extreme —thick, straight, square, unornamented legs—but all of the fashionable furniture is of that stamp—Claw feet have crawled out of fashion & table legs (except being square) resemble those of an Elephant more than any thing else."

Looking for wall coverings, Orlando's mother hasn't "yet visited the Paper Factory," but all the fashionable rooms she has seen, and all those in preparation, "(as far as I can learn) are painted in Art, and of light colours." She thinks such painting would suit the new house better than paper. Yet less than two weeks later in a letter from New York to Orlando's wife, it seems that "Your Uncle has sent 60 pieces of paper with bordering for 4 rooms . . . 30 pieces of one kind intended for your two common rooms—30 pieces of two kinds 15 in each, intended for your drawing & dining rooms —It is not the fashion now to furnish the rooms opening into each other exactly alike."

From the same letter it appears that the piano has been purchased. "Mr. Metz, a celebrated performer, selected it." The price was 300 dollars "and 10 to Mr. Metz for his trouble." Margaretta, the mother, preferred a more handsome piano for $400, but when both the maker and the musician assured her that musically the two were identical, she settled for the less expensive.

When Margaretta and the Senator were next heard from a month later, they were in Baltimore, still shopping for the new house. "Having $128 remaining from your Piano, I thought I would not lay it out to please you better than by purchasing a pair of mirrors." The mirrors were some 30 dollars more than the piano balance, but the Senator made up the difference. The Senator also "purchased two carpets for your two common rooms—44 Yds. each, and one for my room 49 Yds., leaving those for your parlors until some other occasion, and hoping you may be made

John Neagle's 1844 portrait of Orlando,
Jr., (right), his brother Mason, and their
dog Judge, hangs in the back parlor. In
the front parlor the portrait of Orlando
Brown's father, John Brown of Liberty
Hall is by the famous Kentucky painter
Matthew Jouett. The bordered wallpaper
resembles that which was bought for
the two parlors by Orlando's parents.
Orlando bought the brass fender about
1835. The Brown family chandelier is
about 1850, the furniture of the 1820-
1835 period. All the woodwork and ash
floors are original.

comfortable at least during the winter with what he has sent . . . In a box containing my Sunday School books . . . Orlando will find his locks.''

Orlando's wife was Mary Watts Brown, his first cousin, daughter of Dr. Preston Brown, with whom Orlando studied medicine for a time after he came out of Princeton. When he found medicine uncongenial, he studied law at Transylvania, practiced for a few years in Tuscaloosa, Alabama, returning to Frankfort in 1830, and married Mary. She was twenty-two and he was twenty-nine.

In 1833 he became joint proprietor and editor of the Frankfort *Commonwealth,* where his writing attracted the attention of Washington Irving, who thought he should devote himself to literature and not to journalism.

Of Mary's and Orlando's four children, one died early. The two sons who survived were both brought up in the new house, where their portrait together as children with their dog hangs today. Mason was born in 1836, Orlando in 1839. Their mother died in 1841 at Blue Sulphur Springs, Virginia.

"My Dear children," Orlando wrote after Mary's death, "It has pleased God to deprive you of your mother while you are yet too young to feel the loss nor will your memory ever serve to give you much idea of what kind of a woman she was. I have thought therefore that I would leave for you a memorandum that may be gratifying to you in your riper years . . . Your mother was taller than the common height of females in this State, and her figure was most beautiful in all its proportions. Nothing could exceed the beauty of her bust, her waist was delicate, her limbs finely turned and her whole air was light, easy & graceful. Of her features I can give you but a faint idea as the beauty of her face was chiefly in expression although every feature individually was entitled to admiration . . . Her hair was of a clear fresh color approaching to black but not dark enough to be so called, yet in its length and profusion it exceeded any I ever saw. It was more than one yard & a quarter in length and when she let it fall unconfined it would cover her person entirely so that no part of her would be visible through the dense mass that surrounded her on every side. The portrait which you have of her was drawn by an artist not much skilled in his profession at that time and does her great injustice particularly in the mouth & general expression of the countenance. The *drawing* of the picture, as the artists term it, is execrable, and the only part that approaches to a likeness is to be found in the forehead & eyes and the upper part of the nose. But lovely as she was in person, my dear children, all that faded into nothing when compared with the loveliness of her mind as exemplified in the beauty of her walk & conversation. She was constitutionally kind hearted, generous & confiding—above entertaining ungenerous suspicions and naturally frank in her disposition . . . For her musical talents, she was celebrated—The best masters who have ever been in Kentucky informed & every where declared that they never met with any individual who had more talent than she. With but little advantage of cultivation she nevertheless performed on the pianoforte with exquisite skill, taste and feeling . . . It was in graces and accomplishments like these that she came in contact with the world and none of her age received more of its admiration. But you, the pledges of our mutual love, will rather enquire into these virtues that make up the happy home and wish to know how she filled the duties of a wife & mother. Ah, it is here that your fathers heart bleeds afresh and the agony he felt at their separation comes upon him to overwhelm him with grief.''

In 1848 President Zachary Taylor, who as a dashing military hero had excited Margaretta's interest so at Liberty Hall, appointed Orlando Commissioner of Indian Affairs; but again, as with medicine, Orlando found both the job and life in Washington uncongenial. Within the year he resigned and returned to Frankfort. Shortly after, he married Mrs. Mary Cordelia Price Brodhead, by whom he had no children. In 1867 he died in the house that in 1955 was left by his descendants to the Kentucky Dames, who maintain it to perfection as one of their most handsome and evocative possessions.

THE MURRELL HOUSE STORY

The People

George Michael Murrell, merchant, planter, builder of the house
Minerva Ross, his first wife
Amanda Melvina Ross, his second wife
John Ross, Chief of the Cherokee, uncle of Minerva and Amanda

By some legalistic chicanery in the 1830's, Georgia was able to circumvent a U.S. Supreme Court decision that upheld the right of the Cherokee Indians to their historic homeland in the northwestern part of the state; and by this means, after years of trying, the forced expulsion of the Cherokee was begun, with President Jackson furnishing federal troops to expedite the shameful process.

The Cherokee were a peaceable, productive, and enlightened tribe. Many had more white blood than Indian; in fact, their chief, John Ross, was seven-eighth Scottish. It is even possible that their compulsory emigration might have been deferred; but, when gold was discovered in Cherokee country, there was no stopping the expulsion. That was more than the state could stand.

Some unwanted land, called Indian Territory, had been set aside for them in what is now part of eastern Oklahoma, and there, in 1838 and 1839, they were driven, many of them dying on the way. In the Territory their leadership set up a seat of government at Tahlequah, and there they joined western Cherokee who were already there.

Among the voluntary migrants from Tennessee were George Murrell and his wife. He was a well-to-do Virginian from Lynchburg, who in Tennessee had set up quite a mercantile establishment for that time and place and had married Minerva, the eldest daughter of Lewis Ross, Treasurer of the Cherokee and brother of John Ross, the Chief. On arrival in the Indian Territory, the Murrells acquired a log house at a place called Park Hill near Tahlequah, the Cherokee capital. Murrell soon had his new store going, and with large numbers of slaves put a lot of land under cultivation, and got a gristmill and lumbermill in operation.

Murrell had inherited a sugar plantation in Bayou Goula in Louisiana where he and his wife spent their winters and where Minerva died at the age of thirty-six. Some time after her death he married her younger sister Amanda, and in 1844 they built a house that was by all odds the showplace of Park Hill (and still is). Even Chief Ross' very attractive home, Rose Cottage, was no match for the Murrell mansion. It had nine main rooms, each 20 by 20, with 12-foot ceilings, several smaller rooms, a full complement of porches, and a large cellar always well stocked.

One visitor to the house "thought it beautiful because it had red plush furniture and prisms on the chandeliers. There were large mirrors over the curved mantles and the andirons and fixtures for the fireplaces were burnished brass." Another admired "the expensive drapes and the imported curtains around the beds," while another described a screened-in conservatory between the sitting room and the parlor, where "there were a hundred canaries in there among the flowers."

There was a smokehouse filled with hams, beeves and venisons, and a kennel of foxhounds. There is a description of the Murrells at a funeral, quoted by Carolyn Thomas Foreman in her book, *Park Hill*. "On the box of the coach was the negro coachman [who later ran away], with high cocked hat and uniform. The dress of the planter . . . was the old Southern style, while Mrs. Murrell . . . wore a voluminous flounced silk, with the mantle heavily bedecked with spangles which glittered in the sunlight with every movement. I thought Mr. Murrell must be the richest man in the world."

The Murrells and their mansion, like many other opulent pioneers in the Indian Territory at the time, were in striking contrast to the countryside which has been compared to one of Hicks's primitive paintings—a virgin land full of wild animals, simple frontier arrangements, Indians, Negro slaves, and missionaries educated at Princeton who wrote poetry in Greek. Then there were young graduates from Mt. Holyoke who had been sent out by the Board of Missions to teach the Indians, and who invariably married the young missionaries from Princeton.

At the outset of the Civil War, the Murrells left for Louisiana, and then went on to Virginia, where Murrell joined the Confederacy. They took the finest of their furnishings with them, much of which has been returned to the house to give the restoration a fuller flavor of authenticity.

It is a miracle that the house still stands. It was ransacked by raiders on both sides, but never burned, as were so many others in the neighborhood, including that of Chief Ross. He tried but failed to keep his people out of the conflict, and died right after the war.

As the Murrells never returned to their house, under Cherokee law they lost possession. After the war they went to live on the Louisiana plantation, where George Murrell died in 1894, his widow Amanda two years later.

Now once again known by the name that Murrell gave it, Hunter's Home is owned by the State of Oklahoma, assisted by the Oklahoma Dames in its restoration.

Murrell's frontier mansion of 1844, now handsomely restored, stands in a grove of maple and catalpa trees.

The Neill-Cochran house, erected by masterbuilder Abner Cook in the 1850's, was bought and restored in 1958 by the Texas Dames who maintain it as their headquarters and as a Museum House open to the public.

THE AUSTIN STORY

The Houses

The French Legation, 1840
The Neill-Cochran, 1853
The North-Evans Chateau, 1874

The People

Count Alphonse DuBois de Saligny, French Chargé d'affaires to the Republic and builder of the Legation
Colonel Abner Hugh Cook, masterbuilder
Colonel Andrew Neill, 1870 owner of the Neill-Cochran house
Judge T.B. Cochran, 1892 owner of the Neill-Cochran house
Mr. and Mrs. Harvey North ⎱ *builders of the North-Evans Chateau*
Major Ira Hobart Evans ⎰

In 1837, when Sam Houston was serving as its first President, a committee was appointed by the Senate and House of the Congress of the Republic of Texas to search out and recommend a site for the capital. Among the requirements was one that said "no more than $3 per acre;" another that "The said Site shall be [named] the City of Austin."

When Mirabeau Buonaparte Lamar became Texas' second President in 1838, and the committee was still searching for a suitable site, Lamar, on a hunting trip along the Colorado River, came to the little hill town of Waterloo where he looked about him and exclaimed, "Here lies the Seat of future Empire," or words to that effect. And lo and behold, the following year this was the spot the committee picked. So Waterloo became Austin.

Until well into the twentieth century Austin remained a governmental and educational city, and well-to-do citizens at times paid fascinating attention to the architecture of their houses. Twenty-three of the houses, including, of course, the three represented here, were outstanding enough to have been celebrated in a privately and splendidly printed book called *The Minor and Major Mansions in Early Austin*, by August Watkins Harris, the Austin architect-historian. Few if any American frontier cities of Austin's period could have contributed so well to such an impressive portfolio.

No sooner had Austin been made the capital of the Republic of Texas than the French Ambassador in Washington, on word from King Louis Philippe, sent one of his secretaries, Count de Saligny, to Austin to size up the situation. On his return to Washington, the count's report was so favorable that he was named chargé d'affaires to the Republic, with orders to proceed at once to Austin to present his credentials to President Lamar and get things ready for the minister who would eventually be appointed. The house he built remained the French Legation until 1845 when Texas was made a state of the Union.

The house then became the property of the Catholic bishop of the diocese of Texas, who in the fall of 1847 sold it at a loss to a man named Baker; Austin having been somewhat depopulated owing to Indian depredations and Mexican marauders during the war with Mexico. Holding it until order and prices were restored, Baker sold the house to a Dr. Robertson, in whose family's possession it remained until 1945, when it was bought by the State of Texas and put in the custody of the Daughters of the Republic of Texas who invited the Texas Dames to participate in the restoration by furnishing the parlor, "the most opulent room in the house."

No doubt de Saligny had a hand in the finishing up of the house, but the master builder in charge was definitely a man who had confidence in his knowledge of the Creole and Caribbean styles and of the local materials. It is built of a special fine-grained pine peculiar to the nearby region of Bastrop. It appears that de Saligny took over the unfinished shell, agreeing to paint inside and out, put in doors and windows, do the ceilings and paper the walls. All of which he did, except in the way he did the ceilings and inside walls. For instead of plastering, he stretched canvas over the studs and joists, and painted that. When he found that guests were leaning against the canvas walls he simply added chair rails. The canvas walls remain, but now there is wall board behind them.

The plan is admirable: a long, wide hall from front to back, which doubled for dining and dancing. On the front left the parlor, and behind that the study. On the front right the master bedroom and behind that a smaller bedroom. In the attic the servants, in the cellar the wine.

Abner Cook, who came to Austin from North Carolina the same year the city received its new name, became the foremost designer-builder of his day in the capital. Immediately on his arrival he married an Austin girl who had the distinction of bearing the first white boy born in the town. Cook's work is well represented in Mr. Harris' book of Austin mansions, of which the Neill-Cochran is one of the most impressive with its full-height cypress colonnade carted here in sections from Houston by ox-teams at a speed of five miles a day.

The floor to ceiling windows have their original blue glass. The bellows by the library fireplace upstairs belonged to James Madison's mother. Much of the furniture in the room has close associations with early colonial history. Also upstairs are three bedrooms historically furnished. Downstairs the drawing room is French (from New Orleans), the double parlors are Victorian, and the dining room is dominated by a fine Sheraton sideboard.

The French Legation in Austin, built in 1840 as the official residence of Count Alphonse de Saligny, Chargé d'Affaires from the court of Louis Philippe to the Republic of Texas, was constructed in the Louisiana bayou fashion of durable and distinctive Bastrop pine, one of the oldest and most attractive homes in the city. The window glass is from France, the hardware is from England, and most of the furniture is from New Orleans, where the count did his shopping. In the Legation parlor, furnished by the Texas Dames, the armchair was owned by the count, and the portrait over the velvet-lined cabinet is copied from the Winterhalter original at Versailles. The cabinet and the little marble top chess table are of the period of the house. Owned by the State of Texas, the house is in the custody of the Daughters of the Republic of Texas.

166

By far the most ambitious of the three Austin houses shown here is the North-Evans château, now the Austin Women's Club. It occupies a precipitous site, dropping at the left beyond four stories down from the roof. It is a romantic adaptation of the Romanesque style, combining rugged mass masonry in the porches and ashlar masonry in the walls. At the invitation of the Club, the Texas Dames, as charter members, furnished the back sitting room in authentic Colonial as their first domicile.

Cook was commissioned in 1853 to build the house for a man named Washington L. Hill from Columbus, Georgia, who settled in a Texas town, also called Columbus, about seventy miles farther down the Colorado River. He later leased the house to the state as an institute for the blind, the first in Texas. Then toward the end of the Civil War and through the first years of the Reconstruction Era it was used as a hospital for Union soldiers stationed here, many of whom died in a yellow fever epidemic following a flood. The bodies were buried by Shoal Creek on the property, causing a lot of talk in later years about ghosts, even up to fairly recent times.

Right after the Hamiltons moved into their new house Colonel Neill bought the mansion. A native of Scotland and a veteran of San Jacinto, Neill was in his day one of Austin's most prominent lawyers, and his house became the rendezvous of governors, judges and politicians from all parts of Texas. It remained empty for several years after the Colonel's death, which was when *his* ghost appeared, going away when Judge Cochran bought the house in 1892.

The judge put in electricity, replaced the wooden front doors with glass ones, put hardwood flooring over the pine plank flooring downstairs, but left the cool blue glass in the floor-to-ceiling windows. In 1958 the Texas Dames bought the mansion, thus assuring a long bright future to this masterpiece of Abner Cook.

"Sustained by the massive retaining wall with its toes deep-dug into the bed of Crawfish Creek bottom, stepped in terracing to the San Antonio Street level and soaring above it, this French romanesque structure claws into the craglike hillside as do the chateaux which excited the dream of its original owners."

Thus Mr. Harris pays tribute in his archive of Austin mansions to the largest and most romantic of them all.

The site, to let Mr. Harris complete the story . . . "was acquired in 1874 by Mr. and Mrs. Harvey North, who saw in it a seat for the Chateau-home they had envisioned during extended residence in Switzerland and France . . . Before completion of their dream, in 1884 they passed possession of the holding to Mrs. Augusta Evans Gaines, and thence it passed to the hands of Major Ira Hobert Evans in 1892.

"Major Evans it was who brought the dream to fruition, building the imposing stone porches, installing the intricate woodwork, and the mechanical conveniences which had come into vogue . . . The pierced cherry-wood stairscreen, the panelled Texas curly pine wainscot, the flambeau-grained pine sliding doors, the great stone mantel in the front hall with its inscription —'Old books to read, old wood to burn, old friends to talk'—, with the rich art glass of the windows, all appear in full detail, and each is deeply interesting and worthy of study."

The house is now the Austin Women's Club, and in it the Texas Dames furnished the second parlor with authentic Colonial pieces, and used it as their domicile until they bought the Neill-Cochran house. In the room the Bluebonnet picture hangs which the Dames used to secure the adoption of the bluebonnet as the state flower of Texas.

167

THE KILBOURNTON HOUSE STORY

The People

James Stuart ⎱
Nicholas Revett ⎰ *English architects and antiquarians*
Asher Benjamin, American architect
Benjamin Church, builder of the house
Solomon Laurent Juneau, founder of Milwaukee

I n 1762 the publication in England of an elephantine folio volume of plates by Stuart and Revett, called *Antiquities of Athens*, created a frenzied fashion for Greek-like architecture whose reverberations didn't begin to die down until they reached the Middle West of the United States in the 1840's and 1850's. In fact, it can be said that the Greek Revival affected a solid century of architectural taste from as far east in Europe as the Russian provinces to as far west in this country as Wisconsin. Perhaps even farther west, here and there. But anyhow, a particularly charming little relic of that great Greek wave has been left for posterity in Milwaukee.

Stuart and Revett crawled all over the Acropolis with measuring lines and paper and pencils; put down all their dimensions as they carried their tape from temple to temple, then took their findings home to London and had them published.

It hardly mattered that in making their measurements they took a lot for granted. How could they suspect that the Greeks had disposed the parts of their masterpieces by eye, and not by measuring rods? When Stuart and Revett measured the Parthenon from corner to corner, they divided the columns equidistantly, which, of course, we since have learned is not the case. In fact the two Englishmen missed most of the subleties: the faint swelling of the columns, the virtually invisible curves of the cornices, the wonderful asymmetries.

However, the rage that became the Greek Revival would not have been concerned with such subtleties. What the architects and carpenters of the time clamored for was the classical simplicity they saw in Stuart's and Revett's plates and in the flood of builders' plates which followed. It gave them something they could turn out just as well in wood as in stone—even better, and certainly more easily. And it didn't have to be only for churches and banks and other public buildings; it was most wonderful of all for houses.

In his books of house plans, Asher Benjamin, the architect of the Dames's Beacon Street house in Boston, achieved new heights of popularity for both his books and himself by including Greek-like façades and Greek-like details which any carpenter could execute in wood. As a result, Greek Revival houses grew up everywhere, and the Revival became a revival in an almost religious sense.

Like the United States itself, the movement worked its way from east to west. Certain regions took to it more than others. One rich Greek Revival lode can be traced today very clearly along the Mohawk Valley, through northern Ohio, into Michigan, and on into Wisconsin, where, in addition to the Dames's Kilbourntown House, there are other Greek Revival homes open to the public, among them Butternut House in Greenbush, the Grignon House in Kaukauna, and the Cotton House in Green Bay. Of them all, the Kilbourntown is the closest to the pure Greek Revival spirit, the most Asher Benjaminish.

A Greek Revival gem in its leafy Milwaukee setting.

It was built by Benjamin Church, a builder by trade, who came out from the East in 1835, built the first real hotel in Milwaukee, then this house for himself in 1844.

The year before, a trader left this description of the town: "Such a miserable-looking place selected for a settlement I had never seen before. One unbroken series of sand banks, frog ponds, clay hills, river marches, unpretentious habitations of 5000 people scattered in a desultory way. Intended only for waterfowl and wild beasts—not for man's dwelling."

The city-to-be was three separate villages at the time: Walker's Point, set out by Isaac P. Walker on the south shore of Lake Michigan, Juneau Town on the east side of the Milwaukee River, and Kilbourn Town, set out by Byron Kilbourn, on the west side of the river. Between the two sides of the river there was considerable rivalry as to which could first become a city. Kilbourn said they should remain separate villages. It is not remembered what Juneau said, but Juneau is the one who is now remembered as the founder of Milwaukee. He was a French Canadian fur trader who came there in 1818 as agent for the American Fur Company, made a fortune, acquired large tracts of land, built the first store, the first tavern, became the first postmaster in 1835, the first mayor in 1846, then later lost everything, and died in poverty in 1856.

Such was the early background of the house. The Church family lived in it until 1884, when it was bought by a family named Binzel who lived in it and kept it up well until 1922 when the old Kilbourn Town section began to deteriorate, and the house along with it. Then at the instigation of one of the Wisconsin Dames, the Milwaukee Park Commission moved the house to its fine position in Estabrook Park and placed it in the custody of the Dames.

THE REID ADOBE STORY

The People

Don Perfecto Hugo Reid, merchant, ranch owner
Victoria Bartoloméa Comicrabit, his Indian wife

In its beautiful parkland at Arcadia, where palms, live oaks, and eucalyptus are silhouetted against the San Gabriel Mountains, the Los Angeles State and County Aboretum has reconstructed on the Rancho Santa Anita an adobe dating from 1840. It was built by a Scotsman who became a Mexican citizen and a Catholic in order that he might own property and marry in the Mexican province of California. To decorate his new citizenship he pinned the new name of Don Perfecto to the one with which he was christened thirty years before in Renfrewshire, his birthplace.

After two years at Cambridge, Hugo Reid set out in 1830 for Lima, Peru, where he worked at Henry Dalton's Trading Company until he became manager of the company's branch at Hermosillo, Mexico. Several other ventures, in Los Angeles, San Pedro, and back in Hermosillo, occupied him from 1834 to 1837. Then the Don Perfecto period opened in Los Angeles when he was 27, with his marriage and his acquisition of the Rancho Santa Anita as part of the dowry brought him by Bartoloméa (he called her Victoria). She also brought him four children by her late husband: two boys 15 and 13, a daughter nine, and a year-old baby boy. She was 29.

Victoria's grandfather was called "the greatest chieftain in Alta California." She was reared at the San Gabriel Mission, married at 13 to a man of 41, and became the protégée of the aristocratic Señora Eulalia Perez y de Mariné, of Rancho San Pascual (who died in 1878 at the reputed age of 140).

In 1838 Don Perfecto and Victoria built what was to be their town house, *Uva Espina*, or "gooseberry", an adobe "flat-roofed and corridor'd," a few hundred yards from the still-standing San Gabriel Mission. Their country house they built in 1840 four miles away in the vast Rancho Santa Anita property. This, in its present form, was after extensive archaeological exploration, reconstructed on earlier foundations, and is known as Hugo Reid Adobe. The Santa Anita racetrack is well within hearing distance.

The walls are of whitewashed adobe blocks baked in the sun. The flat roof of bullrushes tied with rawhide strips is waterproofed by *brea* from the local tar pits. The floors are of packed earth. All is done as Don Perfecto had it done in 1840.

A high adobe wall creates a patio enclosure containing rush-covered arbors, a beehive adobe oven, a center dip well and bucket, a wine press, dining tables, and benches. Outside the patio are the *jacales,* those beehive-shaped dwellings of bullrushes with cowhide door coverings which were used by the Indian servants.

Reid himself saw very little of either residence during the next four years. For in 1841 he bought the 92-ton schooner *Esmeralda*, making a six-month trading voyage down the coast, then

170

This outstanding adobe restoration, with the San Bernardino Mountains in the background, is owned by the State of California and maintained by the Los Angeles State and County Arboretum. The entire house has been entirely and authentically furnished by the California Dames, the bedroom shown here being an example.

over to Honolulu, from where he returned in 1842 with a cargo whose value was less than the duties on it. After a short coastal voyage the next year he made a trading trip to the Orient, returning in 1844.

In 1847, his health uncertain and his finances none too good, Reid sold the Rancho Santa Anita to Henry Dalton, and in 1849 he naturally joined the rush to the gold mines and did fairly well for a while selling supplies to the miners. He served in the first California Constitutional Convention at Monterey, but, shortly after California became a state, in 1850, he returned to Victoria and *Uva Espina*. By now, at the age of 40, Hugo was being called "Old Reid." While compiling an Indian/English vocabulary and language manual, he died in December of 1852.

Three years later Victoria lost her claim to *Uva Espina*, and almost immediately the adobe was destroyed in an earthquake, whereupon Don Perfecto's widow returned to live with Señora Eulalia, who by her reckoning was then only one hundred and seventeen, with twenty-three years to live—ten years more than Victoria.

Henry Dalton, Don Perfecto's old friend from Lima, had paid Reid $2,700 for Santa Anita, or 20 cents per acre. He called himself Perfecto Hugo Dalton and married Guadalupe Zamorano, daughter of California's first printer. Then in 1875, after passing through many hands, and reduced by now to 8,000 acres, Rancho Santa Anita was bought by Elias Jackson (Lucky) Baldwin for $200,000. A lucky man could win that much in a single afternoon at the racetrack across the road from the adobe.

THE LINCOLN HOUSE STORY

The People

Abraham Lincoln
Mary Todd, his wife

This is the way Lincoln looked to William Herndon, his law partner, biographer, and closest friend: "He was six feet four inches high . . . thin, wiry, sinewy, raw-boned; thin through the breast to the back, and narrow across the shoulders . . . stoop-shouldered. His usual weight was one hundred and eighty pounds.

"When he walked he moved cautiously but firmly; his long arms and giant hands swung down by his side. He walked with even tread, the inner sides of his feet parallel. He put the whole foot flat down on the ground at once, not landing on the heel; he likewise lifted his foot all at one not rising from the toe. He had no spring to his walk."

Mary Todd came of a rich, social, slave-holding family in Lexington, Kentucky. This was seventy miles from the cabin in the same state where Lincoln was born in stark poverty, destined to reach manhood with less than a year's formal education in all. In Mary Todd's private school it was mandatory for French to be spoken at all times. Lincoln never learned a foreign language.

There has been much conjecture about how the Lincolns' life together might have been affected by the famous occasion when Lincoln failed to show up for the wedding that was planned for 1841, about a year before he and Mary Todd were finally married. For, while Mary forgave him when she became convinced that Lincoln's behavior on that occasion was the result of a severe disorder of the mind, it was thought by some that unconsciously she never got over her resentment. Yet a year after Lincoln's death, Mrs. Lincoln told Herndon, "He was the kindest man, most tender husband, and loving father in the world."

A lady relative who lived two years with the Lincolns told Herndon that Lincoln was in the habit of lying on the floor to read with the back of a chair for a pillow. "One evening," she related, "when in this position in the parlor, a knock was heard at the front door, and although in his shirt sleeves Lincoln went to the door. Two ladies were there whom he invited in, telling them in his open familiar way that he would "trot the women-folk out." From an adjoining room Mrs. Lincoln witnessed the ladies' entrance and overheard her husband's jocose expression. Her indignation was so instantaneous she made the situation extremely interesting for him, and he was glad to retreat from the house,—not returning until very late at night, and then slipping quietly in at a rear door."

"I lived next door to the Lincolns for many years and knew the family well," James Gourly told Herndon the year after Lincoln's death. "Mr. Lincoln used to come to our house, his feet in a pair of loose slippers, and with an old, faded pair of trousers fastened with one suspender. He frequently came to our house for milk. Our rooms were low, and he said one day, 'Jim, you'll have to lift your loft a little higher; I can't straighten out under it very well. In his yard Lincoln

The Lincolns made the plateau around the house, and Mary put on the second story, once while Abe was in Chicago.

Lincoln stood in the doorway between the two parlors when notified of his nomination. The furniture of the two rooms has been carefully chosen to reflect the atmosphere and feeling of the Lincolns' Springfield years.

The big wardrobe and the bureau were used by Abraham Lincoln. The bottles were found buried in the backyard, and the wallpaper of light blue and brown is a facsimile of the paper Mary Lincoln chose for the room.

had but little shrubbery. He once planted some rose bushes, to which he called my attention, but soon neglected them altogether. He never planted any vines or fruit trees, seemed to have no fondness for such things. At one time, yielding to my suggestion, he undertook to keep a garden in the rear part of his yard, but one season's experience sufficed to cure him of all desire for another. He kept his own horse, fed and curried it when at home; he also fed and milked his own cow, and sawed his own wood. Mr. Lincoln and his wife agreed moderately well. Frequently Mrs. Lincoln's temper would get the better of her. If she became furious, as she often did, her husband tried to pay no attention to her. He would sometimes laugh at her, but generally he would pick up one of the children and walk off. I have heard her say that if Mr. Lincoln had remained at home more she could have loved him better. One day while Mr. Lincoln was absent—he had gone to Chicago to try a suit in the United States Court—his wife and I formed a conspiracy to take off the roof and raise his house. It was originally a frame structure one story and a half high. When Lincoln returned he met a gentleman on the sidewalk and, looking at his own house and pretending not to know it, inquired: 'Stranger, can you tell me where Lincoln lives?' The gentleman gave him the necessary information, and Lincoln gravely entered his own premises."

This remodeling job was done in 1856, twelve years after the Lincolns bought the house, and cost them $1,300. For the house originally they paid $1,500 in 1844 to the Rev. Charles Dresser, the Episcopal rector who had married them two years before. The only other improvement of any importance which the Lincolns made to the property during the seventeen years they lived in it (it was the only house they ever owned) was the brick retaining wall on the Eighth and the Jackson Streets sides, with a fence surmounting the wall—a very effective feature, placing the house on a level plateau, as it were.

Though herself often the victim of the Mary Todd temper, one of the servants said of Mrs. Lincoln: "She takes no sassy talk, but if you good to her, she good to you." Of Lincoln the same servant said: "He so kind. He chop the wood for fire, and little Robert chop the little wood. When he pass me, he pats my shoulder." What the servant didn't say was that Lincoln secretly gave her an extra dollar a week for taking the Todd temper in her stride.

The Lincolns liked the theater and never missed plays that came to town. Every Sunday Mrs. Lincoln went to church once or twice; her husband hardly ever. Instead he would take the small boys to the office, where the boys behaved like unmanageable monkeys while he worked on his cases completely unconcerned.

Mrs. Lincoln loved to entertain, and at their parties Lincoln wore the fashionably elaborate shirts that his wife, an expert seamstress, made for him. He managed at all parties to segregate the sexes, gradually gathering the men around himself to hear his steady stream of stories. From a neighbor's diary one learns that "after the lecture went to Mrs. Lincoln's for supper." "After tea Mrs. B & self . . . spent the evening at the Lincolns." "At night, attended large & pleasant party at Lincolns." "At large party at Lincolns at night." ". . . went to party at Lincolns last night." "it was the genial manner and ever kind welcome of the hostess," one chronicler recounts, "and the wit and humor, anecdote and unrivalled conversation of the host, which formed the chief attraction, and made a dinner at the Lincolns . . . an evening to be remembered." How Mrs. Lincoln herself felt about one at least of her parties appears in a letter, in the autumn of 1857, to one of her sisters: "I may perhaps surprise you when I mention that I am recovering from a slight fatigue of a very large, and I really believe, a very handsome entertainment . . . About five hundred were invited, yet owing to an unlucky rain three hundred only favored us by their presence . . ."

After his election both the house and the office were so filled day and night with well-wishers and office-seekers that Lincoln, in order to prepare his inaugural address and settle his local affairs, had to find a hideaway in a room over the store of a friend on the city square.

On the last evening that the Lincolns occupied the house they held a grand public levee from seven to midnight. "The house was thronged by thousands," said the St. Louis *Democrat*, "A grand outpouring of citizens and strangers. Mr. Lincoln received the people as they entered, then they passed on and were introduced to Mrs. Lincoln near the center of the parlor. She was dressed plainly but richly with beautiful full train, white moire, antique silk, a small French lace collar, her neck ornamented with a string of pearls. Her head dress was a simple and delicate vine arranged with much taste, but little jewelry and this was well and properly adjusted. She was a lady of fine figure and accomplished address and is well calculated to grace and do honors at the White House."

Early the next morning, in the wintery wet and cloudy dark of a dismal February day, the Lincolns drove over to the station with the boys—Bob, eighteen, who became a successful corporation lawyer in Chicago and president of the Pullman Company; Willie, ten, who died the next year in the White House, and Tad, eight, who lived until he was eighteen. A fourth son, Eddie, had died 11 years before, at the age of four.

The party boarded the special train through a handshaking farewell crowd of friends. In a few moments Lincoln appeared on the back platform and spoke to them. "My Friends—No one, not in my situation, can appreciate my feelings of sadness at this parting. To this place, and the kindness of these people, I owe everything. Here I have lived a quarter of a century, and have passed from a young to an old man. Here my children have been born, and one is buried. I now leave, not knowing when, or whether ever, I may return, and a task before me greater than that which rested upon Washington. Without the assistance of that Divine Being, who ever attended him, I cannot succeed. With that assistance I cannot fail. Trusting in Him, who can go with me, and remain with you and be everywhere for good, let us confidently hope that all will yet be well. To His care commending you, as I hope in your prayers you will commend me, I bid you an affectionate farewell."

On the morning of May 3, 1865, a train draped in black pulled into the Springfield station. It had been on the way from Washington ever since April 21. Twelve days. The slowest and saddest journey ever made on an American railway. Ceremonial stops were made at Baltimore, Harrisburg, Philadelphia, New York City, Albany, Buffalo, Cleveland, Columbus, Indianapolis, Chicago, and God-knows-how-many way stations in between. And finally Springfield.

The house was hung with mourning cloth from top to bottom. The sidewalk and street were filled with people standing there in silence, many in uniform. But Lincoln was carried on to the State House. All was hung with mourning, all the buildings of the square, all the houses of the town.

On the second day a solemn procession, with muffled drums, and with General Joseph Hooker at the head, followed the hearse to Oak Ridge Cemetery, and Lincoln was laid to rest.

The Little Red Brick House was built in 1840 a stone's throw from the site of the Spanish French Fort Miro, and was bought in 1842 by Isaiah Garrett to be his law office. Restored by the Louisiana Dames, Isaiah's office is now their meeting place. Surrounded by collections of historical memorabilia are the spinning wheel brought in by early settlers, two folding chairs carried in covered wagons for the women to sit on around the evening campfire. The chair behind the wheel was carried by a Ouachita Parish boy all through the Civil War, at his mother's insistence.

THE LITTLE RED BRICK HOUSE STORY

The People

Samuel Kirby, the builder
Isaiah Garrett, Louisiana lawyer

When Robert Livingston, our Minister to France, and James Monroe, whom President Jefferson appointed to serve with Livingston, met with Talleyrand in 1803, the Americans had in mind to buy just the region around New Orleans and over to the west coast of Florida, for which Congress had appropriated $2 million.

Imagine the surprise of our two diplomats when Talleyrand said, "How much will you give for *all* Louisiana?" All Louisiana Territory was virtually everything west of the Mississippi; more than the whole United States to the east. But the whole thing was what Napoleon wanted to sell. He had more empire than he could handle. So the bargaining began; and when it ended, the United States was suddenly more than twice as big as it was before. Talleyrand had knocked the Territory down for $15 million.

France had only held the Territory for a little over two years, through a secret treaty made with Spain, and the French flag had been flown over the formerly Spanish Fort Miro for only a week or so when, with the Purchase, the American flag took the place of the French, and the Fort Miro settlement became known as the American Post of the Ouachita, then was shortened to Ouachita.

In 1819, Louisiana became a state, and in the midst of that excitement, the *James Monroe* became the first steamboat to navigate the Ouachita River up from the Red River and the Mississippi, opening up steam navigation between New Orleans and the world. And in the midst of *that* excitement, the name of the town was changed to Monroe, not after the President like all the other Monroes in America, but after the steamboat.

This bit of lore came down from Captain Franklin Garrett, son of the lawyer Isaiah Garrett who had his office in the Little Red Brick House from 1842 on for many years. The house was built in 1840 by a man named Samuel Kirby who, two years later, sold "the new brick dwelling house, kitchen and outhouses and all the improvements" to Mr. Garrett, one of the most eminent Louisiana lawyers of his day. The old Spanish-French Fort Miro was only a few hundred yards away from his office.

At this time Ouachita Parish was a thriving community of well-managed plantations whose proprietors had the time, taste, and intelligence to follow artistic and scientific pursuits. Audubon was attracted here not only by the birdlife but by the sympathetic friendships he formed. When Garrett bought the Little Red Brick House for his office, the town had a population of 4,640, of which 2,188 were whites, 2,439 Negro slaves, and 14 free Negroes. Garrett himself, as a member of the secession convention in 1860, was one of the seven members who refused to sign the ordinance of secession, since, as he was an honor graduate of West Point, it violated his oath of allegiance. Among the major planters in the area there was a two-to-one split against secession. But when war actually came, the whole community was united in support of the South. Garrett's town house was used at one time as a makeshift hospital for wounded Southern soldiers; and his son Franklin became a captain in the Confederate Army.

Although the courthouse, only 300 yards away, was destroyed, the Little Red Brick House was left whole during the war, and remains today a primitive example of frontier America.

THE PLUM GROVE STORY

The People

Robert Lucas, Governor of Iowa Territory
William B. Conway, Secretary of the Territory
T. S. Parvin, one of the Governor's aides
Friendly, the Governor's wife

Iowa was organized a Territory in 1838 by separation from Wisconsin, and on (of all days) the Fourth of July. The double celebration called for twice the oratory, twice the toasting. And, while the temperance movement in the Territory was terribly strong, this was a day, from all accounts, of widespread defection.

All up and down the river towns—Dubuque, Davenport, Burlington—and inland little Iowa City, Iowans were calling for action. Get a government going. The news came through that President Van Buren had offered the governorship to General Henry Atkinson, who knew the region well as an Indian campaigner in the Black Hawk War—but the general didn't want the job. Then word came that the appointment to lead the Territory into statehood had been offered on July 7 to Robert Lucas, twice Territorial Governor of Ohio, and a distinguished soldier. Because Lucas was off politicking it took several days for him to get the news.

The next bulletin at Burlington was that Lucas had accepted the appointment and in a few days would leave Cincinnati for Iowa. Meanwhile Mr. Conway had arrived, and as Secretary of the Territory by Presidential appointment, *he* was the Governor, even presuming to prepare a proclamation apportioning members of the legislature and ordering an election. Iowans by now were impatient enough to pressure him to take these steps for which he well knew he had no authority. There is a lot to show that he was full of ambitions, but nothing to show that he knew the nature of the man who was coming to take over the Territory. Lucas looked a lot like Andrew Jackson and had a lot of Jackson in his nature.

Although low water, encountered coming down the Ohio to the Mississippi, had caused a delay, finally the report came through that the steamboat *Tempest* would arrive the next morning with Robert Lucas on board. That a large crowd was on hand to greet the Governor goes without saying.

"A brisk, erect, dignified figure strode down the gangplank." An authority on Lucas is describing him. "Although only about five feet ten inches in height, Robert Lucas probably seemed taller because of his straight military bearing. His thick wavy hair, frosted by fifty-seven years of intense activity, was combed straight back from his high forehead. Blue eyes, deep-set beneath beetling eyebrows, a slightly aquiline nose, straight firm mouth, all combined to give a somewhat severe expression to his thin face."

When Conway handed Lucas the proclamation he'd prepared, Lucas handed it right back without looking at it. Later in the day he drew up one of his own. When a delegation of Burlington men invited him to a public dinner in his honor he politely proposed that the dinner be postponed until he returned from a tour of the Territory. And as soon as he had settled the more pressing matters waiting for his attention, he started off.

Part of the purpose of the trip was to pick out a place for the capital. One of the river towns seemed offhand the most likely. Dubuque, Davenport, and Burlington were the three most populated places in the territory. Iowa City, which was founded the following year as the capital, was in 1838 nothing more than a small settlement thirty-some miles back from the Mississippi at Muscatine. Des Moines, which became the capital in 1857, eleven years after Iowa became a state, was still wide-open empty country.

Lucas took with him the two young aides he had brought with him from Cincinnati—T.S. Parvin and Jesse Williams. The trip from Burlington to Dubuque was made on the brand-new steamboat *Knickerbocker.* "Fifty handsomely furnished staterooms," Parvin noted in his diary. Captain Van Houton was a "fine chap," whose "energy and activity matched his urbanity and courteous deportment."

They left at two in the afternoon, reached Muscatine, sixty-five miles upriver, at ten that night, too late to go ashore in the dark. But they were making better than eight miles an hour against the current and dodging the sandbars. They had passed Davenport when the Governor and his two aides got up the next morning, and were bucking the Rock Island Rapids, a bad stretch of river at low water. Thirty-five miles up from Davenport, where Clinton is today, they passed some settlers starting a town they planned to call New York. The boat made Dubuque that night, 165 miles and 32 hours out of Burlington, including stops.

Lucas stayed at a temperance house. Where the two aides stayed Parvin's diary doesn't say. It does say that, the next evening, "The Gov. accepted (we refused) an invitation to take tea with Judge King. Said he regretted his 'aids' did not accompany him as there were 3 very fine young ladies—one apiece. So did we," Parvin added.

Several days in Dubuque, then down the river to Davenport, where Secretary Conway, who was waiting for the Governor with some papers, returned by the same boat to Burlington. Lucas and his young men did Davenport for two days, the Governor busy interviewing, the aides sizing up the town.

Parvin and Williams paid a visit to the famous halfbreed translator and negotiator, Antoine Le Claire, an enormous man who spoke fourteen Indian tongues, as well as French and Spanish. Mementos of his career are now to be seen in the Le Claire Room in the Davenport Public Museum, placed there by the Iowa Dames.

In what was called the front parlor of Plum Grove the spinet piano and stool were made in 1800 by N. Sparg of Syracuse, N.Y. Samuel J. Kirkwood, twice governor of Iowa, owned the marble-top table and upholstered side chair. The doll belonged to a granddaughter of Governor Lucas.

The trio drove in a "rude conveyance" from Davenport to Muscatine, thirty miles, stopping en route to interview and stopping for noon dinner with some people named Viole from Troy, New York. "Three grown-up daughters" are noted in the diary, and nowhere in the Territory had the travelers "found anyone living in finer style." Then on to Muscatine, pausing at melon patches from time to time, as this was melon country then as now. They arrived in the dark, and, as a steamboat was due to sail in an hour, they took overnight passage back to Burlington.

"Home sweet home," wrote the weary Parvin, who recorded of the twelve-day tour that "our object had been to view the country . . . examining the claims of various parts for the seat of temporary government and came to the conclusion that for the present . . . Burlington is the place."

Just before the legislature met, one of its members was murdered on the main street of the capital by a prominent lawyer of Burlington, an occurrence that was severely condemned by Lucas at the first session, when he asked for laws against the carrying of concealed deadly weapons.

The whole thing was a three-sided free-for-all between the members, Secretary Conway, and the Governor. The legislators' efforts to pad the payrolls, in which they were abetted by Conway, were consistently vetoed by Lucas. Conway secretly sent in reports to Washington criticizing the Governor's conduct, both public and personal—all turning out to be groundless.

Finally, as Parvin recorded in his diary that day, "the legislature adjourned in confusion. All drunk with few exceptions." Shortly after, Conway died, and an audit of his accounts revealed that "there will be about three thousand dollars to be collected from the securities of the late Secretary Conway, he being, at the time of his death, a defaulter to that amount."

Back at the Governor's home in Piketon, Ohio, his wife, Friendly, was still staying on, reluctant to leave the familiar comforts of Friendly Grove, the Lucas farm, for the rough frontier life of Iowa. Friendly was famous for her "quick witted sallies," her currant pies, and the figure she cut as she galloped about the countryside on horseback. She was been described as "not a great deal over five feet, yet weighing close to two-hundred pounds." Finally in 1840 Friendly worked herself up to making the long roundabout trip by steamboat to Iowa, "to see how she liked it." The year before, her son Edward had joined his father in Burlington, making the journey on horseback by way of Indianapolis and Peoria. He had arrived on his 14th birthday, which he celebrated "by catching three catfish and thrashing a boy who kicked his hound dog."

When William Henry Harrison became President in 1841, Lucas became a casualty of the political appointive nature of territorial governorships, and was removed in favor of a Whig. He stayed on, politically active in Iowa until 1843, when he and his wife returned to Friendly Grove for a year; then he went back to Iowa for good, beginning at once to build his house in a plum grove.

He was hopeful that when Polk became President he would regain the governorship, but he was sixty-four by then, and a younger man was appointed. Though remaining politically active for years, he never held office again. He was a hard-working leader in the temperance movement, the development of the public school system, and the promotion of railways in Iowa. Toward the end he took to putting down, on any blank spaces of paper that came to hand—margins of newspapers, backs of old documents, letters, books—expressions of his hopes of immortality and fiscal salvation. Five weeks before his death he recorded a hymn of hope and cheer on some blank pages of the journal he kept in the War of 1812.

He died at Plum Grove in February 1853. Friendly outlived him there by twenty years. Both are buried in the cemetery at Iowa City, where a monument marks the resting place of the fiery old frontier state maker.

The house the governor built in 1844 is now owned by the state and is furnished and supervised by the Iowa Dames. The "Dolly Madison" spool bed was used by Robert and Friendly. The trunk, bed, deerhide seat and commode were Lucas family possessions. The copper soap kettle, the toaster hanging at the right, the old guns, powder horn and bullet pouch, as well as the tripod kettle are from the Iowa State Historical Society.

The McLoughlin House stands in McLoughlin Park in Oregon City, donated by Dr. McLoughlin to the people of Oregon. It is about thirteen miles south of Portland. Built by the doctor in 1844–45, it is one of the few remaining pioneer dwellings in the region once known as the Oregon country. As with many other early houses in the region, the window sash and doors were probably brought from the East around the Horn. The lumber for this house was no doubt turned out in Dr. McLoughlin's own mill.

THE McLOUGHLIN HOUSE STORY

The People

Dr. John McLoughlin, "Father of Oregon," and builder of the house
Marguerite Wadin McKay, his wife
David McLoughlin, his brother—the Paris David
John McLoughlin, his older son
David McLoughlin, his younger son
Simon Fraser and Alexander Fraser, his uncles
Lewis and Clark, the trailmakers
Captain B.L.E. de Bonneville, fur trader, Mountain Man, and military hero
John Bidwell and Elijah White, leaders of immigrants

John McLoughlin was born in October, 1778, down below Quebec, on the opposite side of the St. Lawrence at Rivière-du-Loup. With his paternal grandfather Scottish, married to an Irish wife, and his maternal grandmother French, he grew up to have a many-sided nature: gentle and passionate by turns, he could drive a hard bargain, manage, command, yet be generous to a fault. In the course of his life he made countless friends together with a fair quota of enemies. Among the latter he himself could often be included.

He was called "Doctor" all his life, yet for the greater part of his career, in which he grew famous and prospered, he had nothing to do with medicine. Make what you want of the fact that as a boy he fell under the spell of two uncles. Simon Fraser was a brilliant British Army surgeon in the Black Watch regiment; Alexander Fraser, a fur-trading wintering partner, or partner in the field, for the North West Company, hot and heavy rivals of the Hudson's Bay Company.

Whichever way he may have been swayed by one uncle or the other, or both, the fact is that he was barely fourteen when he became apprenticed to the famous Dr. James Fisher in Quebec, and for nearly five years studied medicine in this doctor's office. When given his certificate, he went into the employ of the North West Company; and, while he acted partly as a company doctor, it wasn't long before the practice of fur-trading took over his interest entirely, and he never practiced medicine again.

In 1804, the year Dr. McLoughlin took his job with North West, President Thomas Jefferson in Washington selected his friend and private secretary, Meriwether Lewis, to head, with William Clark as his associate, the transcontinental expedition which bears their names. Jefferson's purpose was partly exploration, partly to lay out a land route to the Northwest, and partly to create, if possible, friendly relations with the Indians, but as much as anything else it was to lay claim to the great Oregon Country. At the time this extended from Spanish-held California territory to Russian-held Canadian territory close to Alaska, and from the Rocky Mountain Range to the Pacific.

At Fort Clatsop, near the mouth of the Columbia River, the river that is now the dividing line between the states of Oregon and Washington, Lewis and Clark completed their westward journey. Many miles up the river, at Fort Vancouver, they passed the place where, thirty years later, Dr. McLoughlin was going to greet the immigrants from the East. Closer to the mouth, where the Willamette flows into the Columbia, they passed close to the site of Portland. Ten miles up the Wilamette, at Oregon City, is where he was to build his house, and where, in 1857, he was to die.

By 1809 McLoughlin was doing well at his job with North West, and complaining a good deal about his pay. In 1811 he seems to have formed a common-law marriage with an Indian woman, the daughter of a Swiss immigrant, named Marguerite Wadin McKay, whose husband, a Scottish fur-trader, had deserted her that same year to take part in the fur expedition commissioned by John Jacob Astor that sailed around the Horn, also to the mouth of the Columbia, to where the town of Astoria is today. It was to be up the river from there, some years later, that the McLoughlins' marriage was formalized, with four children growing up: John, Eliza, Eloisa, David.

In 1821, after several climactic years of bitter and violent rivalry, North West and Hudson's Bay combined under the latter's name. Dr. McLoughlin, who had for long been a highly respected wintering partner at North West, became a Chief Factor of the Hudson's Bay Company, with a percentage of the profits, and in 1824 was put in charge of the operation in the important and controversial district of the Oregon Country, with headquarters at Fort Vancouver on the Columbia.

The years between 1824 and 1845 were the ones of McLoughlin's greatest power and influence —the years of the opening up of a new territory, in which he played a principal part—and, at the end, the beginnings of his grief and decline. He was having his troubles with his older son John back in Quebec, but Dr. McLoughlin's mother's family of well-to-do Frasers were there to keep things under control.

The doctor was making money for the company, holding the competition at bay; and immigrants from the East were beginning to filter in. His first greeting was given in 1834 when Jason Lee arrived with his little band of Methodist missionaries.

Capt. B. L. E. de Bonneville, after whom the great Columbia River dam is named, brought the first wagon train over South Pass in the Rockies in 1841, marking the opening of the Oregon Trail. The favorite starting point for the trail was at Independence, Missouri. It followed the Santa Fe Trail for 40 miles, then struck northwest to the Platte, to the junction of the North Platte and South Platte where Omaha is now, then up the North Platte to Fort Laramie and the

This portrait by William Cogswell of Dr. John McLoughlin, which hangs over the fireplace in the parlor of his house, was painted at the height of McLoughlin's career as Chief Factor of the Hudson's Bay Company at Vancouver. At the time he literally ruled an empire stretching from the Rocky Mountains to the Pacific Ocean and from Alaska to California.

present Casper, Wyoming. Some of the toughest parts of the trail were those through the mountains to South Pass and the Colorado River Basin. But Donner Pass, Laurel Hill, and the Cascades were still to come. There was still a long, tough way to go.

What helped the immigrants most on the rugged reaches of the mountains were the Mountain Men, who guided as a sideline while they gathered furs for a fierce livelihood in the forests. It was with the Mountain Men that de Bonneville took up on a two-year leave from the Army (which he extended by two years without leave). He'd been financed by New Yorkers to lead a fur-trading expedition into the rich Green River fur country, and, while he turned out to be a poor risk as a trader, his swashbuckling and wildly colorful personality, courage, and woodsmanship, made him one of the best known figures in the mountains. And when Washington Irving's somewhat overblown *Adventures of Captain Bonneville, U.S.A.,* was published in 1837, the captain's fame reached its peak.

From the South Pass, then, where de Bonneville took through the first wagon train, the trail turned southwest to Fort Bridger (named for another Mountain Man), where the Mormon Trail diverged to the left and the Oregon turned northwest to Fort Hall on the Snake, then along the Snake (the California Trail branching off to the southwest) to Fort Boise, then over the Blue Mountains to Fort Walla Walla and down the Columbia to the lush green valley where the Willamette flows into the Columbia near where Portland stands today.

The first genuine immigrant train, led by John Bidwell, arrived in 1841; another larger one came the next year, led by Elijah White; and in 1843 came the "Great Immigration." Thousands! Most of these were farmers and farm workers, and, until they got established, many of them came to McLoughlin for help, which he gave. For this he was admonished by the company, who wasn't pleased to have its chief representative giving help to settlers who were there to change the country from a fur to a farming economy. But McLoughlin brushed off this rebuke and continued to help the immigrants pretty much as before.

What happened in 1842 was a body blow to Dr. McLoughlin, from which he never entirely recovered. His problem son, John, who had apparently mended his ways, was put in charge of the Hudson's Bay post at Fort Stikine in the Russian territory by Sir George Simpson, governor of the company's North American operations. Even Simpson agreed he was doing well, when suddenly word came that he had been murdered by his men. Simpson's personal investigation, which turned out to have been cursory, caused Simpson to report to the young man's father that the manner of John's death deserved a verdict of "justifiable homicide."

When Dr. McLoughlin had gathered incontrovertible evidence otherwise, he began a series

In the dining room the table and chairs are the original ones sent to Dr. McLoughlin by the Hudson's Bay Company some time before 1832. The rest of the furnishings in the room were also used by the McLoughlin family.

of letters to Simpson so vindictive and abusive that finally Sir George and the Committee of the Company decided that the Doctor's usefulness to them was virtually at an end.

Some time before, as explained by Burt Brown Barker in *The McLoughlin Empire and its Rulers:* "In an effort to protect the interests of the company, McLoughlin had offered to effect a paper transfer of title to the mills at Oregon City from the Hudson's Bay Company to himself, in the hope that the move would lessen the settlers' antagonism. The plan proved to be a trap." And when the company had made up its mind to relieve McLoughlin of his post, as Mr. Barker goes on to say, "Sir George Simpson sprang the trap, and on his recommendation the Honorable Company sold Dr. McLoughlin the mills against his wishes and over his strenuous protests. When it became evident to Dr. McLoughlin that he would be forced to quit his position in the Hudson's Bay Company and manage the mills as his private enterprise, he resigned, reluctantly reconciled to the situation, and began to build a home in Oregon City."

In 1846 Dr. McLoughlin put up his house on lot 6, block 29, of the plat he had had made for the town, and eleven years later that is where he died. When the house was sold out of the family in 1867, it became, with a very large addition in the rear, the Phoenix Hotel. As the neighborhood became industrialized the hotel grew less and less particular, and "gradually," as June Smelser reports in her illuminating little history of the house in the *Clackamas County Historical 1960,* "it grew to be a place of ill-repute . . . and by 1909, when plans were made to move the house, those opposed to the idea put out a pamphlet stating that 'McLoughlin's former home has been for past decades a haunt of shame and disgrace on Main Street. It has been used for vile and disreputable purposes so long that no decent, purity loving citizen can associate it with any good purpose.' "

But fortunately the preservation forces were stronger than the puritanical, for when the Hawley Pulp and Paper Company purchased the property early in 1909 and offered the house free to anyone who would move it away, the preservation forces not only managed to raise the money to move the house, but to move it to a large lot on a bluff overlooking the city which McLoughlin, on his plat, had designated as a city park.

185

THE OAKS STORY

The People

James Hervey Boyd, alderman and mayor, builder of the house
U. S. Grant, general of the Union armies
William Tecumseh Sherman, Major General, U.S.A.
James Lyon Freemantle, Coldstream Guards, war correspondent

May 14 to 16, 1863, were some of the worst days of the Civil War for Jackson, Mississippi. What happened best can be told by Sherman himself.

"I overtook General Grant in person at Auburn, and he accompanied my corps all the way into Jackson . . . McPherson [Union general who had just distinguished himself at Port Gibson on the 11th and was killed July 22 in the battle of Atlanta] had taken the left-hand road toward Jackson, via Clinton, while my troops were ordered by General Grant in person to take the right-hand road leading through Mississippi Springs. We reached Jackson at the same time; McPherson fighting on the Clinton road, and my troops fighting just outside the town, on the Raymond road, where we captured three entire field-batteries, and about two hundred prisoners of war. The rebels, under General Joe Johnston, had retreated northward through the town."

The Oaks is the oldest of the houses which survived the Civil War in Mississippi's capital city. Built when Jackson had a population of less than fifteen hundred inhabitants, it typifies the classic Southern plantation cottage architecture.

Jackson began in 1792 as a trading post established on the Pearl River by a young French-Canadian dancer named Louis Le Fleur. Le Fleur's Bluff, it was called.

Right after the Treaty of Doaks' Stand, when the U.S. bought a large tract of land from the Choctaw, the state legislature of 1821 set aside part of this for the site of a new state capital. The town was founded a year later and named after the hero of the Battle of New Orleans.

When Jackson was just six years old, a typical straggling frontier town, a youth named Boyd came from Kentucky to look around, and, seeing that the place wasn't ready yet for him, went his way, returning to stay in 1834 when he was twenty-three. Eight years later he was elected to his first term as mayor of the town. He was elected twice again, and, when he wasn't mayor, he was an alderman. Then just before he built his little plantation cottage and planted close around it the oak trees, which have by now grown to such an enormous size, he married a girl from Barren County, Kentucky. In their house they had three sons and three daughters. One son, who got his degree at the Princeton Theological Seminary, became a distinguished Presbyterian minister in Michigan and Oregon. One daughter married a man named McGill. The McGills lived on with the parents, and, after the parents died, they lived on in The Oaks, as it was called by now, until they died. A daughter, Mary McGill, lived in the house until the Mississippi Dames bought it in 1960.

The Oaks is the oldest of the four ante-bellum houses in Jackson which survived the destruction of those fearfully hot summer days of 1863. James Boyd and his wife didn't leave the house on either occasion, but before the July bombardment began they sent the smaller children off with a Negro driver and a mule team Boyd had borrowed from a neighbor, and which the Negro never brought back. It is amazing that with cannonballs screaming overhead, the house itself was never hit. The only harm done was when a ball tore through the smokehouse and broke open a big barrel of molasses.

It is said that during the burning of the town in May the Union soldiers stabled their horses in the wide hallway that runs through the house, and bivouacked in the downstairs bedrooms. That was when there was a separate kitchen building across a brick terrace from the hallway, as well as other farm buildings on the grounds, now all gone.

The British officer Freemantle, of the Coldstream Guards, who showed up shortly after Sherman's "visit" in May, came as a war correspondent, and describes Jackson as "a place of great importance. Four railroads meet here," he goes on to say, "and have been destroyed in each direction for a distance of from three to five miles. All the numerous factories have been burned down by the enemy, who were of course justified in so doing; but during the short space of thirty-six hours, in which General Grant occupied the city, his troops have wantonly pillaged nearly all of the private houses. They have gutted the stores, and destroyed all they could not carry away. All this must have been done under the very eyes of General Grant, whose name was on the book of the Bowman House hotel."

One of the citizens interviewed by Freemantle was a Dr. Russell who had saved his property from pillage by seating himself on his veranda, with a loaded double-barreled gun on his knees. "When the pillagers approached," Freemantle reports, "the doctor addressed them in the following manner: 'No man can die more than once, and I shall never be more ready to die than I am now. There is nothing to prevent your going into this house, except that I shall kill with this gun the first two of you who move toward it. Now then, gentlemen, walk in . . . "They didn't walk." adds Freemantle in his driest vein.

The last occupant of the house, Miss Mary McGill, recalls that all through the dismal Reconstruction years the grounds around the house were made colorful and bright by the hosts of unfamiliar wild flowers. She claims they grew from seeds that were in the sacks of feed from which the Union soldiers fed their horses.

In the spectacular pair of parlors in the Andrew
Low House the spirit of its period is emphasized
by the Empire sofa in the near parlor and the two
Sheraton sofas in the parlor beyond. The portrait
is of Mrs. Joseph J. Wilder, second president of
the Georgia Dames, from 1899 to 1913. In the
dining room, with its subtle gold paper and
matching silk damask draperies, Savannahians
entertain in the manner of long ago with grace,
charm, leisure and elegance. Magnolia leaves
usually flank the early 19th-century gold leaf
mirror, above the stately marble mantel. A very
early Kirk silver pitcher is always proudly on
display.

188

The Andrew Low house faces Lafayette Square in Savannah and serves as the very handsome headquarters of the Georgia Dames.

THE LOW HOUSE STORY

The People

*Andrew Low, cotton broker,
        builder of the house*
William Mackay Low, his son
Juliette Gordon, William's wife, founder of the Girl Scouts
William W. Gordon, Juliette's father
Eleanor Kinzie, Juliette's mother
William Makepeace Thackeray, the novelist, a visitor
William Tecumseh Sherman, the Union general, another visitor

The Sheffields were having a Christmas party at their big house in New Haven about ten years before the Civil War, and among the Yale boys waiting in the hall for the girls to come downstairs was Willy Gordon. Willy was a shy, goodlooking boy whose shyness wasn't helped this evening by the cross he bore on the back of his neck in the shape of a wicked boil.

The sound of laughter and whispers from above alerted the young men in the hall, but didn't prepare them for the sudden sight of Nellie Kinzie in her party dress plunging down the bannister, plump into their midst. Anyhow, that was the way Nellie and Willy met.

Eleanor Kinzie was born in 1832 in the frontier village of Chicago. She always said she was the first baby baptized there in a church. This was shortly after her parents, John and Juliette Gordon Kinzie, had returned from the Indian Agency whose story was told in some earlier pages of this book. When Nellie came into her teens it seemed a good idea to the Kinzies to send her to school in New England at Madame Canada's, where the Sheffield girls became her closest friends. When they asked her after the party how she liked Willy Gordon, she said he reminded her of a Methodist parson.

William Washington Gordon was born in Savannah, Georgia, in one of the splendid Regency houses done there by the English architect William Jay. It was in this house that he and Nellie were married a few years after the Christmas party.

Several blocks away, over on Lafayette Square, in about 1848, an English-American cotton merchant named Andrew Low, from Liverpool, built his big dignified Victorian mansion with its hourglass garden in front and its carriage house behind. His first wife died soon after they settled into the house, and his two small daughters went to live in England. In March 1853, while Thackeray was here on the first of his two American lecture tours, Low rescued the writer from the wretched hotel where he was staying and put him up in the mansion.

In a letter from the Low house Thackeray said he was living "in the comfortablest quarters

I shall have between this and Europe . . . O the blessing of quiet, and a clean sweet bed and sleep and all day to myself. . . without hearing the hundred thousand feet of the hotel."

In May 1854 Low married Mary Cowper Stiles of Etowah Cliffs; and in February 1856 Thackeray returned to Savannah to give his lectures on *The Four Georges* and to be Andrew Low's guest again. In a letter from the Low house there are close-ups of the household and of surrounding Savannah.

In a tranquil old city, wide-streeted, tree-planted, with a few cows and carriages toiling through the sandy road, a few happy negroes sauntering here and there, a red river with tranquil fleet of merchantmen taking in cargo, and tranquil ware-houses barricaded with packs of cotton—no row, no tearing northern bustle, no ceaseless hotel racket, no crowds drinking at the bar—a snug little languid audience of three or four hundred people, far too lazy to laugh or applaud; a famous good dinner, breakfast, etc., and leisure all the morning to think and do and sleep and read as I like. The only place I stay in the States where I can get these comforts—all free gratis—is in the house of my friend Andrew Low of the great house of A. Low and Co., Cotton Dealers, brokers, merchants—what's the word? Last time I was here he was a widower with two daughters—there was endless talks between us. Now there is a pretty wife added to the establishment, and a little daughter number three crawling in the adjoining nursery. They are tremendous men these cotton merchants."

The Lows' only son, William Mackay Low, was born the year of Thackeray's second visit. And on his mother's death, seven years later, Willie was sent to England, where he was educated at Winchester and Oxford. "He then embarked," a relative wrote, "upon the exceedingly gay life that a wealthy young Englishman could lead at the height of the Victorian era."

Over at the Gordon house on October 31, 1860, a daughter was born to William and Eleanor. She was named Juliette Magill Kinzie after her mother's mother, who had recently written her book called *Wau-Bun* about her experiences in the Indian Agency days in the Michigan Territory of the early 1830's. But Daisy was the name by which Juliette was known by family and friends for the rest of her life.

"I remember 1864 as vividly as if I had been fourteen instead of three years old," wrote Juliette many years later. "In that year Savannah, which had been besieged for months, surrendered to the enemy, and Sherman's army marched through the city. I can even now feel the thrill and hear the tramp of the tired troops. My colored nurse waked me from a sound sleep, wrapped me in the blanket of my crib bed, rushed with me to the balcony. Here we peeked through the green jalousies, and I saw for the first time real live Yankees, thousands and thousands of them!

"Later in the week General Sherman called on my mother. He had known her in Chicago before her marriage. He asked her if he could be of any use to her, and I remember that he had with him an officer who had lost his arm. He took me on his knee, and with childish curiosity I inquired about the loss of that gentleman's arm.

"Got it shot off by a Rebel! was the laconic explanation.

"I s'pose my father did it," I witlessly exclaimed. He shot lots of Yankees."

Before he left the house the general gave the little girl a packet of sugar. It was the first sugar she had ever tasted. The general had already made another presentation in the following letter.

Savannah, Ga. Dec. 22, 1864

To his Excellency,
  President Lincoln
Dear Sir,
  I beg to present you as a Christmas gift, the city of Savannah with 150 heavy guns and plenty of ammunition; and also about 25,000 bales of cotton.
                  W. T. Sherman
                  Maj. Gen'l

When she was seventeen Daisy was sent to a French school in New York City run with astonishing strictness by the Mlles. Mathilde and Fannie Charbonnier. After two years of intense training in the cultural and social graces, Daisy came home to Savannah ready for her debut. She was a striking beauty, quite unlike the typical Southern belle. She had her mother's quick wit, impulsiveness, outspokenness and tomboyishness. Slender-faced, dark-haired, she was a great success as a debutante, and among the young men whose heart she captured was Willie Low, who during Daisy's debutante days was staying with his father in Savannah. Then Daisy, on her first trip abroad, spent some time with the Low family in England and made best friends of Willie's three sisters.

Daisy was married to Willie Low in Savannah on December 21, 1886. "The wedding was a brilliant event," the paper reported, "with a beautiful bride, and a bridegroom known as 'the handsomest man in Savannah!'" A day or two later on their wedding trip, Daisy's ear, with which she had already had trouble, leaving it partly deaf, became very painful. When the doctor who examined it removed a grain of rice (from the wedding send-off), Daisy was completely deaf on that one side, an affliction she accepted as a matter of course.

The honeymoon couple made their home at Willie's country house in Warwickshire, with a town house in London. And between the two places, with much European traveling, and visits to Savannah at the Low house, Daisy spent the next nineteen years. Her niece remembers Daisy's visits to the house on Lafayette Square. She would arrive, "likely as not unheralded—with an entourage of at least a maid and her two favorite pets, a Pekingese dog and a parrot that everyone else found disagreeable."

Life in England began with great gaiety and stimulation, with riding, hunting, entertaining, and with neighbors Daisy enjoyed, such as the Kiplings next door. Kipling even wrote a poem about her. At her presentation at Court, wearing a dress decked out in feathers with a train six yards long, Daisy describes the three hours it took the procession to pass through seven rooms of the palace, with "everyone very sorry to crowd and push . . . but my train weighed tons and my bouquet pounds, so I disposed of the bouquet by perching it on the bustle of the lady in front of me . . . (who) quite unconscious of the service . . . carried it the length of all the rooms."

But the happiness began to dwindle. Daisy's deafness grew worse, and Willie was far from an ideal husband. So when he died in 1905, "he left a lonely, middle-aged widow without even the consolation of happy memories." Actually she was only forty-five, and not completely without happy memories. It was simply that she had a sense of aimlessness.

Then in 1911 she met Sir Robert Baden-Powell. She became inspired by his Boy Scout movement to create a Scout movement for girls. She began with two groups in Great Britain, one in Scotland and one in the London slums of Lambeth. She drafted friends to take over these two groups while she herself sailed home to get things started in the United States.

As soon as she arrived at the Low house in Savannah she phoned an old friend, Nina Anderson Pope, who had a school there for girls. "Come right over," said Daisy, "I've got something for the girls of Savannah, and all America, and all the world, and we're going to start it tonight."

In the same house, on January 17, 1927, Juliette Low died. Her last year was a year of increasing illness. It was cancer. But it was a year of her most triumphant spirit. She made one final trip to England to settle her affairs. On the way over, ill as she was, she insisted on taking part in the shipboard masquerade, going as the Departed Spirits, draped in a sheet with a pillowcase over her head, and hung at her neck and waist with a dozen empty bottles she had collected.

Juliette Low's American home on Lafayette Square along with its garden has been beautifully restored by the Georgia Dames. At the rear of the garden is the carriage house, Daisy's gift to the Savannah Girl Scouts to have for their headquarters.

In *Baroness Pontalba's Buildings*, by Leonard V. Huber and Samuel Wilson, Jr., one is told that the design of the impressive Pontalba Buildings has generally been credited to the famed Irish architect, James Gallier. But Gallier was supplanted by another Irish architect named Henry Howard, who probably worked over Gallier's original scheme. The Louisiana Dames have their residence here, beautifully furnished in Empire—French, American English Regency and Directoire—in fruitwoods and mahogany.

Baroness Micaela Almonester de Pontalba, from a family portrait in the collection of Baron Alfred de Pontalba. She was red-haired, witty, willful and intelligent.

THE PONTALBA STORY

The People

Micaela Almonester, the Baroness Pontalba, the builder
Don Andres Almonester y Roxas, father of Micaela
Louise de la Ronde, Almonester's second wife, Micaela's mother
Joseph Xavier Célestin Delfau de Pontalba, Micaela's husband
Célestin, Alfred, and Gaston, the Pontalbas' three sons
Baron Joseph Xavier Delfau de Pontalba, Micaela's father-in-law
James Gallier, architect No. 1
Henry Howard, architect No. 2
Samuel Stewart, contractor

Facing each other across Jackson Square in the old quarter of New Orleans stands what is in many ways the most remarkable pair of buildings in the United States. Built between 1849 and 1851, each one the full length of the square, the two Pontalba buildings are identical in design, each with its sidewalk colonnade and each enriched with ornamental ironwork.

In her own way as remarkable as the buildings was the woman who built them, the Baroness Pontalba. It was the foresight of her father, however, which made the pair of buildings possible more than fifty years after his death. Lot by lot, between 1777 and 1781, Almonester, who came to New Orleans in 1770 from his native Andalusia, acquired the five lots on either side of what the French, before they ceded Louisiana in 1783 to Spain, had called the Place D'Armes—their army barracks occupied the sites of the present Pontalba buildings. The place kept its French name until 1851, when it became Jackson Square to celebrate the hero of the 1815 battle of New Orleans, General Andrew Jackson, whose equestrian statue occupies the place of honor in the center.

Almonester cleaned up the debris of the barracks, and on both the St. Peter Street and St. Ann Street sides built houses and stores to rent. He also built a big house for himself on the St. Peter Street side of the square. By the time the baroness was ready to build her dream buildings, the buildings her father had built were ready to be torn down. The three buildings on the third side of the square, which faces across the square to the Mississippi—the St. Louis Cathedral, the Cabildo, and the Presbytère, which still stand to complete this extraordinary civic group—were all three built in their original form by Almonester.

Baron Joseph Xavier de Pontalba was a contemporary of Almonester's, a member of the rich French colony in New Orleans. Micaela was two, and the baron's son, Célestin, was seven, when the Pontalbas returned to France and their estate at Senlis, the Château Mont l'Évêque. Thirteen years later, Micaela's mother and the baron's wife, who were related, contrived a marriage between the fifteen-year-old Micaela and the Pontalbas' twenty-year-old son, Micaela's cousin. In October 1811 mother and son came over to New Orleans, and on the 23rd of the month Micaela and Célestin were married, spending their honeymoon with both mothers on board the ship that carried the four of them to France.

In France certain rifts developed. For one, Micaela, in contrast to Célestin, much preferred Paris to life at Senlis. Questions of inheritances arose as the three Pontalba sons were born. And the conflict of the two opposing personalities began to produce sparks.

The two were living apart when the first explosion occurred. The oldest son, Célestin, always a problem child, had run away at seventeen from military school and gone to live with his mother in Paris. This so enraged the boy's grandfather, already irate at his son's separation, that he disinherited the boy. In an effort to reconcile her child with the family, and get them to take him in charge, she drove out to Senlis.

There she was glad to have a long talk alone with her husband, as she was terrified of the father. In the morning she was getting ready to go back to Paris when the baron came into her room and shot her twice in the chest, but so far from fatally that, after the pistol then misfired twice and he was trying to prime it, she escaped from the room to the floor below, where the maids took care of her wounds until the doctor came. The baron in the meanwhile went to his study where he fixed the pistol and shot himself in the heart, dying at once.

Apart from the chest wounds, from which she quickly recovered, the first finger of Micaela's left hand was shot away and the third finger shattered when she raised her hand to protect herself. By the death of the man who tried to murder her she became the Baroness de Pontalba.

Her marriage with Célestin was dissolved in 1838 at about the time she was building her big town house on the Rue du Faubourg Saint-Honoré, now part of the United States Embassy.

Her mind was also busy with plans for her properties on both sides of the Place d'Armes, and it is reasonable to suppose that she was inspired, as her chroniclers claim, by the example of the Palais Royal in Paris; perhaps too by the arcaded square of the Place des Vosges and the arcades along the Rue de Rivoli. It is hard to believe that the basic conception of the Pontalba buildings was anybody's but her own, however.

Her chroniclers, in their vividly documented story of the baroness and her buildings, describe her cavalier treatment of the two architects involved: first the famous James Gallier, who drew the original plans, and then Henry Howard, the Greek Revivalist, who made certain revisions for her. She appears to have been one of the most fiendish of clients, haggling and pennypinching. Her parsimoniousness in refusing to pay for proper plans, specifications, and surveys was cause for constant bickering with her contractor.

In spite of the fact that she drove everyone crazy (she would put on pants so as to climb ladders up into the upper stories to spy on the workmen), the buildings continued to be her own creation, and proved her to be the true impresario of this fine architectural performance.

The upper Pontalba building was the first to be completed, in the fall of 1850, and the baroness and the two sons who lived with her, Alfred and Gaston, were the first to move in. The lower Pontalba building, on the St. Ann Street side of the square, was finished the following year.

On April 6, 1851, the baroness and her two sons returned to France, where she found her former husband severely ill and everything else in a state of confusion. She took all in hand, put things to rights, and rented a house where she and her sons could take care of him until he recovered his health. In fact, he lived another twenty-seven years, four more than the baroness, who died April 20, 1874, in Paris, never having been back again to her buildings on the square.

After the baroness died the heirs refused to spend money on maintenance, and deterioration set in, reaching its lowest point during the First World War. The Pontalba heirs finally decided to sell. One public-spirited citizen bought the Lower Pontalba building, willing it to the Louisiana State Museum. Three others bought the Upper Pontalba, selling it ten years later to the Pontalba Building Museum Association Inc., which gave it to the City of New Orleans. Then during the New Deal the W.P.A. did a big restoration job on it, as the museum has since done on the Upper Building, which is where the baroness lived and where the Louisiana Dames now have their residence.

THE CAMPBELL HOUSE STORY

The People

Robert Campbell, fur trader, merchant, financier, owner of the house
Virginia Jane Kyle, his wife
Hugh ⎫
Hazelette ⎬ *their sons*
James ⎭
General William H. Ashley, fur trader, politician
William Sublette, fur-trading partner of Campbell

A sickly smalltown boy from Aughlane in Northern Ireland, Robert Campbell, at twenty, turned up in St. Louis in 1824, went for advice about some trouble with his lungs to the best doctor in the city, Bernard G. Farrar, and learned that to cure his condition he should lead a rugged outdoor life. He did what the doctor said. He headed west, won fame as an Indian fighter, made a fortune in the fur trade, and got well.

"His exploits partake of the wildest spirit of romance," Washington Irving wrote. "No danger nor difficulty can appall him."

But about eleven years of this was all he wanted. In 1836 he settled down in St. Louis, and, through his mercantile and financial enterprises, became one of the richest men in the city. At thirty-seven he married a nineteen-year-old girl from Raleigh, North Carolina. When the Mexican War broke out, he was made Inspector General of the Missouri militia, and recruited and equipped four regiments for General Kearney's epic march to Santa Fe. In 1851 he bought one of the best houses in St. Louis, on Lucas Place, where only the elite lived—General Harney, Governor Polk, the Filleys, Ameses, Wickhams, Hitchcocks, Turners, Bentons, Valles, Moffits, Lacklands, the Lucases themselves. The Campbells' guests included General Sherman, Captain Eads, the bridgebuilder, and President Grant, who after dinner appeared with Campbell on the balcony, shaking hands, before a crowd of admirers—though Campbell was a Democrat and Grant a Republican.

The Campbells had thirteen children, ten of whom died under the age of eight, the other three growing to manhood. Robert Campbell died in 1879, his widow three years later. The last of the Campbell sons died in 1938, and Yale inherited the whole estate. And it is a question which makes the better story, Campbell's career on the plains and in the mountains, or what went on with his house after he died.

Just as tobacco was legal tender in colonial Virginia, and whiskey in Kentucky, so was beaver in Missouri when Robert Campbell came there from Ireland. St. Louis paid its bills in beaver, it has been said.

Probably the most successful Missouri trader at the time in this type of legal tender was William Henry Ashley, who came out from Virginia in 1804 when he was twenty-five, made gunpowder, mined saltpeter and lead, and in 1820 was elected Lieutenant-Governor. After his two-year term, he turned fur trader, sending expeditions up the Missouri to the Yellowstone and across South Pass into the Green River Valley. It became his method of operation to hold an annual rendezvous of trappers and traders at any convenient and accessible place, rather than establish fixed trading posts, or "forts."

It was as a member of Ashley's 1825 expedition that Robert Campbell began the therapy pre-
scribed by Dr. Farrar. He became a leader of subsequent expeditions, on one of which he led his
trappers in a fracas with a large party of Blackfeet Indians at what is now the city of Pierre, capital
of South Dakota, on the Missouri. In the course of the fight he rushed out into the open under
fire and pulled a wounded companion back into safety—the famous William Sublette, who later
became his partner in the fur-trading firm of Sublette & Campbell.

The partners went into head-on competition with the operations of the powerful American
Fur Company, owned by the Astors in New York and the Chouteaus in St. Louis, who used the
trading-post, or fort, system as opposed to Ashley's annual rendezvous. The partners' strategy
was to establish forts close to those of the competitors, hoping to lure the Indian trappers away
with better bargains and more whiskey.

In the summer of 1833, Sublette, who had been further up the Missouri with provisions, and
Campbell, who had been on a trading expedition through the Rockies, met by arrangement at
the end of August a little way below where the Yellowstone flows into the Missouri, just inside
the present North Dakota line, and where they had decided to build Fort William, named for
Sublette. Three miles away was Fort Union, the American Fur Company's Upper Missouri out-
fit headquarters. In charge of Fort Union was a man named McKenzie who called himself "King
of the Missouri," a man Campbell couldn't stand.

From September 21, when Sublette took off for St. Louis in the keelboat loaded with beaver
and otter skins from the mountains, Campbell kept a journal, day by day, until December 31,
when he brought it to a close in a mood of despair. The final pages he put down on New Year's Eve
are a resumé of the year.

"I was this day twelve month in New York at the City Hotel making preparations for this trip
—I there enjoyed the pleasures of the Season and was a few days after joined by my Brother and
returned with him to Phila where I remained a short time. I took a farewell of my Brother 18th
Jany proceeded to Pittsburgh—thence to St. Louis where I arrived on the 8th Feb and proceeded
to make some arrangements for our starting there. On the 8th March I was joined by Mr. Sublette
and we set about fitting and hiring men. On the 14th April I left with a company of 45 men for the
Mountains and Mr. Sublette by water with 68 men for this and intermediate places with 2 keel
boats loaded with merchandize—one remained at the Sioux and one came here. I proceeded
directly to the mountains and fortunately sold out our equipment there and returned by the
Yellowstone with our furs. In the Big Horn the skin Boat in which I was sunk and I had like to have
perished. Thrice I went under water and but for an all wise and all merciful God I should never
have seen the termination of this Year. I got safe to shore and succeeded in recovering all but
about 4 packs of Beaver and our arms. Besides I lost my saddle bags &c. I recovered again my boat
and next day was joined by all the Crow Indians—and here again I must acknowledge my depend-
ence on God who inclined those Indians to treat me kindly and return most of my beaver when
they had us completely in their power. And I may here observe that these same Indians 17 days
after at the instigation of the American fur Co. robbed Mr. Fitzpatrick of all he had with him, but
of themselves afterwards returned animals for nearly all they had taken.

"I proceeded on down to this place where I arrived on the 30th of August and found Mr.
Sublette who had got here the day previous. We took the next day to select a suitable place to
build, and having pitched on this place we set to work. But to my mortification Mr. Sublette was
taken sick and barely recovered when he left me on the 20th Sept. for St. Louis with the returns
I had brought down—and I heard afterwards he had got as far as little Mo and was much recovered.
I may date my trouble from my arrival here. I had every thing to construct—I had to make a Fort
build ten Houses dig a well and make an Ice House not yet built but all is in the fort to construct
it. I have 5 carts made and the materials for six more. I have harness for as many—the stuff out for
2 mackinaw boats. I have made 4 canoes and a Perogue, and have established 50 miles above here

The house was built in 1851, a fairly typical city house of the fifties, the architect probably William Fulton. The bay on the side with the lattice porch above is a nice note. In Mrs. Campbell's bedroom, furnished by the Missouri Dames, the bed is a Victorian monument. The wallpaper was chosen by the Campbells, the portrait is of Campbell's brother Hugh, and the rug is Aubusson. In the parlor the candelabra on the left were brought from Paris by the sons. The mirror and window cornices are goldleaf backed with diamont dust, and all the furniture is virgin Victorian.

where I made a Fort and 4 houses and have sent up the Yellowstone to do like there. All this work requires much attention and is attended with immense troubles. Even the finding in provisions so many men, so badly provided with animals as we were, was enough trouble for one man. I can safely say as unhappy a time as this I have never before passed during my life. What is worst our prospects are not good for McKenzie has hired our interpreters and bribed them whilst they were here to betray us. But he must answer for this so soon as I get one to whom I can leave this business in charge. . . . ."

Actually, there was a good man Campbell could leave in charge—William Almond, a Virginian, whom he had sent to start the fort up the Yellowstone; and Campbell could meet his partner in St. Louis, on Sublette's return from his February meeting in New York with the American Fur Company people. It was a sensible arrangement Sublette had made. The fort-by-fort idea didn't really work. The Indians simply played one company against the other, and the companies used the Indians for the same purpose. But the nuisance value of the Sublette-Campbell scheme was what brought American Fur to terms. The new deal separated the two companies' activities altogether geographically. American would take the Upper Missouri territory, the partners would take the mountains.

At that, Campbell only stayed in the mountains another year or so. When he next went back to St. Louis in 1836, he went back to stay. Once there, after a four-year courtship he married Virginia Kyle, whom he'd met in Philadelphia at the house of his brother Hugh. Hugh told Robert at the time that she had already been "four times courted and twice engaged." A happy marriage ensued nevertheless.

When Virginia died, two years after her husband, the youngest son, James, was twenty, Hazelette was twenty-two, and Hugh was thirty-three. The house was thirty. It was furnished the way it had been furnished from the time Campbell bought it, the way it stayed during the tenure of the sons, and identically the way it is furnished today. Nothing was ever changed. Nothing. And no one ever threw anything away. It remains the same rich rosewood and walnut, black horsehair, and flowered-carpet Victorian it was in the 1850's.

James was the only son who went to college. He graduated in the class of 1880 at Yale and took a law degree from Harvard in 1882. In 1890, in Paris, returning from a trip around the world with his two brothers, James died.

In 1903, when Hazelette was forty-five, he suddenly became mentally ill and lived the remainder of his life, thirty-five more years, on the third floor of the house in the care of a male nurse. At the time his brother became ill, Hugh was fifty-six, a bachelor with no relatives to help him get away from the house. His extremely retiring nature was made morbidly more so by the character of Hazelette's illness, which in those days was looked upon by many people as a disgrace.

When there was talk, two or three years after Hazelette's death, of tearing down the house, a group of St. Louis citizens, who understood the municipal as well as the social and cultural value of historic preservation, set out to save the house *in toto*, for everything there was still intact After all, what would the house be without the furniture, or what, for that matter, would the furniture be without the house? There was going to be an auction, so they had to move fast.

They raised enough money for the furniture, which made five vanloads to put in fireproof storage, then began a desperate race with demolition to save the building. At that moment Pearl Harbor made fundraising for old houses seem to many an almost unpatriotic diversion from war-bond buying. Fortunately, there were people who were able to do both. Yale had already offered the house to the Campbell House Foundation for a fraction of its value, and, when the owners of St. Louis' largest department store donated $10,000, the building was in the bag. Spick-and-span, with all the furniture back in it where it belongs, and with many of Virginia Campbell's dresses on display, the house was opened to the public in 1943.

THE MINTHORN HOUSE STORY

The People

Jesse Edwards, builder of the house, founder of Newberg
Dr. Henry John Minthorn, physician, teacher, uncle of Herbert C. Hoover
Laura Ellen Miles, the doctor's wife
Herbert C. Hoover, the 31st President, as a boy

Jesse Edwards was an enterprising Quaker farmer of Plainfield, Indiana, with a wife and four children, when a Quaker preacher, returning in 1880 from a Quaker settlement in Yamhill County, Oregon, spoke at meeting with such enthusiasm of both present and future possibilities of the fresh young state that Jesse sold his farm and set out with his family on the Union Pacific.

"Each coach," according to our chronicler, "had a large stove at one end where meals could be cooked, the car seats could be adjusted into beds, but each occupant had to bring his own bedding." It was summer, and "travel preparations called for meats to be well cooked and stored in heavy crocks. Vegetables were scrubbed and carried in flour sacks, and quantities of bread were baked."

The train took eight sooty days from Council Bluffs to San Francisco, and often the men and boys would run alongside as the train puffed and panted up the steep mountain grades. The rest of the way, by the steamer *Orient*, was considerably cleaner and more comfortable, and soon the Edwardses were made welcome at the Newberg settlement, where Jesse built his house the following spring, the oldest house still standing in the town.

By the winter of 1884, an academy building of twelve big rooms, two full stories, and a mansard tower was going up in the middle of the eighty acres of Jesse's best field, and Dr. Minthorn, who had come out from West Branch, Iowa, in 1882 and bought the Edwards house, was made superintendent, his wife becoming one of the teachers. And on the rolls was a boy who signed himself "H. C. Hoover." Everybody called him Bertie.

The boy's father had died four years before, and his mother, a sister of Dr. Minthorn, three years later, the same year that the Minthorns' son had died. So the doctor and his wife arranged for young Herbert to come and live with them as a son. And soon "in Iowa all arrangements were made. At the age of ten Herbert Hoover travelled with his roll of bedding and a large lunch basket well loaded with ham, chicken, bread, and meat pies, which he divided with the family who looked after him during the trip to Oregon. Dr. Minthorn met him at Portland and drove him in a buggy to Newberg, twenty miles to the south."

"The day I arrived at Newberg," Hoover recalled, "Aunt Laura Minthorn and her three daughters, my cousins, were making the pear-butter supply for the winter in a wash-boiler over a fire in the yard. I had never eaten a pear before. I was asked to stir the butter and urged to eat as many pears as I liked. I liked them. But after two days of almost exclusively pear diet I didn't eat pears again for years."

Burt Brown Barker, who was a schoolmate of Hoover's and a boyhood friend, tells about how a new world opened in Newberg for the young emigrant. "He became a regular member

199

The house where the late Herbert Hoover lived as a boy with his foster parents, Dr. and Mrs. Henry J. Minthorn, in Newberg, Oregon, couldn't be more evocative of the early settlements of the Northwest. The Oregon Dames help with the maintenance of the house and grounds. According to Dr. Burt Brown Barker, biographer of Dr. McLoughlin and president of the Herbert Hoover Foundation in Newberg, the dining room table is the second oldest and best known in Oregon; the oldest and best known being Dr. McLoughlin's in Oregon City. The chairs belonged to Vannie Martin, Hoover's favorite Sunday school teacher. The china (100 pieces) is copper lustre tea-leaf ironware.

of a warm family which included three girls. He was given regular chores to do such as sawing, splitting and carrying in wood for three stoves, milking the family cow, feeding and caring for the doctor's ponies and hitching them up periodically, and at times going along on visits to patients in the country. In later years he wrote, 'They were profitable journeys to me. The doctor was mostly a silent, taciturn man, but still a natural teacher. He taught me much of physiology, health, and sickness . . . With this background of sporadic talks from him, the long tedious drives over rough and often muddy forest roads became part of my education.'"

Bertie stayed at Newberg until the Minthorns moved in 1889 to Salem, where the doctor had organized the Oregon Land Company, and where young Hoover became the office boy who also drove prospective customers out to see the various properties of the company.

As he learned so much about health and sickness from Dr. Minthorn, he learned typing from the office stenographer, bookkeeping from the bookkeeper, and the rudiments of politics from the town politicos who gathered every evening in the office to discuss and argue by the hour.

When a mining engineer came to Salem, young Hoover spent every minute he could spare away from work making geological surveys into the hills with this new friend, from whom, while he didn't learn to be a mining engineer, he did learn that a mining engineer was what he wanted to be. And it wasn't long before he left the Minthorn family and went to Leland Stanford. And from 1929 to 1933 he learned what it was like to be President.

200

The Governor Ramsey mansion in St. Paul.

THE RAMSEY HOUSE STORY

RAMSEY, ALEXANDER (b. near Harrisburg, Pa., 1815; d. 1903), lawyer. Congressman, Whig, from Pennsylvania, 1843-47. Removing to Minnesota, 1849, as newly appointed territorial governor, he opened an immense area in the south of the territory to settlement by negotiating treaties with the Sioux, 1851. At the end of his term, 1853, he entered business in St. Paul, Minn., and served as governor of the state, 1859-63. As U.S. Senator, Republican, from Minnesota, 1863-75, he made important contributions to postal reform. He was U.S. Secretary of War, 1879-81, in President R.B. Hayes's cabinet.

Concise Dictionary of American Biography, N.Y., 1964

IT was during his second term as Senator that Ramsey began building what he rightly called his mansion house, designed by the St. Paul architect Monroe Scheire in the favorite mansion style of the times—French Renaissance, topped of course by a mansard roof. It has walls two feet thick of Minnesota limestone, porches and floors of Minnesota pine, blackwalnut woodwork, and door panels of the paler butternut for contrast.

The large parlor, or drawing room, measuring 20 by 40 feet, has a bouncing floor for dancing, and there was a great canvas the size of the floor which could be brought down from the attic after all the furniture was taken out, and stretched tightly wall to wall over the rug. The canvas could be waxed to a high shine, and the dancers would wear shoes resembling ballet slippers.

From the St. Paul *Daily Press* for November 23, 1872:

"Hon. Alex Ramsey's elegant residence on Exchange St. is approaching completion. Mrs. Ramsey gave a very fine entertainment and banquet to the workmen on the building on Thursday evening last. . . . Everything passed off very pleasantly and agreeably."

The next big event was announced in the *Daily Press* on December 17:

"A musical sociable will be given at the residence of Mrs. Ramsey . . . [Her] well known taste and skill provides the whole evening's entertainment, and on this occasion throws open to the public for the first time her new and elegant residence."

"$75 was realized for the House of Hope sociable at the Ramsey residence," reported the St. Paul *Daily Pioneer* on December 21.

The Ramseys entertained many guests of prominence during their lives together in the house —military men, college presidents, and, of course, politicians galore. Probably most important were Rutherford B. Hayes and his wife, who made two visits—in 1878 and 1886. When the President came in 1878 to open the State Fair, the directors of the fair made it clear to the Ramseys that, while Mr. and Mrs. Hayes would spend the night and have breakfast with the Ramseys, they would be entertained for dinner at a large public banquet. Mrs. Ramsey stayed home, while everybody else, servants and all, went to the fair. At dinner time, the fair party returned to the Ramsey house with the news that the banquet plans had fallen through. No servants, no telephones, no stores open, and only leftovers in the big icebox. Mrs. Ramsey was frantic. But her spirits rose when she discovered several dozen prairie-chicken legs, and building on this she managed to produce a dinner that delighted the whole gathering. The next year the President made her husband his Secretary of War—and, for ten days, his Secretary of the Navy.

The woodwork of the great parlor, which became a ballroom in a few hours' notice, is black walnut. The marble mantels were made in St. Paul, but the fireplaces were never used. The chandeliers are of Bohemian crystal. The Steinway concert grand was a gift to the Governor from his brother Justus in 1872. Most of the furniture is of the family.

The California Dames' Octagon House is one of the rare relics of a short-lived craze for eight-sided homes which left its mark much more on the East than the West, making this example even more rare. Built in 1861 in the late Gold Rush era, it was one of the last homes in San Francisco to be electrified.

THE OCTAGON HOUSE STORY

The People

William C. McElroy, builder of the house
Harriet, his wife

A round the 1850's a phrenologist named Orson Fowler was having considerable success and influence with a book of plans and principles called *A Home For All*. It extolled the virtues and explained the advantages of the octagonal house. Thousands were built before the fad died out, and several hundred still stand in various parts of the country.

One of the advantages claimed for it over the rectangular house was more space to the same amount of wall (a circular house, of course, would offer perfection in that respect). The trouble was that off-rectangular houses presented difficulties and awkwardnesses in construction and planning. Rooms could be rectangular all right, but the builder was left to cope with a lot of triangular spaces in between. It was also claimed that "they offered less resistance to the wind," and received "more direct sunshine in a region known for its fog."

It would be reasonable to suppose that this last claim could have caused at least five octagonal houses of record to be built during the fifties and sixties in San Francisco, of which the California Dames' Octagon House is one of the two remaining examples. It was built in 1861 by William C. McElroy, a miller, on land bought two years before by his wife Harriet. The wife, at least, lived there until 1892, for in that year she made application to the Spring Valley Water Company for connection with its system. Up to that time she had used a well in the yard.

After 1893 the house had a variety of tenants, who must not have minded its unusual interior

In the reception room, the chest against the staircase between the 1790-1800 Massachusetts Sheraton side chairs, is an 18th-century coromandel china lacquer from New England. The 18th-century mahogany sideboard is Philadelphia Hepplewhite. The dropleaf table under the Trumbull portrait of Washington is New England Chippendale, 1760-1780. The center table is a Sheraton tip-top of 1780; its stenciled chairs Hitchcocks.

In a window embrasure of the reception room the handsome sofa is a Duncan Phyfe. The Louis XVI George Washington chair is from the Robert Morris home in Philadelphia. The two corner cabinets contain Luster and Staffordshire china.

arrangements, for no changes from the original scheme were made. However, the house continued to be owned by the McElroys or their descendants until 1923. Due to the loss of all records in the earthquake and fire of 1906, the legislature passed the McEnerney Act under which property owners in San Franciso had to clear the title to their property. Mr. McElroy's daughter, Emma Van Duzer, and her husband brought suit to acquire title in early 1908. In 1924, when it was bought by the Pacific Gas & Electric Company, it was one of the few houses in San Francisco still not wired for electricity. It was rented to three elderly sisters named Riley while the company tried to make up its mind about using the site for a substation. The ladies lived lives of virtual recluses, rarely letting themselves be seen for almost twenty-five years. Toward the end of their occupancy a reporter happened to see a little white-haired woman on the steps by the mailbox. He asked her how she liked living in an Octagon House. "I do not care for it at all," Miss Riley replied, "It is very badly arranged and very inconvenient to keep orderly and clean."

When the company in 1950 finally decided not to build a substation on the site after all, and as the now-empty house was beginning to be harried by the vandalism of the neighborhood children, they agreed to sell it to the California Dames for a nominal sum if the Dames would take it away, which the Dames did, having it inched across the street on rollers, restoring and furnishing it as a museum and meeting place.

One of the relics in the house is a letter from Mr. McElroy well worth quoting in part. It was found in 1953 in a tin box sealed in the wall beside the staircase leading to the "Widow's Walk," when the electricians were wiring the house for the first time. It is dated "San Francisco, July 14, 1861." "This Octigon House was built and owned by Wm C. McElroy and his wife Harriet S. McElroy and is intended as our privet Residence, we have only one daughter aged nine years, my wife is a native of Lancaster, Pa. and her maden name was "*Shober*" (aged 40 years) I am a native of Virginia ("aged 42 years") and we are a very good looking old Couple and pretty well off in this worldy goods. My wife landed in this city in 1849 and I arrived here in 1851 and . . . were married in this City . . . The young man that you observe in the picture Herewith inclosed is our Nephew Master Saml A. Wolfe an artist by profession, we are in hopes that he will be in a more Respectable business by the time that this paper is discovered . . . We are sorry to be obliged to inform you that our Glourious Union is about being disolved, in fact *Seven* of the *Southern* States have already pulled out inconsiquince as they say that the Northern States have Ellicted a *Black* Republican President and of course opposed to Slavery and this is the true cause of the quarrel the Presidents name is Abreham Lincoln Commonly Called "*Old Abe*" This City has incresed in the past thirteen years from a population of Three Tousand souls in 1849 to about Ninety Thousand in 1861 and continues to increse with Gian Steps we have had Since 1849 regular Steam Ships between this City and the City of New York by way Panama N. Granada but the Genl Government have made arrangements for carrying the mails overland by way of "*Salt Lake City*" and we have at this time Try weekly mails as well as Two Poney Expresses Each week across the Continent in fact but for the troubles going on in the Atlantic States we would have Obtained a Grant for a Pacific Railroad and obtained the assistance of the General Government in making it over the Continent for myself I have given all hope up of that .

"The Gold Mines of this Country was discovered in the year 1848 and have proved very profitable the average yeald for Summer has been about Fifty Millions of Dollars."

"Look which ever way you will and you observe happiness prosperity and wealth—it has always been the Subject of remark by new commers that they never saw so much Enterprise as the people of California have, the whole state of California only contains a white population of about Four Hundred Thousand Souls, and we number at this time about seventy five thousand Chinamen . . . "

THE McALLISTER HOUSE STORY

The People

Major and Mrs. Henry McAllister, builders of the house
General William J. Palmer, the major's Civil War commander and founder
*   of Colorado Springs*
Henry McAllister, Jr., the son

It was in 1806 that Captain Zebulon Montgomery Pike, on an exploring expedition for the Army, sighted the peak in the Rocky Mountains whose summit was named after him, though he didn't climb it. At the foot of Pike's Peak, in the town of Colorado Springs, founded there in 1871, Major McAllister built his house in 1873, the year of the panic. It was the same year that President Grant, serving his second term, visited Colorado, and at Central City walked from his stagecoach to the Teller House on a pavement of silver bricks. Colorado was still a territory. In 1876 it became the 38th state, which is why the flag with thirty seven stars in the McAllister house is such a nice historical touch.

Henry McAllister was born in 1837 near Wilmington, Delaware. His Quaker parents moved soon after to Philadelphia, where Henry lived until 1862, when he joined the 15th Pennsylvania Cavalry, commanded by Colonel (later General) Palmer. Henry quickly rose to the rank of sergeant; ending the war as a major on General Palmer's staff. Their ages were identical to the day.

In 1872 Major McAllister was asked by the general to come to Colorado Springs to be a director of Palmer's developing company, called Fountain Colony (later the Colorado Springs Company), which managed just about everything in this new town.

One of McAllister's first moves was to buy a lot and begin building a house before going back to Philadelphia to fetch his wife and infant son. His architect was a Philadelphian too— George Summers, who had been brought to Colorado Springs by the company in the hope that the people, who were already in a house-building fever, would hire him instead of committing the customary architectural atrocities.

In a general way there were three kinds of houses being built in this country at the time: "cottages," "villas," and "mansions." The names more or less suggest the architectural fashions of the 1870's; and, while a "villa" like the McAllister house has more appealing qualities to make it attractive today than the majority of our present split-levels and ranches, the houses of the centennial period could, without some architectural restraint, go to quite alarming lengths, especially in the building booms of frontier towns. Even the wild ones, however, often now seem documents of strange delight, and a relief to modern monotony.

The McAllister house was built twice as substantially as it was meant to be, due to the fact that an unusually strong windstorm, which uprooted trees, blew off roofs and blew down chimneys one night, made the Major so apprehensive that he gave orders the next morning to double the thickness of the brick walls. This despite the fact that the bricks were all brought by train from Philadelphia, or so it has been stated.

Major McAllister's "villa" of 1873 in Colorado Springs.

As nice as the house was with its big yard and white picket fence, there were still no near neighbors when the McAllisters moved in. "It was all open prairie," an oldtimer has written, "and many times when Mrs. McAllister was baking bread, Indians would come to the kitchen door to beg." And westward pioneers were still piling through. "Often at sunset, two or three covered wagons would drive in across the way and camp for the night. Mrs. McAllister would go over and talk to them, and invite them to get water at her well . . . They would be gone the next morning."

It was the year after they moved in that the grasshoppers came—the great grasshopper plague of 1874. The chronicler describes how "almost everything was eaten up," and how Major McAllister, who was determined to keep them off his garden, "hired a boy to wave a wand at them. It looked as though they would eat the boy and all," was the way he put it. "They filled the wells, spoiling the water. The sides of the houses were black with them."

The chronicler has this further incident to record from 1878, when the Denver & Rio Grande was starting to build its tracks through the Royal Gorge. "They found armed opposition from the Santa Fe," he relates, "who wanted the right of way for itself. Armed camps were set up by the opposing forces, and Major McAllister was asked to take the rifles, which had been stored in a closet in his house, down to the railroad's camp." He doesn't say which railroad: simply that "he drove down through Dead Man's Canon to the entrance of the gorge," and there he leaves him.

By then it was 1906. There were two grown daughters, Mary and Matilda. Henry, Jr., went to Swarthmore, became a lawyer, married a Long Island girl at Jericho in 1896, was district attorney during the Cripple Creek strike and trouble in 1904, and moved that year to practice law in Denver.

General Palmer, now very rich, but too crippled to attend the regimental reunion in Philadelphia, invited all the surviving members to come to Colorado Springs, all expenses paid. Two hundred and eighty came from the East alone, in a private train. The entire Antlers Hotel was taken for them for the six days of their visit. On the last day they had their parade, with the general leading the procession in his specially built White Steamer. Then they all had dinner at the general's mansion and left for home.

Mrs. McAllister died in the house in 1912, the Major in 1921. Matilda inherited it and lived there until she sold it to Shepard's Citations. In 1960 the Colorado Dames acquired the property through the generosity of El Pomar Foundation in cooperation with Shepard's Citations. The objective was to preserve one of the few earliest houses still standing in the town. The Dames have fully restored the house and its gardens, and have furnished the house with late Victorian pieces.

THE HOTEL DE PARIS STORY

The People

Adolphus François Gerard, alias Louis Dupuy, the builder
Sophie Gallet, his housekeeper
Jay Gould, Russell Sage, George Jay Gould, and five other luncheon guests

On October 12, 1846, a baby christened Adolphus François Gerard was born at Alençon, the lace town in Normandy. For centuries the sons of the family had been soldiers. But this boy's widowed mother decided her youngest son was going to be a priest instead, and before he could be called up for military service she sent him to the nearby seminary, where he stuck it out until he was twenty. Suddenly he decided at mass one morning that he wasn't cut out for the priesthood, and without a by-your-leave struck out for Paris.

Down to a few francs on his arrival, he took a dishwashing job at a big hotel where he persuaded the chef to take him on as an apprentice. He felt he'd found his real *métier*, as indeed he had, and was well on his way to chefdom when a legacy of $50,000 fell upon him from a rich relative. It took him only a few months to gamble and give it away. And having, at this point, temporarily at least, also lost his taste for hotel cookery, and finding that in a boat's kitchen he could work his way to America, he sailed for New York.

If Adolphus had only known, he would have worked his way right out to Colorado. For while the gold-rush fever there had subsided, silver mining was making fortunes, and a place called Georgetown, just west of Denver, was the greatest silver camp in the world, with a population of 10,000, (which today has dwindled to something like 400).

But no: Adolphus stayed on in New York, which was still suffering from the effects of the Civil War, and, instead of sticking to his culinary career, tried his hand at journalism. This he did partly by using a natural bent for writing and partly by helping himself generously to the writings of others, then palming off the pieces as his own. This worked for a while, until an editor at *Frank Leslie's Weekly* caught on; and Adolphus, by some very nimble footwork down the office stairs, and by catching the ferry to Brooklyn, barely missed going to jail.

In Brooklyn he hurried down to Fort Hamilton and enlisted in the cavalry, getting sent first to Fort Riley, Kansas, for training, then on to Cheyenne, Wyoming, where in the summer of 1869, fed up with army life, he bought a suit of civilian clothes from a peddler for $25 and deserted.

He took his time to Denver, hiding by day, hiking by night, and growing a good disguise on his face. In Denver, with his new look and a new name—Louis Dupuy—he first got a job sorting out buffalo hides, and on the side took to writing letters to the editor of the *Rocky Mountain News*. When he began making the letter column with his bright and neatly penned observations, the editor offered him a job as roving reporter to cover the mining camps.

With a large figure of Justice on the roof, the name and crossed flags emblazoned on the wall, and ornamental ironwork decorating the front, Louis Dupuy's hotel has airs and graces typical of many a provincial French hostelry. Much of the bedroom furniture was made in or near Georgetown, especially for the hotel by the husband of Louis' heiress-to-be. Victorian was still the rage. In the dining room, as throughout the hotel, the ceilings, borders and walls were decorated by Louis himself. The mirrors were backed with diamond dust. The fountain was copied from an Italian original. The shades of the two statuette chandeliers have been attributed to Tiffany's. The sideboard was made for the room, the china in the corner cupboard is de Haviland, and the floor is made of alternating boards of walnut and maple.

First he bought a burro he called Fleurette. Then he loaded her with camping equipment and rations, heading first for the Printer Boy mine, from which he sent a piece to the *News* on placer mining. Then on to the silver camp of Breckenridge, sending another piece from there. The next camp on Louis' calendar was the biggest and boomingest of all—Georgetown, close by Loveland Pass and Berthoud Pass, named, respectively, after the president and chief engineer of the Colorado Central Railroad—Georgetown, the place he should have headed for when he first landed in New York. He could still have been calling himself Adolphus François Gerard, and saved himself a lot of time.

Georgetown was the second largest and possibly the most prosperous city in Colorado. Everybody had money, but there wasn't a decent place to eat. Why Louis didn't quit his reporting job at once (which he did anyway) and open a restaurant can be explained only by the fact that he chose instead to become a silver miner, and stayed one for several years until he was almost killed in a powder explosion. When the surgeon who saved his life discharged him from the hospital he told Louis never to go into a mine again.

Finally he took a step in the right direction, the first since he had left the seminary. Some say he got a job in a bakery and some say in a rough little restaurant. Whichever it was, he soon owned the place and was making it pay so well that he was able to build his own restaurant-hotel, which took him two years. Even so, with everything having to be hauled by wagon from a railroad fifty miles away, it was a miracle.

He gave it 11 big bedrooms, three large living-room libraries, a great dining salon, an enormous kitchen. In the two oversize bathrooms the cased-in tin tubs were said to be the deepest ever made. Every room in the hotel except the dining salon had a marble-bowl corner washstand with hot and cold running water; there was steam heat throughout; as well as the finest of Wilton carpeting. The furniture was all hand-carved black walnut, and the whole hotel was lit by gas.

Outside he gave ornamental heads to all the doors and windows. He grooved the plastered walls to resemble straight-course masonry; he gave the upper windows a gallery effect with lace-like iron; and he crowned the main street façade with the most fanciful cornice he could find.

At one end of the roof he placed a heroic iron figure of Justice holding her scales above the crossed flags of the United States and France in proper colors, and at the other end an iron stag. Above the granite gateway to the courtyard he laid a crouching lion. And under the cornice across the front he fastened his great metal sign that proclaimed it *Hotel De Paris*. The mistake of the capital D must have been made at the foundry. Louis knew better than that. He almost always printed it correctly on his menus.

He filled one rock-walled cellar room with bin after bin of imported vintages and the finest spirits he could buy; the other big room with beeves, muttons, venisons, and game birds galore, refrigerating it with ice water that he piped in from a nearby glacier.

Actors, singers, authors, lecturers, bankers, and silver magnates were among his guests. Even grander guests were the traveling salesmen, who made it a point to reach Denver by Friday so they could take the afternoon train to Georgetown for a weekend of Louis' hospitality.

One March day in 1879 there appeared unannounced a party of nine whose wealth at the time totalled hundreds of millions, a good part of it in the possession of two members of the group—the millionaires Jay Gould and Russell Sage—but sizable hunks in the hands of Gould's son, George Jay, Sidney Dillion, president of the Union Pacific, W. A. H. Loveland, president of the Colorado Central, and two big Boston bankers, Oliver Ames and Capt. G. H. Baker. With these powerful figures in giant railroading enterprises were the two finest brains in railroading, Gen. Grenville M. Dodge, chief engineer of the Union Pacific, and E. L. Berthoud, chief engineer of the Colorado Central. The party had driven to Georgetown from a special train on which they were making an inspection trip, and they let Louis know they were hungry.

210

What he prepared for them as they stayed their appetites with oysters, celery, and olives around his largest damask-covered table, was his regular luncheon menu for the day: stuffed grouse, venison cutlet, asparagus with browned butter, a salad, frozen punch for desert, and his own special coffee, from which he'd removed the caffeine. With the lunch he served them his fresh-baked French loaves and tall cold bottles of his vintage Moselle . . . Remember, this was still a rough remote frontier town: it had been only two years since hostilities had ceased in Colorado between the whites and the Indians.

Regardless of how Louis' distinguished guests are said to have raved about his luncheon, it is more interesting to think of how much Louis enjoyed preparing a luncheon for nine men and no women. In the early days of the hotel he did have a worshipful love affair by mail with a young girl, who wouldn't answer his letters. Whatever it was, he afterward gave every sign of being a misogynist. With one exception. He was devoted to Sophie Gallet, the widow of the Creole cabinetmaker who had made most of the hotel's furniture. For twenty-two years, from her husband's death to her own, she lived and worked in the hotel.

Louis died in 1900. Being treated for a fever, his doctor told him to do without his daily ice-cold bath. Waking up delirious one morning in October, he disobeyed the doctor and died two days later. He left everything to Sophie, who died five months later. She and Louis lie buried together in Alvarado cemetery down the canyon. A granite shaft marks their grave.

Sophie left the estate, which in addition to the hotel included a lot of Georgetown real estate and a great ranch stocked with cattle at Middle Park (all estimated at $100,000), to a host of relatives in France who preferred to sell at a sacrifice for cash.

Mrs. Sarah Burkholder in 1903 bought the Hotel De Paris for $10,000. At her death her daughter, Mrs. Hazel McAdams, took it over intact to keep it as it was, hoping that someday it would be a museum. Then in 1954 the Colorado Dames came along and bought it for that very purpose, starting its restoration in 1954.

At the banquet in 1875 to celebrate the opening of the hotel, Louis Dupuy spoke these words to his invited guests (all men): "Gentlemen: I love these mountains and I love America, but you will pardon me if I bring into this community a remembrance of my youth and my country . . . My friends, if in after years someone comes and calls for Louis Dupuy, show them this little souvenier of Alençon which I built in America, and they will understand."

THE NEW YORK MUSEUM
HOUSE STORY

The late Richard Henry Dana, Jr., who designed this house in the late 1920's and the early 1930's for the New York Dames, was a traditionalist of unusual taste and talent; and, in doing this house, he performed a tour de force. It functions to perfection both as a museum and as a working-headquarters house in which the public rooms provide exquisite backgrounds for the rarest of 18th-century furnishings. Into the house itself and as elements of the various rooms, Mr. Dana skillfully quoted features from at least ten famous colonial houses.

The façade is his free translation of the house at 34 Wall Street, long since gone, that was lived in during the Revolution by a British commander, General Dodo Henry Knyphausen. The marble floor in the entrance hall he adapted from the one in the 1745 Nelson House in Yorktown, Virginia, and the fireplace and overmantel here he adapted from the 1740 John Marsh House in Wethersfield, Connecticut. The hall arch was inspired by the one in Carter's Grove, near Williamsburg; the stairs by the ones in the 1740 John Hancock House in Boston.

In the Queen Anne waiting room off the entrance hall (the architect's favorite), the pine chimney breast mantel and overmantel are an original English Chippendale example, brought from the Thompson House, Centerville, Maryland, which was built about 1760. The rest of the woodwork is not original, although much of the wood is old. The wallpaper is handpainted, called Bamboo and Morning Glory, c. 1760. The paper was made in England, painted in China and returned to England; it was originally in Hornby Castle, Yorkshire, which belonged to the Duke of Leeds.

In the second-floor hall, the door frames were fashioned after those in the Miles Brewton House in Charleston, South Carolina; and in the third floor hall the Palladian window that breaks the wall is a copy of the one at Mt. Airy in Virginia.

The rest is Mr. Dana's own interpretation of all that he felt was finest in 18th-century American interior treatments. Filling the rooms, and setting them off, are more treasures than there are pages here even to catalogue them. There is space for a mere taste, in the picture on the opposite page.

The great members' withdrawing room on the second floor,
illustrated here, with its repeating ends in which shell
niches flank the fireplace, is reminiscent in many details
of the stately interiors of the Pepperrell family mansions
at Kittery Point, Maine, c. 1740, while the cornice was copied from that in the Schuyler Mansion at Albany, New
York. The piecrust table, the Martin Van Buren wing chair,
Irish Chippendale tables and Karabagh rugs are notable.

Balancing the members' withdrawing room above is the
ballroom in the back, where a feature is the fine musicians'
gallery composition fashioned after that in the John Vassal
House in Cambridge, Massachusetts.

III

THE OLD POWDER MAGAZINE

Charles Fraser, chronicler of Charleston people and places between the Revolutionary and Civil wars, writes of poking around in the old Powder Magazine in about the year 1800 and finding a pair of full-length portraits "leaning face to face against the wall, with an old coach wheel pressing on them, and covered with dust."

The portraits turned out to be of that "stubborn dull" Queen Anne and of George I who succeeded her in 1714, oddly enough the year the Powder Magazine, as it stands today, was built. The supposition was that the portraits, like many other relics of Charleston Loyalists, were placed in the magazine at the outbreak of the Revolution by English sympathizers "to hide the evidence." A painter himself, Fraser judged the portraits to be the work of Sir Godfrey Kneller, who lived in London from 1675 to 1723 and was appointed court painter in 1688.

When Fraser came back to the magazine a few years later the heads and shoulders of both portraits had been cut from the canvases. Fraser himself then sliced a neat rectangle of canvas containing the Queen's hand resting on the crown of England, framed it, and presented it to Charles Manigault, then owner of the building, whose family used the magazine for many years as a wine cellar.

As architecture the ancient building is a curiosity, its forms inside and out possessing an aspect both medieval and modern. Fraser called it octagonal. Actually it is almost square, 32 feet by 35. Two gables fill each side of the hip roof, and the eight-gabled structure does give the impression of an octagon. The South Carolina Dames, who own it and maintain it as a museum, use it as their meeting place. As such, with its massively arched, cryptlike interior, it is probably unique.

It was built as part of the fortification system of early Charleston, and through somebody's oversight, or indifference, it was placed without permission on land belonging to one of the first settlers, named Buretell, whose grandsons, Ralph Izard and Nathaniel Broughton, in 1740 petitioned the King's Council "that the public had built a Magazine on their Lott by wich means the said lott and four other adjoining . . . were Intirely Rendered useless." The property, including the magazine, was later recovered by the family and maintained by them from after the Rev-

olution until the South Carolina Dames acquired it in 1901.

It was originally planned as protection against attacks of the French, Spanish, and Indians, who were an occasional threat until 1770, when its military use was discontinued. The Revolutionary War then reactivated the magazine until 1780, "when the town was closely invested by the British . . . and General Moultrie informs us," writes Fraser, "that a thirteen inch shell fell and burst within ten yards of it." After that occurrence the powder was removed to a "better place of safety," and following the evacuation of the British in December 1782, the building was returned to its private owners.

In the spaces between the vaulted ceiling and the tile roof tons of sand were packed to protect the powder. The English tile floor in the picture is a copy of that in St. Michael's Church around the corner. The heavy wrought-iron door was the original entrance. On the hanging lanterns the arms of sixteen Colonial governors of South Carolina are painted on the glass. Over the fine tambour Chippendale desk from England, of about 1780, hangs an early watercolor of Medway Plantation House, built in 1686 and the oldest house in South Carolina. The portrait here is of Sir Nathaniel Johnson, who was governor of the province when the Powder Magazine was built. The South Carolina Dames raised $500 to have it restored. A copy hangs in the Magazine.

ton had waited along Brandywine Creek near Chadd's Ford, Pennsylvania. Howe and Cornwallis had turned the American right flank, under General John Sullivan, and Washington had ordered a retreat to Chester. Leaving a holding force at Wilmington, Howe went on to take Philadelphia. This was to be Washington's worst winter—the one at Valley Forge.

After a larger new church was built beside it in 1840, the little Meeting House was used as a Sunday school, the boys meeting upstairs, the girls down. The last church service of any kind in it was held on January 17, 1878. The building was then rented to the Historical Society of Delaware, which used it for meetings and to house historical collections until the land was needed for the new public library. The little Meeting House then was moved out to Wilmington's Park Drive, where it became the headquarters of the Delaware Dames. Part of the restoration was the removal of the second floor, where the boys had had their Sunday school class—a great improvement, for now it is all a fine high-ceilinged downstairs room for the Dames.

THE FIRST PRESBYTERIAN MEETING HOUSE

Churches don't always remain houses of worship forever. Some get turned into schools, dwellings, art galleries, settlement houses; some get turned into theaters. As churches, they are ready for all emergencies. The British occupied Wilmington in Delaware after the Battle of the Brandywine on September 11, 1777, and used the little Presbyterian Meeting House as a hospital and prison for their American captives.

Before the battle, Howe's army had advanced on Philadelphia from Elkton, Maryland, where it had disembarked in the Chesapeake after sailing around from New York. Hopelessly outnumbered, Washing-

GADSBY'S TAVERN

"On May 27 [1749] . . . the *Maryland Gazette* announced that the lots in Alexandria [named after the
two brothers Alexander who owned most of the site]
would be sold to the highest bidders on the 13th of
July. To have all the parcels laid off by that time,"
as recounted by Freeman, "the regular Surveyor,
John West, Jr., most advantageously used young Mr.
Washington as an assistant. George worked fast. By
approximately the 17th of July, he had finished his
part of the survey and had drawn a plan of the
town." George was seventeen at the time, and a
seasoned surveyor.

On the second day of the sale, Charles Mason, a
tailor of the town, bought lot 45 (half an acre), and
by 1755 had opened a coffee house on the premises;
it was the smaller of the two connecting brick buildings now known together as Gadsby's Tavern which
ennoble North Royal Street at Academy. The larger
building on the corner was put up in 1792 as an
annex to the Coffee House, and was called the City
Hotel by the then owner, John Wise. In 1796 Wise
leased the whole property to a talented tavern-keep-
er from England named John Gadsby—a clever
move on Wise's part, for during the 12 years of
Gadsby's management the place became one of the
most popular, and expensive, dining establishments
in the country.

Alexandria had long been known for the stylishness
of its early houses contemporary with the Coffee
House, and its fame grew as street after street became filled with fine Federal houses of the City
Hotel period.

With Mount Vernon only a few miles away, Gadsby (and Wise before him) was host on countless occasions to George Washington, as when the *Gazette* reported in February 1798 that "Yesterday
we celebrated as the Birth Day of our fellow citizen,
George Washington. The day was ushered in by a
discharge of cannon. In the evening there was a
splendid ball at the City Tavern at which George
Washington was present."

Dorothy Kabler describes how "the General came
again to Gadsby's Tavern [that November] when he
stopped en route from Mount Vernon to Philadelphia.
The Independent Blues uniformed company met
him at the turnpike and accompanied him to the

old hostelry where he had dinner. His order was
canvas-back duck, hominy and madeira wine, with
a chafing dish on the table to keep the meal hot.
Following the meal, George Washington stood on
the steps of the large building while the Independent
Blues passed in review before him." His last cash-
book entries for expenses at Gadsby's are dated
April 5 and 30, 1799. In November he declined the
invitation to him and Mrs. Washington to take part
in the Winter Assemblies. "Thank you for this mark
of attention. But alas! Our dancing days are no
more." He died on December 14 at Mount Vernon.

To save it from threatened destruction, the beautiful ballroom was transplanted in 1917 to the Metro-

politan Museum, which also acquired the doorway from which Washington reviewed the Independent Blues. This doorway, however, was bought back from the museum in 1949 by Colonel Charles Beatty Moore and his wife, a Virginia Dame. And while all the organizations concerned with the restoration are listed in the Acknowledgments it may be of interest that what enabled the Alexandria Post of the American Legion, which owns the tavern, to pay off its indebtedness of $14,000, when the Department of the Interior, in 1929, refused to help, was a battery of slot machines in the basement.

THE OLD SCHOOL HOUSE

The most important name connected with the Old School House is that of John Woolman, a Quaker saint, but a wordly one, who was born here in Mount Holly in 1720 and died of smallpox on a pilgrimage to York, England, in 1772. For much of his life he did tailoring and shopkeeping from his house; he farmed his land; he became expert at writing wills and other legal documents. He could do simple doctoring, he taught school, and he kept a voluminous journal that was first edited by Whittier. Among his published works is *Some Considerations on the Keeping of Negroes.* When he was twenty-three he was recorded a minister by the Burlington Meeting, adding preaching to his other activities. He married Sarah Ellis in 1749.

In all his undertakings he devoted his life to a Gandhi-like godliness. He discouraged his customers from buying beyond their means; he would not draw up a will of a slaveholder who planned willing his slaves into further slavery. A passionate abolitionist, he traveled great distances, on foot and horseback, in attempts to make slaveholders see the evil of their ways.

When he taught school he taught it in the Old School House, then as sparkling new as it is sparkling old today. The school was built as a cooperative and altruistic enterprise on the part of 21 shareholders, who chipped in seven shillings and six pence per share when later on there was a stove to buy and repairs to be made.

It was the custom then for the schoolmaster to bill the child's parents every so often for his schooling: "To Schooling Thy child, seven shillings six pence."

Some parents paid the schoolmaster for the child's share of the firewood which Woolman brought in from his woodpile.

By his preaching, writings, and by word of mouth, Woolman was almost as well known in England as here, and, when suddenly in 1772 he was inspired to visit England (where there were slaveholders, too), there was nothing to do but go. Although he could well afford a cabin, he elected to travel steerage with the crew in the cold and wet. In England he didn't ride but walked from place to place in all weathers. He was asking too much of himself, and by the time he reached York he was in very bad shape. Fortunately, he stayed with affluent Quakers who could give him every care and comfort. Too weak to resist smallpox, however, he came down with the disease, and in a few days was dead.

In 1815, thirty-three years before public schools were open in Mount Holly, the surviving heirs of the twenty-one shareholders deeded the Old School House over to the Female Benevolent Society. It was that Society's altruistic plan to teach "in a public school [privately owned] all the poor children of Mount Holly and its Vicinity gratis." The building began to be called the "Free School House." In many other places at that time such a school was called a "pauper school." After 1848 the building was rented for use as a private school by a succession of various teachers, and once in a while was used by a neighboring public school for its overflow. Finally in 1951 the Female Benevolent Society presented the school to the New Jersey Dames for preservation and restoration—a fascinating and moving memorial to Woolman and those benevolent females of Mount Holly.

The arched ceiling follows the original line of the handhewn arched beams; the great fireplace was reconstructed from internal evidence. The crane came from a local farmhouse. On the schoolmaster's desk, beside the candlestick, are two wooden sanders for blotting sand, and an apple for the teacher. On the desks are blown glass inkwells, hornbooks, quill pens, and frameless slates. Among the early books is a schoolmaster's record book once used here, which rates pupils for "Alphabet in Sand, Writing on Slate, Writing on Paper, Reading on Boards [hornbooks perhaps], and Reading from the Bible."

THE OLD BARRACKS

"In time of war the rules and customs of war must govern." By this pronouncement, the Eaal of Loudoun, in command of His Majesty's forces in America for the Seven Year's War, from 1755 to 1763 "arbitrarily abrogated and rendered in effective the Mutiny Act." Among other things, this act provided that British soldiers should not be billeted with, or in any way forced on, private householders. Much to the consternation of Trenton residents, due to the leeway Loudoun had given the Mutiny Act, "soldiers were soon quartered largely in private houses of the town . . . Sometimes ten or fifteen were quartered in one small house." There were no organized American troops at the time.

Winter was the worst time for the citizens, for, because of the way these colonial wars were usually fought, the heavy fighting was done in the more favorable seasons, and winter became the big billeting time.

In *The Old Barracks at Trenton*, Alden T. Cottrell has a complaint brought forward by Joseph Yard, one of the prominent citizens of Trenton, which gives a graphic picture of the billeting practices, which disregarded all the rights of privacy.

The complaint reads in part that "Houses had been fixed upon in Trenton for such of His Majesty's Forces as should be quartered there; not withstanding, that a Captain of one of the Companies of the Said Forces came to his house with some soldiers in order to quarter one of these; which the said complainant refused, and requested to know his Authority, but the said Officer showed him only a list of the Inhabitants of the Town; and soon after, the said Officer taking a Musquet in his Hand, rushed against the said complainant and forced his Way into the House, and put in one of his Soldiers; who after some stay went away, leaving his Baggage; That towards the Evening of the same Day, an Officer came again to his House with a File of Musquetiers, in order to replace the said Soldier, under Pretence that he had been turned out with his Baggage; tho' no such Thing had been done, and told him he had sufficient authority from Lord Loudoun for what he did; and then said Officer went into every Room of said Complainants House, and then ordered one of his Serjeants to see that the soldier was lodged in a good Feather-Bed in the House or expect Punishement; and that in the Evening of the same Day a Serjeant came and brought another Soldier, and left in the House of this complainant."

"In March 1758 a series of petitions," Mr. Cottrell tells us, "was presented to the legislature setting forth the evils of the situation and suggesting 'the building of barracks.'" A committee was appointed to report on the matter, recommending that barracks to house 300 men each be built not only at Trenton, but also at Burlington, Elizabeth, New Brunswick, and Amboy.

The report was accepted, and in May work began on the Trenton barracks. "The building was constructed of native undressed stone," as described by Mr. Cottrell, "two stories in height with cellars under the whole and covered with a shingle roof projecting over the balcony which extended out from the second floor around the entire court. The building was plastered throughout and contained open fireplaces.

"Kitchens were provided in the basement of the south wing and the entire property enclosed by a wooden fence. It was completed in December 1758. During this month an addition two-and-a-half stories high was erected at the east end of the north wing to be used exclusively by commissioned officers . . .

"The original sum of £1400 approved for each of the five barracks was found to be insufficient and subsequent appropriations were made so that ultimately £2600 was appropriated for each one. The final accounts for building and furnishing were all rendered and approved in November 1760, except for those at Trenton. These accounts were not finally settled until April 1764. They included £385 and 16s paid by the State Treasury to the officer Severns, a Commissioner whose vouchers could not be checked because he had 'absconded the province' . . . .

"Joseph Yard was made one of the Barrackmasters at Trenton, whose duty it was to keep the buildings and furniture in order and the troops supplied with 'wood, candles, vinegar, salt, and other necessaries'.

"These supplies were distributed in accordance with a very definite and exacting schedule. The commanding officer, chaplain, surgeon, and each captain were entitled to receive a weekly allowance of half a cord of wood; the subalterns (sergeants) and every twelve men half a cord of wood weekly between October 1 and May 1 and one-quarter cord for the remaining period of the year. The guard room was entitled to double the allowance of the subalterns. Each man was entitled to two gills of vinegar weekly, four pints of 'small beer' were allowed daily and, in place

of beer, molasses could be substituted. Although at first the Barrackmasters were limited to an annual expenditure of £300, this limit was later removed and they were given discretionary powers in the amounts to be drawn annually from the treasury for supplies . . .

"The first troops of the British Army to occupy the Old Barracks were part of the Inniskilling Regiment of Foot composed almost exclusively of Irishmen. There were about 700 men in the regiment and when they were quartered in New Jersey beginning in early November 1758, they were divided between Trenton and Burlington. The regimental uniform was scarlet with facings of blue and racoonskin caps."

After the close of the War in 1763 the Barrackmasters were directed to sell the furnishings and rent the buildings, but this didn't work too well. The cost of keeping the buildings in repair was greater than the income from rent. The outbreak of the Revolution, however, did away with that difficulty.

First it was filled with British prisoners of war, then with Colonial troops. For two short weeks, when Trenton was in British hands, it quartered the Hessian mercenaries, most of whom were taken prisoner by Washington in the Battle of Trenton. From then until the end of the Revolution it was constantly being occupied by American troops passing through Trenton.

Of the five barracks originally built, only the Trenton Barracks remain standing today. After the close of the Revolution the barracks were sold and the barrack rooms divided into private apartments, which resulted in considerable deterioration. That they are

standing and handsomely restored is largely due to Mrs. Beulah A. Oliphant, who in 1899 organized a committee of women called the Purchase Fund Committee, which raised the money to buy the south wing of the building from the Trenton Society for the Relief of Respectable Aged Widows and Single Women, who had occupied it for almost fifty years.

It was Chancellor Edwin Robert Walker who in 1911 suggested that the building exterior be restored to its original state. It is owned by the State of New Jersey, and is in the custody of the Old Barracks Association. In it the New Jersey Dames have their headquarters.

While the interior now consists of many rooms handsomely furnished (by other patriotic organizations in addition to the Dames), and museum rooms of priceless Revolutionary relics, none of the original barracks aspects within are left.

In the dining room furnished by the New Jersey Dames, the table is a walnut Chippendale of 1760. The matched pair of side chairs are Chippendale, of 1765, as is the third chair; while the fourth, against the wall, is considered by authorities to be the work of Eliphalet Chapin. Under the 1765 Chippendale looking glass of mahogany and gilt is a Queen Anne style table of 1710-1720. Notable among the silver and china in the cupboard is a cream pitcher of the 1790's (fourth shelf from the top)' made by Abner Reeder, a well-known New Jersey silversmith who worked right here in Trenton.

THE LITTLE CEDAR GROVE CHURCH

Oxen with their cloven hoofs provided a time-honored technique for kneading clay before it was ready to be molded and baked into bricks. It was a trick brought from North Carolina by the settlers of southeastern Indiana when William Henry Harrison was Governor of the Territory. It was in 1811, just at the time of Harrison's fight at Tippecanoe (in northwest Indiana) with the famous Tecumseh's brother, the Shawnee Prophet, that the Little Cedar Grove Church was built of bricks made in that fashion. The War of 1812 was about to break out, and not far from the church Harrison's troops would soon be marching north along the Ohio line to their victory at the Battle of the Thames above Detroit, in which Tecumseh himself was killed.

When the present church was built, it replaced an earlier one of logs which had long been outgrown. The fact that a series of earthquakes that same year had shaken the neighborhood has given some grounds for the story that this occurrence caused the speeding-up of the construction by putting the fear of God into the hearts of the congregation.

A few Indians were still about, and this, in turn, has given rise to a less likely legend that the church was heated by a charcoal fire in an open pit in front of the pulpit, so there wouldn't be smoke to call the attention of hostile Indians to the fact that services were being held. The trouble with the story is that the unvented fumes would be more deadly than the Indians.

The truth is that the church stands as its own story. If it hasn't made history, it has seen a lot of history being made, and in that sense *is* history. Other churches, holding larger congregations than the hundred and sixty people who crowded into this one, were being built of bricks made by machinery and of timbers not hewn by hand. This one for a while was used only once a year, and after the Civil War it was never used again as a church. In 1912

corner of the old village common. It is not surprising that many members of the present community are descendants of the emigrants from Massachusetts.

The emigration took place in 1805. Three small parties were sent ahead, the first in March to plant corn, the second in May to start building a gristmill, a sawmill, and cabins, and the third in June to survey the land for settlement. The main groups went out in the fall, in five installments, spaced far enough apart to avoid overburdening the overnight facilities, such as they were, en route. It was a six- to seven-weeks' trip, the pace being set by the heavy farm wagons drawn by oxen.

From Granville, near the Connecticut border, the wagon trains and horseback riders struck out at oxen speed across the northern Connecticut counties; went down the Housatonic to the Fish Kill road, ferrying across the Hudson to Fort Edwards where Washington had his headquarters; then moved across northern New Jersey to Easton, Pennsylvania, and on to Harrisburg, beyond which they picked up the well-traveled Philadelphia-Pittsburgh highway to Washington, Pennsylvania; then traveled on to Wheeling and Zanesville, and finally to the site of the new Granville, their home-to-be.

it was bought by the Brookville Historical Society, which saved its life, and since then the restoration has been made complete, due in large part to the Indiana Dames.

SAINT LUKE'S CHURCH, GRANVILLE, OHIO

About the year 1800 a population explosion took place in and around the town of Granville, Massachusetts. The number of children being born was out of line with the local food-producing resources, and when the town count, normally less than a thousand, reached 2,309 in 1800, it created a crisis in the community. What saved the situation was a mass emigration to the newly opened Ohio country. In a few years the population was down to 1,500 and today Granville is a thriving village of several hundred.

Granville, Ohio, with a population of about 3,000, could easily be mistaken today for a New England town, and a charming one both by the lay of the land and the looks of its very New England-ish architecture, typified by Saint Luke's Church on one

There was more corn than they could eat, though the gristmill, sawmill, and cabins were still not ready. But the lots were laid out; the choice ones were for sale, and the others were to be free. If the settlers didn't get just what they wanted at first, they could always swap. And, while they were an intensely religious lot, they didn't overlook the fact that the extra corn could be turned into whiskey. In fact, distilling became the first important industry.

These settlers from New England were all Congregationalists, and it wasn't until 1823 that a schism in the church led to a division into two congregations: Presbyterian and Episcopal, and to the building in 1837 of the Episcopal Saint Luke's. This break occurred when the Congregational minister, Ahab Jinks, gave permission to his contractor, Lucius Mowrer, to lay bricks at the parsonage on a Sunday. The Episcopalians went along with the practical-minded Ahab, and when it came time to build Saint Luke's, it was Mr. Mowrer's contribution of $2,000 which gave the big push to the project. The total cost was $7,200, which included a 1,000-pound bell, an $850 organ, and a $100 chandelier.

It was a thriving parish for the first twenty-five years, then in 1863, when the Granville Female Seminary, with 140 Episcopal students, moved to Mansfield, a long twilight period began. Saint Luke's hobbled along, sometimes using lay readers and sometimes being closed with nobody to preach. Then in 1930, the Ohio Dames completely restored the church, and it is again a growing and prosperous parish, thanks to the Dames and to Mr. Jinks's letting the men lay bricks on a Sunday. As Ahab tried to explain to his congregation, winter was coming on, and if the bricklayers didn't work seven days a week, the wet mortar would start freezing and the parsonage would have to be put off until spring.

THE SHAWNEE MISSION

"They were all on horseback, and although they had blankets they had laid them aside as they rode along, and were naked when they arrived. One especially was an object of interest. He was a fine looking boy,

ten or twelve years old, well proportioned, and his whole estate, real and personal, was a red string of the thickness of his finger tied round his waist, He was an orphan, and the missionary bought him from his friends. The price was one blanket."

Thus a visitor at the Shawnee Mission in April, 1841, describes the arrival at the Mission of a party of Indian boys, accompanied by two Kansas chiefs (fully dressed in Indian garb) and a man from the mission.

"The boys were soon dressed," the visitor went on to say, "and appeared quite pleased with their new home; but, poor fellows, when it came to dressing themselves the next morning, they were at their wits end; for, when discovered, they were busily engaged in arranging their pantaloons, wrong side out, and the forepart behind. The next thing was to give them names. This done we all repaired to the dining room for breakfast."

In 1841, the mission consisted of the west building, built in 1839 to be the superintendent's quarters and dining hall, and the east building, just being completed the year the Indian boys arrived. This became the boys' dormitory. The north building, to be the girls' dormitory, was completed in 1845. Shops and farm buildings were part of the establishment during the days of the mission's activity which ended in 1862. But these three are the only ones still standing; all three are now restored and are administered by the Kansas State Historical Society, which in 1939 published a chronology of the mission compiled by Martha B. Caldwell, whose researches are responsible for much of the history set forth here.

In the introduction to this chronology, the then secretary of the Society provides the background by explaining that "Nearly all the early missions in Kansas were a result of the removal of Eastern Indians into the territory, beginning about 1825. The most important is the one we now somewhat incorrectly call the Old Shawnee Missions among the Shawnees. It was a Methodist mission established in 1830 by the Rev. Thomas Johnson near Chouteau's trading post, not far from the present town of Turner in Wyandotte county. It became outstanding because of the Shawnee manual labor school organized with money received from the church and from the federal government.

"In 1839 Johnson began building on the present site in Johnson county, and the school became an establishment of two thousand acres, containing three large brick school buildings and thirteen smaller buildings, with an enrollment of nearly two hundred Indian boys and girls. For years it was an outpost of civilization on the Western frontier. The Santa Fe and Oregon trails passed near its doors. Many of the great figures of the old West were entertained here. In 1854 it became the executive offices of the first governor of the territory of Kansas. The legislature convened here to pass the first terri-

torial laws. It was the scene of many conflicts between Antislavery and Proslavery parties. During the Civil War the buildings were barracks for Union troops and in 1864 a battle was fought across the mission fields."

According to Nyle Miller, speaking as secretary of the Society in 1964, "the Rev. Johnson was a very fine citizen, a good missionary, in fact considered one of the best of the many who came to Kansas in those days. His establishment, Shawnee Mission, was the largest and best organized and had the largest enrollment of any of the missions."

It was Johnson's habit, in making his visits to the various other missions, to scatter Kentucky bluegrass seed from his saddle bags as he rode along. It was his bride who rode the horse in 1830 when he came to his first Shawnee Mission, while he walked alongside.

Johnson insisted on a firm regime. "The whole school retired to bed, as a general regulation, at 8 p.m. and rose at the ringing of the large bell at 4 a.m. There were three meals a day, and the whole school and all connected with it ate at the same time at two long tables that would accommodate nearly two hundred persons."

Assembly for meals followed a pattern just as strict. "The signal . . . was given by the ringing of a bell that was fixed upon the top of the dining hall. At its sound, the Indian boys and girls formed in line in front of their quarters, the east building, the boys leading; and, upon entering the dining room, the boys took their places at one table, the girls at another, and the whites at another. Then, all standing, Mr. Johnson, with his knife handle struck the table three times for silence preceding the blessing, then one rap to be seated. At the close of the meal, he again struck the table once and the boys filed out, and the girls followed; then, arising himself all passed out. At the morning and evening meals, however, the single rap was the signal for prayer, all kneeling."

The best description of the school is contained in a letter from one of the teachers in 1850. "I am much pleased with the school. The girls are perfectly quiet and easily managed. They were never known to sauce a teacher and are quite affectionate and kind, harmless and playful. The male school is taught by two young gentlemen.

"I live in a stately brick house that has thirteen rooms, all very conveniently arranged. I have a very neat room with window blinds and nicely carpeted floor and as nice a stand and as good a bed as I ever wish to have."

Johnson was caught in the middle on the slavery issue. A Southerner, he was sent out by the Missouri Conference of the Methodist Episcopal Church, so, as the President of the Kansas Dames points out, "It was quite natural that the should be pro-slavery and own many slaves of his own. And since Shawnee Mission was established in Kansas just a mile west of the Missouri—Kansas border, it was in an environment more pro-slavery than anti-slavery."

Johnson moved his home in 1857 from the west building at the mission closer into town to a "fine old Southern colonial house with side-lights and fan-lights at the front door."

In 1861 Lincoln was inaugurated, the war began, and the following year the mission was suspended. Then at midnight on January 2, 1865, Johnson heard some men calling from the front yard. From the doorway, he could hardly see them in the shadow of the trees. They asked the way into Kansas City, While he was giving them directions, they rushed at him, but he got inside and locked the door, only to have them fire at him through the door. A bullet through one of the sidelights caught him, and before his wife could get to his side, he was dead. He was buried southeast of the mission buildings in the mission burial ground.

THE 18th-CENTURY ILLINOIS HOUSE

"*New France* (as the French now claim) extends from the Mouth of the River *Mississippi*, to the Mouth of the River *St. Lawrence*, by which the French plainly show their intention of enclosing the *British Settlements*, and cutting us off with the numerous Nations of *Indians*, that are every where settled over the vast Continent of *North-America*."

That is how Cadwallader Colden, Surveyor General of New York, sized up the situation in 1724, and while the French penetration caused considerable trouble to the English colonies at times, it had defects that doomed it to fail, and by 1763 it had in fact failed completely. In Illinois, for instance, where it probably gained a greater foothold than

anywhere else north of New Orleans, hardly a trace of the penetration remains today. A restoration or two, a few French names, but nothing else, which makes the typical Illinois French *habitation*, faithfully reconstructed and furnished at the Chicago Historical Society, such a vivid memento of the days when French was the white man's language in the whole Illinois country.

These houses made ideal dwellings for the French settlers in their frontier villages. Their components were all light in weight and easily assembled. The walls were made of cedar posts planted upright, not quite touching, and filled between from floor level to roof with a mixture of mud-clay and chopped straw, called *bousillage* or *pierrotage*. The system was essentially the same as that used in the somewhat later and ever-so-much-larger Bolduc House at Ste. Genevieve, described earlier, where the components, by comparison, are extremely heavy. These little French settlers' houses were designed to be quick and easy to build.

The steeply pitched part of the roof was a cap to cover the house walls. The more flatly pitched part sheltered the porch, or *galerie*, that surrounded the house to provide weather protection for the house walls, as well as warm-weather shade. The houses stood well off the ground, and because of their cedar-post construction required no conventional foundations and adapted readily to the irregularities of the site.

If the French penetration had been as well thought out as the *habitations*, there might conceivably

have been a different story to tell. The tight and arbitrary supervision that Louis XIV and his ministers exerted over the daily lives of their subjects in New France placed the French settlers in an almost ridiculous situation. They were told by the government in France which crops to grow, and how to grow them. They were forced to follow French tradition in everything they did. If a settler wanted to erect a dovecote outside his door he practically had to get permission from Versailles. The French settlers had no freedom to adapt themselves to their new environment: the English settlers along the seaboard took such freedom as a matter of course.

Another problem for the French penetration was the distance from the mouth of the St. Lawrence or the mouth of the Mississippi to, say, the settlements of the Illinois country. How was it possible in any practical way to protect 1,500 or more miles of the waterway-overland route via the St. Lawrence and the Great Lakes, or, for that matter, the Mississippi? The forts the French built were, for the most part, flimsy affairs, the garrisons wretchedly equipped, and the discipline of the soldiers deplorable. And finally, how could the French fail to foresee the inevitability of the seaboard colonies expanding and exploding over the mountains and occupying the Mississippi valley as soon as it became expedient?

The soldiers were recruited from a very simple and uneducated class. They frequently were not paid. As a result, they often took to the woods to earn a little money from trapping and trading and

to join in the life of the Indian tribes. But it is generally conceded that the French handled the Indians far better than the British, and remained unconquered by the British in the Illinois country for this very reason. The commandants, with a few exceptions, were very brave. It is quite a miracle that they managed to hold the Mississippi River region for a hundred years with only a handful of soldiers and little help from home.

The feats of French exploration are among the great American epics, the operations of their fur traders are still among our favorite tales, the *voyageurs* were perhaps the most picturesque personalities in the whole history of New France, and houses like the *habitation* here were strokes of frontier genius. But the penetration itself never reached the point of true colonization. It may not be too much of an oversimplification to say that at best it had elements of a beautiful adventure.

THE DENVER ROOMS

When the fine brick house built by Joseph Russell in Providence in 1772 was being torn down in the 1930's, its paneling had four separate buyers. The Brooklyn Museum got the first-floor living room and the staircase, the Minneapolis Art Museum and the Museum of the Rhode Island School of Design got the rooms they wanted, and one of the Rhode Island Dames had the good fortune and judgment to buy the full-paneled drawing room, the half-paneled dining room, the stately arched entrance hall, and the stair hall with its Palladian window on the landing. The first three purchases were installed in their respective museums and the Rhode Island Dame's paneling was stored away in the loft of her mother's barn.

Russell built his house at 114 North Main Street where he could keep an eye on his ships, which were in the rich East Indies trade. As Antoinette Downing observes in her *Early Homes of Rhode Island* it "was one of the first Providence mansions to reflect the true Georgian style." It was square, three-storied, and had a low hipped roof with a small balustrated summit and a splendid Corinthian doorway taken verbatim from Plate XXXVI in Batty Langley's *Compleat Builder's Assistant* (London, 1738), one of the most popular handbooks (it went through four editions) for 18th-century master builders, both here and in England.

It was a very stylish old house they tore down, and it was a happy thing that at least the paneling of the rooms, which were as stylish as they come, could be preserved, distributed now among museums in New York, Rhode Island, Minnesota and—Colorado. For in 1946 the Colorado Dames decided they would like to install a suite of Colonial rooms in the Denver Art Museum; and, to make a long story short, they finally heard about the Russell rooms in the loft of the Rhode Island Dame's mother's barn, and were able to buy them. And as the Brooklyn Museum wasn't using the staircase, the Colorado Dames were able to buy that too.

It is a stunning suite of rooms, restored and fitted with extraordinary skill and patience (it took two years) by a deaf-mute master craftsman named Joseph Wilkes, employed by the museum. The furniture and furnishings, largely donated by the Dames, their friends, and friends of the museum, are as fine as the rooms; altogether it is one of the most important Colonial settings and collections to have been transported west of the Mississippi.

Connected with the Colonial Suite are an early 19th-century bedroom and an 18th-century kitchen, both reproductions, but with authentic furnishing of the periods. And a fascinating extension is the cabinetmaker's Sample Room, with original paneling from Connecticut, and containing the outstanding Stacey Collection of the small scale-model furniture which cabinetmakers' salesmen used in the old horse-

and-buggy travel days as samples from which customers could order the full-size originals. All in all, one of the Dames's most entertaining cultural contributions in the country.

As was customary in the great Providence houses of the period, a flat arch made an architectural separation between the entrance hall in front and the stair hall in back. Ordinarily supported by brackets, the arch here is supported by engaged columns, all integrated with the dentilled cornice. The stairs, with their twisted Chippendale balusters, consist of two runs and a landing; the landing is lit and decorated by a large Palladian window. The settee is Hepplewhite, about 1780; the Queen Anne chair dates from about 1740; and the tall clock under the landing was built by Randolph Storm in Lancaster, Pennsylvania, in 1790.

In the half-paneled Russell dining room, the portrait of Sir John Erskine, the famous 18th-century professor of Scots law at the University of Edinburgh, is by John Singleton Copley; the mahogany dining table and chairs are English, about 1780; the wine cooler is English, about 1770. Also late 18th-century are the side table, the English bracket clock, the English brass chandelier, the American Hepplewhite mahogany sideboard, and the Lowestoft fruit bowl.

THE 18th-CENTURY DRAWING ROOM IN SEATTLE

In 1791 Commander George Vancouver, with his lieutenant Peter Puget, set out from England to survey and explore the northwest coast of America. He came by way of the Cape of Good Hope, Australia, New Zealand, Tahiti, and the Hawaiian Islands, following pretty much the course he had taken in 1776 with Captain Cook on Cook's unsuccessful venture to find a passage through to the Atlantic. Vancouver arrived off the coast in 1792 and stayed until 1795. He charted all the important approaches, including the course to the Straits of Georgia and Juan de Fuca, on either side of Vancouver Island (named after him) and leading into Puget Sound (named after his lieutenant). He made a landing at Restoration Point, so named then to commemorate King Charles' restoration to the throne.

It was during the days of Vancouver's explorations

around Seattle that most of the furniture now in the Washington Dames' 18th-century drawing room in the Seattle Art Museum was being used by American families along the eastern seaboard; much of it had been brought from England by the colonists.

The portrait above the mantel, painted by Copley, is of General Cadwallader Colden, whose somber words about the Franch menace introduced the story of the Illinois Dames' 18th-century French exhibit. Flanking it can be seen one each of a pair of hurricane sidelamps and Chinese Export birds. The Sheraton style fire-screen, with three-way extensions, is about 1790. The Chippendale wing chair, with its gout stool, is about 1760. The portrait by Joseph Badger (1708-1765) of Mary Greenough is paired with one of her sister Elizabeth on the right-hand side of the rare Chippendale style cabinet of about 1760.

CHARLESTON IN CINCINNATI

In about 1942 the late Duchesse de Talleyrand-Perigord née Lela Emery of Cincinnati, came into the possession of the drawing-room woodwork from a Charleston, South Carolina, house that had been torn down. Oddly enough, the dealer from whom the duchess bought the room had never been able to identify the house. Nor have any Charlestonians. Even Samuel G. Stoney, author of *Plantations of the Carolina Low Country*, the best-informed low-country historian, and an architect as well, had been unable, as of early 1965, to locate the house. The nearest Mr. Stoney had come was that the house stood in the vicinity of Mazyck and Beaufain Streets, and its date was "very close to 1820."

At any rate, the duchess turned the woodwork over to the Cincinnati Art Museum, which stored it away until 1957, when the room was reconstructed by the Ohio Dames under the museum's direction. The furnishing was a joint undertaking of the Dames and the museum. Two plans of procedure were considered. The first, endorsed by a well-known authority, proposed furnishings of the American Federal period, 1780 to 1810. A second authority on restoration held that "furniture and accessories too closely related in date tend to lose the semblance of reality," and suggested the use of furniture representing a longer period of acquisition, since many families undoubtedly continued to preserve inherited pieces along with their own purchases. This latter plan made sense, and became the plan which was followed.

The Queen Anne style walnut wing chair dates from about 1720. The rug is a Herat of the early 17th century. The mahogany chest of drawers with ball-and-claw feet and the American bird-cage table both date from 1760-1780. The Washington is the Rembrandt Peale "port hole" portrait. The side chairs are Connecticut Chippendale, and the armchair and mirror are Philadelphia pieces. The urns and the porcelain in the corner cupboard are Chinese Export, the tea set is Worcester, and the ball-shaped kettle is by Richard Bayley, London 1736.

THE EARLY WEST IN OMAHA

It was the day after Christmas in 1854. The Acting Governor of Nebraska Territory opened a letter from the Surveyor General's Office in Washington, asking in effect: where *is* Omaha? and please to circle it on the map, as well as any other villages there

may be. One was Bellevue, a few miles down the Missouri from the settlement of Omaha. Bellevue had been made the territorial capital October 16, the day the ailing Samuel Burt of South Carolina had taken office. But in two weeks Burt was dead. The territorial secretary, according to law, took over as Acting Governor, and on December 20 moved the capital to Omaha, where it stayed until Lincoln was made the capital when Nebraska became a state in 1867. Today Bellevue has a population of about 9,000 as against Omaha's 350,000—the Acting Governor's choice.

The Acting Governor was Thomas B. Cuming, a bright young man from Michigan, who was twenty-five when he was appointed territorial secretary by President Pierce. He became Acting Governor again in 1857, just in time to prevent the capital from being moved to nearby Florence, which has long since been swallowed up by Omaha. And he was Acting Governor once again, in 1858, when he died.

About a year after Cuming brought his bride to the Territory in a covered wagon, he built what has been described as a little Gothic cottage, one of the first in Omaha, and in a window facing the Missouri the young couple lit a copper lantern every night to lead travelers across the river. The next year a man named Charles W. Hamilton arrived from New York in Omaha by mistake. He had meant to go to St. Paul, but he took the wrong boat. He married the sister of Cuming's wife, became president of the United States Bank, and survived his brother-in-law by thirty-eight years. In striking contrast to Hamilton's peaceful progression from bookkeeping to financial prosperity, Cuming's brief career in Omaha was packed with pioneer political turbulence. It had barely begun before it was over.

Now in the rose marble Joslyn Memorial Art Museum, as part of a fascinating permanent Early West Exhibit, sponsored and supported by the Nebraska Dames and covering the Omaha century from 1852 to 1952, a Cuming-Hamilton Room contains furni-

ture and other possessions of the two connected families, including the copper lantern from the Cumings' cottage.

The exhibit continues with a lively collection of architectural fragments from early Victorian cottages like the Cumings', giving the visitor a glimpse into the background of later Victorian elegance, with photographic enlargements of the Balbach and Redick mansions, whose owners helped make Omaha history.

Judge John I. Redick in particular, who lived until 1906, and who figured in the famous affair of the Omaha Claim Club in 1856, while Cuming was still alive, makes early Omaha come to life.

Dissatisfied with the Government's limit of 160 acres to be entered by one man, the Claim Club members organized to defend their right to enter twice that amount of land. Whatever the legal reasoning behind the club's strategy, and whatever the misunderstanding was which caused the Claim Club to call a meeting to denouce what they called Redick's "treasonable language against the Club," Redick decided to attend the meeting.

"I laid in a revolver that day," Redick recounts, "loaded it, and put it in my pocket. The meeting was held in The Pioneer Block, and the first speech was made by A.S. Hanscom, the president . . . in a very reasonable, moderate way. He was followed by Michell, of Florence . . . very abusive of new people . . . coming in to break down local institutions. Then a man from Bellevue . . . followed by John M. Thayer . . . in a tone similar to that of Michell . . . Thereupon I came to the front, and for ten minutes I dwelt upon the advantages of the Territory of Nebraska . . . its glorious future . . . and that I had had no intention to reflect upon the Club . . . that I had not been correctly reported. I added that I knew every man present was at least an ordinarily brave man, and with that I produced my revolver . . . took out my watch . . . and said, 'I denouce the man who has thus misrepresented me, as a liar, coward

and sneak, and will give him one minute to come out and face me.' As the time ticked off, no one moved, and when I announced that the time had expired, there was a burst of applause, and I was convinced that I had nothing to fear."

A ROOM FOR ANTOINE LECLAIRE

In a series of permanent historical exhibits at the Davenport Public Museum there is a room devoted to Antoine LeClaire, born 1797, died 1861. Dominating the room filled with his personal possessions is the portrait of LeClaire which plainly pictures both his physical immensity and the power of his personality. He kept track of his weight. In 1844, at forty-seven, he weighed 385 pounds; in 1849 he was down to 368; and a year later he had shrunk to 355. His height was five feet eight.

He was the natural son of a French-Canadian

blacksmith and a Potawatami Indian woman. It is said that he could speak fourteen Indian languages, in addition to English, French, and Spanish. He spoke English with a French accent.

As a young man he became in a sense a protegé of William Clark, of Lewis and Clark fame, who was U.S. Commissioner of Indian Affairs as well as Governor of Missouri Territory, and who saw to Antoine's education. By the time he was twenty-one, he was a government interpreter among the Indians. He attracted the trust and friendship of all the tribes to such a remarkable degree that his success as a negotiator was unequalled, and so grateful was the Sauk tribe for all the good advice Antoine had given them, and all the good faith he had shown, that, in drawing up the treaty between the tribe and the United States authorities in 1832, the Sauk tribe insisted that it be allowed to insert a token of the respect, gratitude, and affection the tribe held for LeClaire. In the treaty this token took the form of a square mile of land where Davenport stands today, another square mile where the city of LeClaire now stands, and still another square mile (for Mrs. LeClaire) where part of the city of Moline is today across the Mississippi in Illinois.

LeClaire's potency as a promoter and proprietor turned out to be even more impressive than his skill as a negotiator, with the result that his square miles of unimproved land turned into towns and then into cities, and he and his partner, George Davenport, grew to be very rich men indeed. LeClaire would have been richer if he had been able to curb his runaway generosity. Partly because of this particular trait, he became by far the most popular figure in this whole frontier region.

When the railroad, whose coming he had probably done more than most to make possible, came through, the first locomotive bore the name "Antoine LeClair" in large gold letters. On one side of the engine was a bust of LeClaire; on the other a bust of Pocahontas. And when the Iowa State Bank put out paper currency in various denominations, the five-dollar bills bore the likeness of Antoine LeClaire.

In the crash of 1859, as banks and businesses failed, LeClaire, now the richest man of the community, tried to bolster his friends' finances with his own, and, while he was able to stem the bankruptcies, the strain was physically too much for a man of his obesity. He had already had one stroke. Now he had another, and this one was fatal.

"Davenport has never seen a ceremony more imposing than that with which the first settler was buried," the paper reported. "Business was almost suspended, and the sidewalks crowded with spectators, as the body of the man who had been seen in the streets almost every day for thirty years was carried in solemn procession to its long home."

THE BENNINGTON MUSEUM LIBRARY
A Postscript

Anybody who has just been writing a book that tries to relate certain houses and other landmarks and arrangements to their places in history, and to the people concerned, will be keenly aware of the various sources to which he has gone to get his information. Letters, diaries, memoirs, newspaper files, local records, and the sites themselves have given him a more intimate, vivid, and flavorsome notion than anything else of the people, places, and happenings he has been trying to describe. Encyclopedias of various kinds which could be kept at hand have constantly gotten him started and kept him going. Histories, biographies, genealogies, pictures, and maps have been an essential part of his sustenance. And because libraries could make almost all of these things available, libraries have been his greatest blessing.

It is appropriate that such a book should close with a library—a historical library at that, one that the Dames—the Dames of Vermont—have furnished and that they help to maintain.

Good old Vermont! When the Continental Congress in 1776 refused to recognize her as the 14th colony or state, she simply proclaimed her own independence (calling herself New Connecticut but gradually being known as Vermont). She performed all the offices of a sovereign government She coined her own money, set up her own post offices, naturalized her own new citizens, and appointed her own ambassadors. There was even talk for a time of annexing herself to Canada. Finally, however, in 1791, she entered the Union, on her own terms, becoming, as she had wanted to be fourteen years before, the 14th state.

The library is part of the Bennington Museum, an important fixture of the famous old town, with an attendance in 1964 of 65,000. Among the 4,000 volumes in the library there are, of course, many on American history, a large section devoted to genealogy and family history, files of the Vermont *Gazette*, published in Bennington from 1783 to 1879, a section containing a large collection of Vermontiana, and myriad local and state records from the far past to the present, all on open shelves. Handsomely and comfortably furnished, it is a charming little paradise for the writer, the student, the researcher, and the delver in pedigrees. It couldn't be a better place with which to end a book—*this* book.

HOUSE LOCATIONS

ALABAMA

The Fort Condé-Charlotte House
104 Theatre Street
Mobile

ARKANSAS

The Noland House
214 East Third Street
Little Rock

CALIFORNIA

The Hugo Reid Adobe
Los Angeles State and County
    Arboretum
301 North Baldwin Avenue
Arcadia

The Octagon House
2645 Gough Street
San Francisco

COLORADO

The McAllister House
423 North Cascade Avenue
Colorado Springs

The Providence Colonial Rooms
Denver Art Museum
1343 Acoma Street
Denver

The Hotel De Paris
Georgetown

CONNECTICUT

The Wethersfield Houses

    The Webb House
    211 Main Street
    Wethersfield

    The Deane House
    203 Main Street
    Wethersfield

    The Stevens House
    215 Main Street
    Wethersfield

DELAWARE

The First Presbyterian Meeting
    House
Park Drive
Wilmington

DISTRICT OF COLUMBIA

Dumbarton House
2715 Q Street, N.W.
Washington

FLORIDA

The Ximenez Fatio House
20 Aviles Street
St. Augustine

GEORGIA

The Andrew Low House
329 Abercorn Street
Savannah

ILLINOIS

The 18th Century French Illinois
    House
Chicago Historical Society
North Avenue at Clark Street
Chicago

The Lincoln House
Corner of Eighth & Jackson Streets
Springfield

INDIANA

The Little Cedar Grove Church
Route 52
Brookville

The Harmonist House
New Harmony

IOWA

The Antoine LeClaire Exhibit
Davenport Public Museum
1717 West 12th Street
Davenport

Plum Grove
Iowa City

KANSAS

The Shawnee Mission
Shawnee

KENTUCKY

Liberty Hall
Corner West Main & Wilkinson
    Streets
Frankfort

The Orlando Brown House
Wapping & Wilkinson Streets
Frankfort

LOUISIANA

The Little Red Brick House
520 South Grand Street
Monroe

The Pontalba Apartments
532 St. Peter Street
New Orleans

Oakley
Audubon Memorial Park
St. Francisville

MAINE

The Tate House
1270 Westbrook Street
Portland

MARYLAND

Mount Clare
Carroll Park
Baltimore

MASSACHUSETTS

55 Beacon Street
Boston

The Martin House
Stony Hill Road
Swansea

The Plymouth Memorial
Plymouth

The Quincy Homestead
34 Butler Road
Quincy

KANSAS

The Shawnee Mission
Shawnee

MINNESOTA

The Ramsey House
265 South Exchange Street
St. Paul

MISSISSIPPI

The Oaks
823 North Jefferson Street
Jackson

Evansview
107 South Broadway
Natchez

MISSOURI

The Bolduc House
U.S. Route 61
Ste. Genevieve

The Campbell House
1508 Locust Street
St. Louis

NEBRASKA

The Early West Exhibit
Joslyn Art Museum
2218 Dodge Street
Omaha

NEW HAMPSHIRE

The Moffatt-Ladd House
154 Market Street, West
Portsmouth

NEW JERSEY

The Old School House
Brainard Street
Mount Holly

The Old Barracks
South Willow Street on State
    House Grounds
Trenton

NEW YORK

The New York Headquarters
215 East 71st Street
New York

The Van Cortlandt House
Van Cortlandt Park
New York

NORTH CAROLINA

The Joel Lane House
728 West Hargett Street
Raleigh

The Burgwin-Wright House
224 Market Street
Wilmington
and
St. Philip's Church
U.S. Route 17
Brunswick

The Fourth House
450 South Main Street
Winston-Salem

OHIO

The Charleston Room
Cincinnati Art Museum
Eden Park
Cincinnati

The Kemper Log House
Cincinnati Zoological Gardens
Cincinnati

St. Luke's Church
Granville

OKLAHOMA

The Murrell House
Tahlequah

OREGON

The Minthorn House
Newberg

The McLoughlin House
McLoughlin Park between 7th &
  8th Streets
Oregon City

PENNSYLVANIA

Wheatland
1124 Marietta Avenue
Lancaster

Stenton
18th & Courtland Streets
Philadelphia

Pottsgrove
High Street
Pottstown

RHODE ISLAND

Whitehall
Berkeley Avenue
Middletown

The Hopkins House
Corner Hopkins & Benefit Streets
Providence

SOUTH CAROLINA

The Old Powder Magazine
79 Cumberland Street
Charleston

The Hanover House
Clemson College
Clemson

TENNESSEE

Travelers' Rest
Farrell Parkway
Nashville

TEXAS

The Austin Houses

  The French Legation
  Robertson Hill
  East Eighth & San Marcos
  Austin

  The Neill-Cochran Museum
    House
  2310 San Gabriel Street
  Austin

  The North-Evans Château
  708 San Antonio Street
  Austin

VERMONT

The Bennington Museum Library
Bennington

VIRGINIA

Gadsby's Tavern
North Royal Street at Academy
Alexandria

The Settlement of Jamestown
Jamestown Island

Wilton
Wilton Road
Richmond

WASHINGTON

The 18th Century Drawing Room
Seattle Art Museum
Volunteer Park
Seattle

WISCONSIN

The Kilbourntown House
Estabrook Park
Milwaukee

The Old Indian Agency
Portage

GREAT BRITAIN

Sulgrave Manor
Sulgrave
Northamptonshire

INDEX